Offshore Financial Centers, Accounting Services and the Global Economy

David L. McKee,
Don E. Garner and
Yosra AbuAmara McKee

QUORUM BOOKS
Westport, Connecticut • London

Library of Congress Cataloging-in-Publication Data

McKee, David L.
    Offshore financial centers, accounting services and the global economy / David L.
McKee, Don E. Garner and Yosra AbuAmara McKee.
        p.   cm.
    Includes bibliographical references and index.
    ISBN 1–56720–310–8 (alk. paper)
    1. International business enterprises—Accounting.   2. International finance.
I. Garner, Don E.   II. McKee,Yosra AbuAmara, 1948–   III. Title.
HF5686.I56M384   2000
657'.8333—dc21   99–059832

British Library Cataloguing in Publication Data is available.

Library of Congress Catalog Card Number: 99–059832
ISBN: 1–56720–310–8

First published in 2000

Quorum Books, 88 Post Road West, Westport, CT 06881
An imprint of Greenwood Publishing Group, Inc.
www.quorumbooks.com

Printed in the United States of America

The paper used in this book complies with the
Permanent Paper Standard issued by the National
Information Standards Organization (Z39.48–1984).

10 9 8 7 6 5 4 3 2

In order to keep this title in print and available to the academic community, this edition
was produced using digital reprint technology in a relatively short print run. This would
not have been attainable using traditional methods. Although the cover has been changed
from its original appearance, the text remains the same and all materials and methods
used still conform to the highest book-making standards.

Contents

Acknowledgments

Over the course of this project the authors have benefited from opportunities to present portions of their work as papers at various professional meetings and conferences. Conferences at which presentations were made included those of the American Society for Business and Behavioral Sciences, the American Society for Competitiveness, the Decision Sciences Institute, the International Academy of Business Disciplines and the Western Social Science Association.

The authors are grateful to their respective institutions, California State University, Stanislaus and Kent State University for significant travel support. They are also appreciative of the support of Diane Williams of the Department of Economics at Kent State University for significant assistance with the final preparation of the manuscript.

Introduction

In the waning years of the twentieth century advances in transportation and communications have supported the emergence of a truly global economy. The scope of that economy has been broadened in theory at least by the demise of the Soviet Union and with it the decline of socialism as a viable alternative on the international scene.

The new global climate of free enterprise has brought with it a proliferation of offshore financial centers that presumably have important roles to play in the emergent global economy. With respect to that global economy the most significant role for the centers in question appears to be the facilitation of international business and finance.

It is their interest in the facilitators of international business that has drawn the authors to the current project. This volume builds upon earlier research regarding the role of major international accounting firms (McKee and Garner, 1992 and 1996; McKee, Garner and AbuAmara McKee, 1998 and 1999). The present intent is to continue the study of the role of major international accounting firms and their services in the processes of business facilitation in the locations that host them and beyond. By focusing the investigation upon the role of the accounting firms in offshore financial centers it is hoped to gain a better grasp of the real or potential impacts of the firms in the global economy and, of course, in the jurisdictions that host them.

The volume is divided into four parts. Part I beyond the current overview provides the general background or foundation for the specifics to follow. In it the positive functions of offshore financial centers are reviewed with special emphasis upon their hosting of international services. Care is taken to point out what attributes are needed by jurisdictions hoping to succeed as offshore financial centers. Examples of the involvement of the major accounting firms in such centers are also included.

In Part II the focus shifts to a more detailed assessment of what the major accounting firms are actually doing in offshore financial centers. Space does not permit an appraisal of what the firms are about in every identifiable offshore center. Thus a selection of centers from various regions of the world will be considered. The first chapter of the section is focused on selected Caribbean and North Atlantic centers. Included are Antigua and Barbuda, the Bahamas, Barbados, Bermuda and the Cayman Islands.

Following that chapter, the focus switches to Europe where jurisdictions were selected so as to stress the current role and future prospects of accounting services in the types of offshore centers that are emerging today. Centers such as Switzerland, Liechtenstein and various continental jurisdictions were not included, since their business climates and the roles of the service firms that they house are rather well known. Instead, the centers to be studied include the Channel Islands, the Isle of Man, Gibraltar, Malta and Cyprus.

The final chapter of Part II reviews the operations of accounting firms in a selection of jurisdictions located in the Persian Gulf, the Indian Ocean and the Far East. In the Persian Gulf the centers selected include Bahrain and the United Arab Emirates. Mauritius and Seychelles were selected from the Indian Ocean. In the Far East Singapore and Vanuatu are included.

In Part III the emphasis switches to a description of the legal and institutional environments facing business operations in general and the accounting firms in particular in offshore financial centers. The centers featured are those that were discussed in Part II. Thus the organizational structure to be found in Part III resembles that of the previous part.

In the final section of the volume, Part IV, the activities of the firms in the various jurisdiction previously discussed are highlighted and reviewed with an eye to assessing their overall impacts. Through this section it is hoped that the role of the offshore centers and their hosted accounting firms in the global economy will be made clearer.

Part I

The General Frame of Reference

Chapter 1

The Role of Offshore Financial Centers

Historically offshore financial centers have been seen as a mixed blessing for those concerned with international finance and its affect upon the world economy. Financial professionals and economists have often seemed to be overly concerned with various questionable activities that have rightly or wrongly been presumed to be accommodated in the offshore centers. It seems more realistic to presume that the offshore centers would find it difficult to sustain themselves through time, barring more positive functions in the world economy.

The present authors suspect that the centers in question, through the activities they house, are actually facilitators of various international activities. Indeed it appears as though the leading participants in the global economy, whether corporate or public, are in need of various services provided by or through offshore financial centers. This chapter will provide introductory support for that thesis.

OFFSHORE CENTERS AND THE WORLD ECONOMY

Accompanying the genesis of an actual world economy, various service groups have been cast in the mantra of facilitators of international business. Of course, this role in international business transactions is far from a completely new activity for various service groups. The involvement of banks and insurance companies in international matters can be traced at least as far back as the Mercantilists. Nonetheless, recent improvements in transportation and communications have contributed greatly to the strengthening of the global economy, while simultaneously expanding the demand for an ever broadening menu of international services.

Historically such services have been housed in a small number of world capitals, such as New York and London, and more recently Tokyo. Recently, however, the activities in question have followed the needs of their business clients and have established themselves in various locations on a worldwide basis. Such activities have emerged in various major urban areas around the world. By doing so they have become better able to satisfy the needs of clients in various domestic economies and have assisted in the expansion of those economies.

Surpassing what might be termed domestic service enclaves, various service centers have been generated, with their main functions designed to facilitate international business. Historically, the most obvious examples arose in Europe. Included were such jurisdictions as Liechtenstein, Luxembourg and, of course, Switzerland. Even during major conflicts such as World War II, Switzerland was regarded as an international business and financial center, facilitating a wide range of business activities that might very well have been impossible without it. Hindsight being what it is, the part played by Switzerland and perhaps a handful of similar jurisdictions seems obvious today. Certainly, the accomplishments of such principalities signaled their importance as facilitators of a wide range of international transactions.

As was suggested elsewhere, "the emergence of Eurodollars to prominence as an international medium of exchange has actually led to a proliferation of financial centers geared towards the needs of the world market" (McKee, 1988, 126). However, "the reality of international exchange in the 1960s and 1970s continued to be one where the 'openness' of economies to international competition remained constrained" (Johns and LeMarchant, 1993, 4), mainly due to nation-states and their political systems (Lindbeck, 1975, 29, quoted in Johns and LeMarchant, 1993, 4). Johns and LeMarchant were delicate in their description of the issue (quoting Picciotto, 1983, 11) as a "growing 'territorial non-coincidence between an increasingly interdependent international system and the traditional . . . national state' " (4).

According to Johns and LeMarchant, each national market was replete with barriers interfering with access by foreigners, not to mention access by domestic practitioners to the international trading system (4). In fact those authors suggested that "the combined national friction structures of the major industrial onshore trading nations, from which and to which the main global exchange flows emanate and gravitate, constituted an 'international friction matrix,' the overt and covert characteristics of which diverted, destroyed or created profitable invisible and visible trade activities" (4).

The authors in question identified U.S. banks as the progenitors of the radical reorganization of international finance, through their reactions to specific changes in U.S. monetary and balance of payments policies during the 1960s (13). Such policy adjustments they saw as the stimulus for a two-stage series of banking migrations. During the first stage various onshore free financial markets emerged beyond the United States in traditional financial centers "that took a relaxed attitude to the establishment of what became Eurodollar markets" (13). Such new markets were described by the authors as providing an extranational channel for multinational banks to intermediate the flows of capital through national boundaries, unregulated by national rules and operating procedures (13). These international developments certainly increased the demand for various facilitative services.

Additionally, Johns and Le Marchant alluded to the "selective transformation of particular tax havens . . . into fairly sophisticated offshore financial centers" (13–15). They outlined the setting up of a network of onshore external financial centers and onshore-related offshore centers. According to them, those locations were spatially interlinked by air travel and telecommunications (15). "A new invisible secondary trading system, global in scope, was thereby forged; a new tier of circuitry and conduitry provided to facilitate the global velocity of international funds, to cater to the growing and changing needs of multinational business, whether private, corporate or institutional" (15).

As has been suggested elsewhere "banking and financial services have a major share in the general role of the facilitator" (McKee, 1988, 126). Banks have been lending large amounts of money for various developmental projects, while simultaneously servicing the needs of multinational firms (Johns and Le Marchant, 1993, 15). There appears to be little doubt that the needs of both the banks and their clients are contributing to the continuing expansion of business service offerings.

Johns and Le Marchant have suggested that the new offshore financial network included 36 jurisdictions by the end of the 1970s (15). Those authors identified three types of geographical locations—inland enclave states, coastal enclave states and island states (15). They saw such enclave states as establishing a worldwide pattern of what they called satellite clusters, compatible with four main business time zones. (16).

The four clusters enjoyed time zone linkages to major global/regional capital markets. The Western Hemisphere was served through the New York epicenter by the Caribbean and the Central American Basin. European enclaves, coastal enclaves and independent islands were included in the London epicenter. The Asian-Pacific region and Oceania were served within the Tokyo time zone by Hong Kong, Singapore, Vanuatu and Nauru. The final cluster was composed of Persian Gulf jurisdictions providing service to Middle Eastern oil countries (16).

Of course since advances in transportation and communications appear to have made the system of financial centers mentioned above viable, it may be reasonable to ask whether continuing improvements in such linkage facilitators may cause the system to become redundant. For such a system to have emerged to begin with, it seems clear that much more was required than the mere improvement of international linkages. There are various ways in which the financial centers that have materialized are facilitating both business and economic linkages. If those centers can continue their successful facilitative functions, then they should be able to survive and prosper.

Some of the newer financial centers are located in emerging nations "where they have begun to replicate various functions that were traditionally the preserve of centers such as London or Zurich" (McKee, 1988, 126). Among such centers, both their success and their degree of involvement vary widely. According to Johns and Le Marchant the offshore network by the end of the 1970s was comprised of four primary centers, 11 secondary centers, four transitional secondary centers and 11 peripheral tax havens (1993, 17). Those authors explained that each region had a minimum of at least one primary offshore center for surplus and resident funds. Listed among such centers were Panama, Switzerland, Bahrain and Hong Kong (17).

In addition to such primary centers Johns and Le Marchant described secondary centers that acted as "turntable" centers supporting and encouraging international invisible activities. In the Caribbean region they pointed to locations such as Bermuda, the Bahamas, the Cayman Islands and the Netherlands Antilles (17). In Europe they identified Luxembourg, Liechtenstein and the Channel Islands, and in the Persian Gulf the United Arab Emirates (17). In the Far East they listed Singapore and Vanuatu (17).

Regardless of where in the world such centers are located, it seems clear that they depend upon the understanding and acceptance of onshore economies. Johns and Le Marchant pointed to development viability relying "on the tacit/complicit passive attitude of one or more onshore economies" (18). It seems safe to say that the functions of the majority of international financial centers would be seriously limited were it not for an implicit agreement among major nations to avoid impeding them. The implication appears to be that major nations have decided that the benefits to be gained from facilitating the operation of the global economy outweigh the real or imagined problems stemming from the avoidance of certain laws or institutional understandings involving individuals or corporations who are utilizing the advantages offered by various offshore financial centers.

The air of secrecy that appears to pervade the activities of offshore financial centers may well slant or obscure any real understanding of the functions of such centers with respect to the global economy. Offshore financial centers are often considered to be synonymous with tax havens and in a related oversimplification are viewed as safe havens in which to launder or hide funds generated by questionable means. Indeed offshore financial centers have been viewed as settings for corruption and illicit transactions.

Ingo Walter has documented a variety of determinants of the demand for secret money (1990, 50–51). Beyond tax evasion and money laundering Walter referred to ordinary business and confidentiality motives, as well as capital flight, bribery and corruption, smuggling, the violation of securities laws, fraud and government undercover activities.

Presumably, most of the factors referred to by Walter are far from encouraged or supported by government agencies and legal establishments in most nations. Nonetheless, the press and other media in various wealthier nations have recounted various machinations involving money manipulations that have taken place with the assistance of financial specialists in various offshore financial centers. Occasional incursions on the part of legal authorities from wealthier nations notwithstanding, it seems as though the secret money industry is alive and well, and offshore financial centers, where it may be finding support, appear to be expanding in number.

It is not the intent of the current investigators to indict the industry or offshore banking centers. Instead it is presumed that such centers perform various functions in the world economy beyond those listed above and that it is those functions that support the ongoing operation of the financial centers, rather than a permissiveness or naivete on the part of governments confronted with the peculiar specifics that emerge on an ongoing basis.

Hopefully, it is an understanding of the positive inputs from offshore financial centers vis-à-vis the world economy that deters the wealthy advanced nations from applying constraining pressures towards them that might curtail the entire spectrum of their activities. Walter has generated a helpful understanding of the negative aspects of the secret money industry through his investigations. Nonetheless, as he has suggested, there are sufficient legitimate reasons to justify the actions of both individuals and businesses seeking confidentiality in their international dealings (51).

Corporations have never been noted for openness concerning their operations. A "close to the vest" posture on the part of corporations active in the global economy may as easily be driven by a defense of markets as by more questionable motives. Without making excuses for questionable practices housed in offshore financial centers, it might be helpful if the positive functions of such centers in the global economy were better understood.

No one would dispute that secrecy is a part of what clients hope to gain from the services of financial professionals located in offshore jurisdictions. According to Walter the desired secrecy is supplied in two ways. "One is domestic bank secrecy laws, which bar insight by national and foreign authorities alike" (187). The second source for secrecy stems from blocking statutes "which effectively prevent the disclosure, copying, inspection or removal of documents located in the host country in compliance with orders by foreign authorities" (187).

Walter suggested that the provision of secrecy in offshore locations may embrace the actual blocking of legal depositions related to litigation being considered or actually in progress elsewhere (187). He was careful to indicate that various nations not seen to be tax or secrecy havens "have comprehensive blocking statutes to guard their sovereignty from the extraterritorial reach of foreign authorities" (187). His listing of such jurisdictions included the United Kingdom, France, South Africa, West Germany, Australia, Norway and Canada.

Offshore financial centers have been known to be materializing in emerging nations (McKee, 1988, 126). The success of operations in such centers varies widely. "Some are recognized as successful players in world financial markets, while others are viewed with some skepticism (126). As has been noted elsewhere, various nations have been attracted to the idea of offshore banking as a potential developmental stimulus (126).

Walter suggests that "countries with very small open economies have often embraced the financial secrecy business as a way of promoting economic development (1990, 188). With some exceptions he identifies such jurisdictions as being geographically isolated and possessing narrow production bases geared towards a few commodities generally destined for export (188).

For such jurisdictions he identified two ways to become a financial center (188). One was to become a functional center with transactions actually occurring and value added emerging in both design and delivery of financial services (188). Examples cited by Walter included Geneva, Zurich, London, Singapore, Bahrain and Hong Kong. The other route was to become a booking center where transactions are documented but the value added is created elsewhere. As examples of such centers he included the Bahamas, Cayman Islands, Seychelles and Vanuatu (188). Among prerequisites for becoming a booking center he stressed the need for a favorable tax climate together with a benign regulatory and supervisory environment (188). Beyond such matters he saw an important role for financial secrecy. Potential benefits included induced employment, fiscal contributions and "positive linkage effects to firms and industries that service the financial sector" (188).

"There is no question that international financial services of various types do play the role of facilitators in the expansion of economic activity in emerging nations" (McKee, 1988, 126). However, there are no guarantees for specific jurisdictions, and indeed the creation of additional offshore financial complexes may offer very modest potential gains to would-be hosts. As has been noted elsewhere, "new aspirants must be seen by prospective customers as capable of improving on services already offered elsewhere" (126).

This requirement may be a somewhat less formidable barrier to entry in an international economy in which the demand for financial services is increasing. A greater need for services in existence is fueling the demand increases, as is the expansion of the service menu. In 1988 Kazumasa Iwata suggested that "the past decade has seen marked progress in the integration of world financial markets and the internationalization of finance" (148). According to Iwata, the latter factor comprised four elements: "cross-border trade in financial flows; the internationalization of financial instruments; the multinationalization of financial intermediaries; and the internationalization of currencies" (149). It would appear as though all such factors have a potential for expanding legitimate business opportunities for offshore financial centers.

During the 1970s cross-border trade in financial flows was dominated by syndicated loans to non–oil producing countries (149). He saw such loans as facilitating the recycling of OPEC surpluses through the international banking system. In the 1980s the crisis caused by the debt problem in Mexico "caused the mainstream of international financial flows to shift from developing countries to advanced economies" (149). A boom in international portfolio investment and securities ensued (149).

According to Iwata, financial services included insurance, banking, brokerage and services facilitating commodity and other goods trading. Insurance companies dealt with transportation insurance, general insurance and reinsurance, while banks provided consulting services and the management of portfolio investment. Banks also provided credit and payment facilities for customers across the border (149). "Brokers engage in arbitrage, commissions, chartering and leasing" (149).

It seems clear that the types of activity discussed by Iwata would fit within the offerings of offshore financial centers. From the menu outlined he selected two dimensions of financial services. One was financial intermediation, including both the payment mechanism and the market maker. "International financial intermediation connects the demand for funds by ultimate borrowers in one country to the supply of funds by ultimate lenders in another" (149). In this manner primary securities become indirect securities through the services of international financial intermediaries. Alternatively, the international market makers "engage in the international transaction of securities among market participants of different countries" (149). It seems clear that such operations may well be occurring through offshore financial centers.

Iwata saw securitization to be blurring the distinction between the financial intermediation business and that of the market maker. He was careful to suggest that financial services are related not exclusively to banking and dealing but also to investment management as well as to leasing and consultancy (149). It seems clear that such matters may be well within the venue of various practitioners and specialists located in offshore facilities.

In Iwata's view "international trade in financial services covers three aspects of the internationalization of finance" (150). To begin with he spoke of cross border trade in financial flows. Such flows were considered to be the necessary accompaniment for international trade in goods and non-financial services (150). The growth in trade volume expands the range for the exchange of financial services, generating an exchange trade in bonds and equities and the financing of the imbalance of the current account among countries (150).

Iwata saw the second aspect of international trade in financial services as the "internationalization of financial instruments arising from the integration of the world financial market" (150). He saw this as being illustrated by a rapid increase of international bond issues configured in various currencies. The emergence of trade in financial services was considered by Iwata to be the third aspect of internationalization.

It seems clear that Iwata was explaining a very legitimate and important aspect of the business of offshore centers. "Financial services at the retail level are provided through establishments in the different clientele countries like many services that are traded internationally" (150). He was accurate suggesting that the sale of such services requires local offices and branches. With regard to the banking business, he pointed out that international banking produces a cross-border trade in financial services.

Although Iwata does not refer to offshore financial centers in this context, the importance of his insights to such settings seems clear. He goes on to explain that "international financial intermediaries seek maximum laxity of regulations and minimal tax burdens in determining the location of their activities" (150). He sees such intermediaries as arbiters of different regulatory and tax systems among countries. They facilitate international tax arbitrage on investment and saving, thus reducing the capital cost of business investment in an open economy (150). He recognizes the possible involvement of a certain type of offshore financial center—"the tax haven facility provided by a number of developing countries increases the locational diversification of international financial intermediaries" (150).

Various legitimate international business endeavors are restricted by both laws and customs in regard to transactions that penetrate the borders of sovereign jurisdictions. It appears as though facilitating such ventures may well be an important area for various groupings of business services operating either in or through offshore financial centers. Business services designed to facilitate international trade are growing phenomena in the world economy. A trade in those services can easily fall victim to the restrictive laws and customs of specific jurisdictions.

Undoubtedly, impediments to international business and financial services are also impediments to the activities that such services are intended to facilitate. As early as 1988 Geza Feketekuty defined a barrier to trade in services as "a government measure that creates an obstacle to the sale of services produced abroad" (131). He recognized that "since the movement of services across a border is largely invisible, it is generally useless to put up barriers to trade in services at the border" (135). Feketekuty was undoubtedly correct in suggesting that barriers, if erected, should be at a point where the government can exert some control (135).

It has not gone unnoticed by the present investigators that the emergence of services that may be undesirable to the governments of various nations is a phenomenon that is eminently controllable. When concentrated in a relatively small number of offshore financial centers, such services appear to present rather obvious targets. The continued existence of such concentrations, not to mention their seeming increase in both quantity and magnitude, raises an interesting question. Traditionally, attacks on activities in offshore centers have been aimed at various criminal endeavors of the sort referred to by Ingo Walter (1990) and much less frequently at various international faciltative services.

Speaking of barriers to service trade, Feketekuty suggested that governments can limit or at least attempt to limit various factors. Included is the purchase of the foreign exchange needed to cover imported services. Governments may also limit the movements of population, information, goods and money across their borders. They can limit the sale of services by foreign business within their borders and the employment of foreign service workers. Beyond that they can limit the consumption of services needed to meet regulatory requirements (135).

Feketekuty recognized that a government normally "cannot control international trade in services purchased abroad" except through "a comprehensive foreign exchange control system," or by establishing "comprehensive controls on the consumption of services," or perhaps by establishing "a comprehensive system for controlling the movement of all the information, people, money and goods" (135). Such a government would also need to establish a system for obtaining information concerning foreign exchange transactions, as well as information concerning "the information, people, money and goods crossing the borders," not to mention the consumption of services.

As implied earlier, governments may be much less interested in controlling various business-related services housed in offshore financial centers than a cursory appraisal may imply. If the services in question actually do facilitate business operations in the global economy, it may not be in the best interests of governments to attack them.

It is conceivable that the removal of banks from offshore financial centers may improve domestic tax receipts in various nations. The actual impact of such an action may be less than obvious. In a similar vein the removal of offshore insurance options may increase potential business for insurance firms in various nations. The impact of such a procedure upon various major corporations may be somewhat more difficult to assess. The elimination of offshore ship registration will certainly adjust the flagging of merchant fleets, but how such an action may affect ocean transport and the multinational firms that employ it remains to be seen. Certainly, the elimination of offshore financial centers would generate significant repercussions in the global corporate community. In the face of potential impacts it seems hardly surprising that the major trading nations display little enthusiasm for a confrontational posture towards offshore financial centers.

Beyond efforts to discourage obvious criminal activities generated in offshore financial centers, major nations or their law enforcement agencies have little taste for curbing or controlling activities based in those centers. Business and financial services available through offshore centers have assumed major roles as facilitators of activities in the world economy.

Today, various smaller developing nations are turning to the hosting of international services as an important addition to their expansion programs. Few would suggest that there are no limitations to such service concentrations as foundations for economic development. Certainly, very small jurisdictions attempting to host offshore services may not be successful. However, various successful centers have emerged and others are building. Realistic appraisals of the positive potential for such centers and their activities would be helpful.

SUMMARY AND CONCLUSIONS

The rise of international services as facilitators of business in the global economy appears to be contributing to the expanding importance of offshore financial centers. Johns and Le Marchant have identified three types of locations as offshore centers—inland enclave states, coastal enclave states and island states. Such centers should be able to prosper as long as they house service functions designed to facilitate international business.

It seems clear that most offshore financial centers would have little to offer the global business community in the absence of a willingness on the part of major nations to avoid impeding their operations. This may mean that certain questionable activities may sustain themselves in such centers, but the positive facilitative pursuits that the centers house are far more important.

According to Walter (1990, 188), there are two ways in which jurisdictions become financial centers. One is as functional centers where transactions actually occur and value added emerges in the design and delivery of financial services. The other is as booking centers where transactions are recorded but the value added is created elsewhere.

In a global economy that is experiencing an increasing demand for financial services and where major progress is occurring in integrating global financial markets and internationalizing finance, there may be growing interest in such centers. Various legitimate international ventures are impeded by laws and customs of nations whose borders they breach. Business service groups operating in or through offshore centers facilitate such ventures.

Such service groups in offshore centers would appear to be obvious targets for the governments whose borders are being penetrated. The fact that little is being done to target such services or their hosts suggests a recognition on the part of governments of the importance of the services in question and the centers that house them.

Chapter 2

The Centers, International Services and the Accounting Firms

The relatively recent emergence of a truly global economy has brought with it the need for major corporate players to find ways to pursue their legitimate business goals in the face of the rules, regulations and institutional anomalies in place in a wide range of jurisdictions. One way in which the corporations and other business interests have responded to such operating difficulties has been through the use of what have come to be termed offshore financial centers and the services that have become available in and through such locations.

This chapter is concerned with services offered through offshore financial centers with emphasis on those aimed at facilitating international business. It will begin with a brief overview of the development of offshore business activity. Following that, the role of offshore financial centers will be considered. In that context the international service revolution, which has been fueled by technology, will be discussed. Services and their providers in offshore environments will be considered, with particular emphasis on the rise of advisory offerings, most especially those that have become the preserve of major international accounting firms. The intention is to provide a better understanding of the facilitative roles of the accounting firms in offshore financial centers.

THE DEVELOPMENT OF OFFSHORE BUSINESS ACTIVITY

It has been suggested that offshore business can be established with the intention of servicing three main transnational sectors (Johns and Le Marchant, 1993, 22). The sectors involved are the personal sector, the corporate sector and the financial sector (22). The sectors in question are thought to have various reasons for developing offshore activities. Beyond tax motivated transactions Johns and Le Marchant included safe haven protection, explaining that this could include protection from onshore inflation rates or repercussions from domestic political instability. Other possible transactions included the avoidance of regulation and a desire for the freedom of operation for business (22).

Johns and Le Marchant pointed to the avoidance or minimization of taxes as another important motivation behind the creation of offshore business (1993, 22). Quoting Wisselink (29), they defined international tax avoidance as "the reduction of tax liability through the movement or non-movement of persons or funds across tax boundaries by legal methods" (22). In this vein the authors identified four combinations of activities. To begin with they mentioned the emigration of natural or legal persons complete with all or part of their income sources or assets (22). Following that, they referred to the movement of taxpayers without all income sources or assets (22).

Third, they spoke of the movement of funds alone, most commonly involving the shifting of income and profit or the establishment of base companies (22–23). Finally, they referred to cases where neither persons nor funds move, which they explained covers situations following an earlier move wherein a taxpayer does not return or repatriate funds beyond an intended temporary move (23).

The authors in question have identified two types of tax avoidance activity. The first is tax planning consistent with the spirit and letter of the law, while the second takes advantage of unintended legal or administrative loopholes (23; and Gordon, 1981, 60–61). Another set of motives for developing offshore activities may have to do with escaping legal obligations by fraudulent means (23). Such activities are referred to here in the interests of completeness and are not pertinent to the central thrust of the current investigation.

Irrespective of the driving forces pushing individuals and businesses to carry out offshore operations, there are a variety of factors that such practitioners will generally look for in choosing a setting for their operations. It is the factors in question that support the success of specific offshore centers. The necessary ingredients have been summarized by *Euromoney* (Supplement, May 1989, 8). Among ingredients considered significant for the success of offshore financial centers, that publication placed the absence of direct taxation at the top of its list, while at the same time conceding that jurisdictions with low taxes or tax treaties may be successful as well.

Second on the *Euromoney* list was "no restrictions on the use of foreign enclaves or the free movement of funds in and out of the territories" (8). Among other important concerns were a guarantee of client confidentiality, preferably protected by legislation and the local court system. *Euromoney* was of the opinion that governments in offshore centers should welcome and encourage offshore activities by assisting the functioning of intermediaries through flexible regulations and minimal constraints and formalities. Although favoring the expeditious processing of official documents, *Euromoney* notes that "a complete absence of regulation is a handicap not an asset" (8).

Additional support for offshore financial centers should include "a solid cadre of professionals . . . including lawyers, accountants and bankers" and "some well-known major international institutions" as well as a well-educated local labor force (8). *Euromoney* also pointed to a need for an adequate physical infrastructure, including such things as telecommunications, skilled help to maintain and repair equipment and adequate office space (8). The magazine also indicated a need for a reliable and impartial legal system and went as far as to suggest that relevant legislation should be clear and unambiguous and designed with an eye to minimizing uncertainty and arbitrary administrative rulings (8–9).

Centers hoping to succeed as offshore or international business hosts should be conveniently located with easy air access from major cities. In the same vein such centers require suitable accommodations and meeting facilities (9). A pleasant environment was also cited as helpful, as was a respectable image and freedom from scandal (9). "The jurisdiction should enjoy political and social stability in order to instill confidence among investors and their agents" (9).

As it stands, it seems quite obvious that there is a significant demand for the services provided through offshore financial centers. Various economists share the opinion that services expand "as businesses need to tend to their relations with more and more governments" (Harrison and Bluestone, 1988, 74). Frequently such relations stem from government regulation of corporate operating procedures (McKee and Tisdell, 1990, 33–34). Beyond that they may also involve tax matters or the international transfer of financial assets (34).

Frequently offshore financial centers are housed in smaller jurisdictions. In fact offshore financial and business activities are proliferating in such locations. Some of the potential benefits from becoming a financial center were enumerated by Ingo Walter: "indexed employment, fiscal contributions and positive linkage effects to firms and industries that service the financial sector" (1990, 94).

"It seems rather clear that among the services multinational enterprises purchase through offshore financial centers is distance from various government rules and regulations" (34). What that distance actually amounts to may be difficult to measure. However, the provision of such distancing is an intangible facilitating service that has major impacts upon the size and operating effectiveness of the global economy. The providers of international services operate in or through various offshore centers because the needs of their clients support such operations.

The transactions of multinational firms or other international practitioners in various locations can be run through the books of financial intermediaries or subsidiaries in offshore financial centers (34). Such procedures may well be able to adjust tax liabilities and repatriate larger profits. "Captive insurance enables major corporations to insure themselves against certain risks, thus evading cumbersome insurance regulations and high commercial premiums" (34).

By the parking of funds, banks may well be able to circumvent domestic onshore regulations with an eye to improving speculative opportunities in foreign exchange markets (34). "The positioning of actual banks or deposit desks in offshore locations may provide banks with a greater potential for deposits in the form of flight capital, estate moneys, and other funds attracted by the service of secrecy" (34). Incorporation opportunities present additional avenues for removing funds from the visibility of onshore operations.

Beyond various factors referred to earlier as significant for the successful functioning of offshore financial centers, *Euromoney* listed various other issues (May 1989, 9). Among issues deemed to be significant were such things as the use of the dollar as local currency, the cost structure of the host jurisdiction, labor laws and regulations, and whether or not the center in question has a proven track record and offers a variety of services (9). *Euromoney* has suggested that "there appears to be a point at which some offshore centers acquire a critical mass or independent momentum, having secured a good reputation, and a steadily expanding clientele" (9). It goes without saying that the size and nature of the service menu offered is also important.

With respect to the transnational corporate sector, Johns and Le Marchant have suggested, quoting an OECD committee, that the interest of corporate players in using tax havens is not so much a desire to avoid or reduce taxes but rather the economic necessity for cutting costs, taxes included, to bearable levels, where the laws of nations are uncoordinated and laws internal to individual nations are inconsistent with respect to their dealings with international business (1993, 26).

Those authors pointed out that a firm's decision to go offshore needs careful consideration from the standpoint of net tax efficiency (26). However, they acknowledged other potential advantages that may be derived. Among those were "the cash flow advantage that may be gained from tax deferral; the lower country risk from the financial center's own political stability; and greater security from the effects of onshore vicissitudes of economic policy . . . following general elections" (26).

According to Johns and Le Marchant, non-tax benefits in the cost category include lower operating costs resulting from being able to avoid expensive onshore employment protection laws. In addition, they listed higher onshore manning scales, social security payments and pension requirements, as well as the capability of avoiding onshore constraints and costly procedures (26).

The authors referred to three basic means of what they labeled "transnational profit engineering" that can profit from an offshore setting in their quest for building transnational income. The means in question were profit creation, profit diversion and profit extraction. Under the first category they referred to setting up a commercial business in a low-tax location for either domestic offshore activities or international ventures. Speaking of profit diversion, they meant endeavoring to direct pre-tax income and profits away from a high-tax setting. By profit extraction they meant "the mitigation of post-tax profits in a high-tax jurisdiction via a strategically located subsidiary in low tax jurisdiction in order to gain maximum 'treaty-shopping' benefits from specific tax treaty provisions between the two countries" (26).

Speaking of small island states, the authors in question saw little opportunity for internal profit creation from either offshore domestic economy–directed invisible activities or, with limited exceptions, from visible trade development of component assembly (27). They saw the extent for offshore non-resident participation as related to special legislation directed towards particular offshore globally focused niche industries. Examples included shipping registers, ship chartering, aircraft basing, film making, property development, cross-border equipment leasing, employment companies, mining and oil production and development and writers' royalties (27).

It appears to be evident that the governments of smaller and perhaps even poorer jurisdictions would be unlikely to attract such activities by simply displaying a welcoming attitude. "Large firms can place components of their production processes in numbers of locations throughout the world, constrained only by the profit potential of their operations and by the transportation, communications, and other service cadres necessary to realize such potential" (McKee and Garner, 1992, 94).

Stephen S. Cohen and John Zysman saw such changes as generated at least in part by "a technological revolution spreading across major segments of manufacturing services" (1987, 80). Those authors saw what they described as the beginning of a new industrial era in which the convergence of computers and the technology of communications is giving birth to a new infrastructure (Cohen and Zysman, 1987, 18; McKee and Garner, 1992, 94). Although Cohen and Zysman were speaking about the United States, their analysis certainly applies internationally. Their type of sustained competitiveness vis-à-vis established or aspiring offshore financial centers appears to presuppose a state-of-the-art telecommunications infrastructure and the business service firms needed by corporate players using such offshore centers.

The "marriage between the technology of telecommunications and computers is altering the industrial and business landscape in revolutionary ways," and "the role of various sophisticated service subsectors in the accelerating processes of change can hardly be ignored" (McKee and Garner, 1992, 94). Groupings of business services in offshore financial centers, facilitated by improved transportation and communications technologies, have been developing major roles in the world economy. These services have collectively grown into major players in the economies of the offshore financial centers that host them and the centers for their parts are assuming major importance in the global economy.

"By extending markets and providing more flexibility in production chains services have dramatically altered the processes of production" (McKee, 1988, 115). In fact some services "contribute to facilitating the passage of materials, personnel, and financial assets through national boundaries" (McKee and Garner, 1992, 94). Technological change has improved the efficiency, not to mention the reach, of such actions.

Peter Robinson is of the opinion that technological change, in addition to affecting markets and products, has had profound impacts on international business operations (1989, 43). He sees functions as becoming easily shiftable from place to place (43), perhaps footloose in the terminology of spatial analysis. If his assessment is accurate, the pressure points in the global economy that have come to be known as offshore centers can easily experience changes in their importance. The improvements in transportation and communications that encouraged their functions can easily encourage the emergence of rivals. In such a global economy the satisfactions of the concerns of corporate customers will be the foundation for the success and continued viability of such centers.

Referring to multinational corporations, Johns and Le Marchant have suggested that such organizations have access to an intra-firm transnational financial system, permitting them to move funds and accounting profits among units in order to practice tax system arbitrage, financial market arbitrage and regulatory system arbitrage (1993, 29). Those authors suggested that this can involve strategic switching and the offshore placing of funds.

As examples of such activity they listed transfer pricing, invoicing and reinvoicing, share exchanges and "the positioning and realization of capital gains in a tax haven from the disposal of overseas assets" and upstream loans (29–30). This of course suggests major reasons for interest on the part of multinational corporate players in offshore financial centers. Such centers would seem to offer significant advantages to corporations.

Despite the fact that various questionable activities have been identified in offshore financial centers, it is clear that such locations serve various positive functions in the global economy. They provide for the legitimate service needs of a wide range of international business enterprises. Although many of the services offered appear to be aimed at circumventing the institutional and legal encumbrances maintained by various nations, those same nations seem prepared to accept such services and the settings that host them as ongoing realities.

SERVICES AND THEIR PROVIDERS IN OFFSHORE ENVIRONMENTS

The needed infrastructure and the other components of an acceptable offshore financial center have been considered. It is clear that such centers are hosts to various facilitative services and that those services are having domestic impacts in host jurisdictions as well as international impacts. Beyond such understandings it would be useful to provide more detail on the nature and extent of service menus and their providers. That information would hopefully be a basis for a better understanding of the role of such centers and the services they host, not to mention the potential for the expansion of those services and their host.

Johns and Le Marchant have enumerated these basic areas of financial service development (33). They listed international banking services, investment funds and "other financial niche products associated with transnational business" (33). With respect to banking they identified the banks as central role players providing specialized technological knowledge for financial profit creation activity and the promoting of the accumulation process stemming from profit diversion and profit extraction activities (33–34). They see the banks as providing a diversified range of personal and corporate services, often using a number of specialist associate subsidiary companies (34). Among such services they list portfolio loans, discretionary portfolio management, foreign currency fund floatation, mortgages, guaranteed deposit accounts in most major currencies, and the management of salary dispersal schemes (34). Beyond those services they include investment and cash management, insurance brokerage, expatriate financial services and company registration and trust formation services (34). Certainly the banks are in a position to provide wide-ranging services to the international business community.

It is true historically that banks have been the most visible providers of international services in offshore financial centers, however, there are various other service professionals located in those centers. Among such providers, the major international accounting firms have been very prominent and have been expanding both service menus and the number of offices through which such menus are being offered. It is hoped that an examination of their offerings in offshore financial centers will supply a more complete view of the functions of facilitative services in the world economy.

Improving technology has had significant influences upon the effectiveness of the accounting firms, not to mention the expanding range of services offered by them. Seemingly there is "little doubt that improvements in information processing, the ever increasing role of computers, and continuing improvement in information networking are really the factors that have been so successful in internationalizing their operations" (McKee and Garner, 1992, 96).

The mobility of activities and the efficiency of international linkages that technology has generated have had major impacts upon the ability of the accounting firms to serve customers in multiple settings. "If the firms can rely on information technology and computerized operating techniques that can be accessed internationally, they can provide the level of service that might have been slow in emerging in settings where basic accounting expertise is in short supply" (96).

The effectiveness of accounting firms housed in offshore financial centers is reinforced by the technological infrastructure common to such centers. In fact, the infrastructure in question may be instrumental in attracting the accounting firms to locations with offshore ambitions. A symbiosis may exist in which the accounting firms may have positive impacts upon the jurisdictions that host them.

The possibilities for such a symbiosis has been strengthening, since beyond their traditional range of accounting services the firms are offering an expanding range of consulting services that may well have technological impacts upon the economies to which they are applied (97). "Such impact may be quite extensive, presumably limited only by the extent of consulting services offered and, of course, by the skill of those offering them" (97).

Writing in 1989, Nicolas Jequier and Yao-Su Hu stressed the importance of the embodiment of technology in investment and production in different sectors of the economy (86). Certainly "accounting firms facilitate such embodiment in various ways" (McKee and Garner 1992, 98). They provide standardized international services to business customers by use of their own technological networking, and through their ability to establish themselves in various settings, they assist in international transfer of technology "which seems an inevitable accompaniment to the operations of multinational manufacturing firms" (98).

A recent supplement to *The Economist* highlighted the importance of management consultancy or "the advice business" (March 22, 1997, 3). The major accounting firms were seen to be important participants in that business. In listing the top 25 management consultancy firms in the United States, the publication gave first place to Andersen Consulting, followed by McKensey & Company. The following five places in the consulting hierarchy were held by members of accounting's Big Six. Indeed, the only member of that elite accounting fraternity failing to be ranked among the top 10 consulting firms was the pre-merger Price Waterhouse, which held the eleventh place in the ranking (4).

Of course, all of the accounting firms listed as high ranking consultants by *The Economist* are international in scope with offices in a wide range of jurisdictions. As will be seen in the present volume, through the expertise of their consultants, they are important facilitators in the world economy. They are involved in many of the issues and procedures referred to earlier in the current discussion. Much of what they have to offer is well based in various offshore financial centers. By functioning through such centers it appears as though the accounting firms are providing themselves with strong positions of international influence.

Support for the hypothesis that the accounting firms are assuming major roles in the global economy can be found in what *The Economist* has posited as stimuli to the expansion of consultancy. Leading the list of fueling elements behind the boom in consulting has been the impact of major economic changes including globalization and deregulation (4). Those adjustments can be assumed to offer impetus to the consulting activities of accounting firms, not to mention their more traditional services.

In addition to globalization, *The Economist* mentioned reengineering and downsizing, as changes with positive impacts on consultants. Certainly, the major accounting firms appear to be well positioned through their international networks as well as their strategic locations in established business capitals to take advantage of such changes. Where they do so their significance in the world economy increases.

The Economist referred to the growing importance of information technology as a stimulus to consulting activity. In addition they cited the convergence of technologies such as computers and telephones (4). The accounting firms have been said to be expanding their influence through improved technology (McKee and Garner, 1992).

In the view of *The Economist*, consultants have to have a global scope (6). Support for that contention was seen in the fact that the most successful companies are global and thus require a similar scope from their consultants (6). *The Economist* described such firms as wanting consultants able to provide "seamless services" that can cross borders (6). If such services are included in what the accounting firms are offering, it seems logical that they are available in or through offshore financial centers.

The Economist sees the major accounting firms as best placed to take advantage of globalization, since they have had offices around the world for decades (6). Yet that publication sees the firms as franchises of national partnerships, as compared to fully integrated global companies

(6). If this is a correct assessment, both the firms and their clients, not to mention the international economy, stand to benefit from the operation of internationally oriented offices in offshore centers.

The efforts put forward by the accounting firms towards becoming truly global have been seen as a frequent detriment to their relations to their auditing functions (6). *The Economist* suggests that all consultancies find that globalization causes problems (6). Among such difficulties they see the most obvious as being the establishment of an intangible product in a new market, especially when such a market may be dominated by family firms, wary of outsiders (6). Other problems revolve around creating staffs in various locations and the balance between local and "Western employees" (6). Clearly, such difficulties may be potentially less severe in an offshore center where an intentional international emphasis exists. An examination of the specifics of the operations of the accounting firms in offshore financial centers should improve the understanding of how they function in the global economy. In addition, it should provide additional evidence of the role of the offshore centers themselves in that global economy.

A FINAL OVERVIEW

Johns and Le Marchant have suggested that offshore business can be established to service three major transnational sectors: the personal sector, the corporate sector and the financial sector (1993, 22). In addition to the driving forces motivating offshore transactions, there are factors influencing where they locate. High among locational factors is an attractive tax climate. According to *Euromoney*, the ability to move funds freely is ranked second behind the tax climate (Supplement, May 1989, 8). Beyond the friendly regulatory environment and the efficient processing of documents, the magazine cited the availability of professional assistance, including lawyers, accountants and bankers. It also specified the need for a well-educated labor force and a good physical infrastructure. Aspiring centers would also require good transportation, communications linkages with the global economy and adequate accommodations for business visitors.

With the business climate as described above, there appears to be a growing market for services offered in and through offshore financial centers. Such centers are developing in smaller jurisdictions. According to *Euromoney*, offshore centers appear to reach a point where momentum can carry them, provided that they are offering a sustainable service menu (9).

In the case of small island states Johns and Le Marchant suggest the potential of globally focused niche industries. However, businesses in search of hosts for their endeavors have a wide selection of jurisdictions from which to choose. Their choices have been expanded greatly by advances in transportation and communications. Speaking of small island states, Johns and Le Marchant suggested the potential of globally focused niche industries.

Advances in transportation and communications have also dramatically increased the number of industries harboring segments that are relatively footloose internationally. It appears to be obvious that various business services of the sort to be found in offshore financial centers are enjoying expanding roles in this new international climate.

Business services are extending markets and providing more flexibility in production change, and some are contributing to facilitating the passage of material, personnel and financial assets through international boundaries (McKee and Garner, 1992, 94). How well offshore centers fair in such a world will depend upon how well they serve as platforms for needed facilitative services.

It seems clear that offshore financial centers are serving various positive functions in the global economy. They are supplying the legitimate service needs of a wide range of business enterprises. Despite the fact that many of the services in question may be aimed at circumventing the laws and customs of numerous nations, those jurisdictions appear ready to accept the services in question and their hosts as ongoing phenomena.

According to Johns and Le Marchant, banks have been providing a wide range of services (1993). It may well be that the banks are the most visible providers of international services in offshore financial centers, but such centers host many other professional services, among which are those provided by the major international accounting firms. Those firms have been expanding both the breadth of what they offer and the locations or offices through which they operate.

Like multinational firms in general and their other service providers, the accounting firms have benefited from the technological revolution and most especially from computers in their efforts to internationalize their operations. Certainly, the technological infrastructure, so evident in offshore financial centers, adds to the operating efficiency of the accounting firms located in such centers. The accounting firms are providing standardized international services through the use of their own technological networking. By offering their service menu in and through offshore financial centers they are strengthening their own impacts in the global economy, which at the same time supports the role of offshore financial centers in that economy.

Chapter 3

Offshore Financial Centers and the Accounting Firms in a Global Perspective

In its first two issues, *Offshore Investment* devoted considerable space to offshore financial centers (September and November/December, 1986). In describing the functions of such centers, that publication stated that it is "at its simplest . . . to provide international banks and businesses with foreign bases which are not hostage to the whims or fiscal piracy of high-tax governments, and which allow international trade to be pursued with the minimum of bureaucratic restriction" (September 1986, 34). Even today that description appears to offer a reasonable preliminary appraisal of why such centers have emerged and are continuing to emerge and proliferate.

In introducing its coverage of offshore financial centers, the magazine described the offshore world as a secondary trading system, global in scope, and vital to transnational private business. Indeed, it declared that the offshore world has rewritten the geography of world finance (34). Succinctly, it stated, "Changes in political policy, tax rates, inflation and exchange control restrictions are domestic factors which can distort trading conditions for individual companies" (34). An explanation for the genesis and proliferation of offshore centers followed. "The need to remain competitive internationally creates the private sector demand for a stable alternative—which offshore centers now provide" (34–35). This observation remains cogent if the operations of existing and emerging offshore centers are to be understood.

In its second issue, *Offshore Investment* continued its review of offshore centers (November/December, 1986, 34–37). All told, 42 jurisdictions were listed as either primary or secondary centers. In the Americas, embracing the Caribbean Basin and Central America, fifteen jurisdictions were listed, including the United States. Among the centers considered as primary were the Bahamas, Bermuda, British Virgin Islands, Cayman Islands, Costa Rica, Netherlands Antilles, Panama and the Turks and Caicos Islands. Secondary centers included Anguilla, Antigua, Barbados, Jamaica, Montserrat, St. Vincent and the United States (35).

In Europe primary centers included Cyprus, Gibraltar, Guernsey, Isle of Man, Jersey, Liechtenstein, Luxembourg, Netherlands and Switzerland. Among jurisdictions listed as secondary centers were Campione, Greece, Ireland, Malta, Monaco and the United Kingdom. In the Far East Hong Kong, Nauru and Vanuatu were listed as primary, while secondary centers included Cook Islands, Macau, Philippines and Singapore. The Middle East and Africa boasted five centers, which included Liberia, Bahrain, Israel, Seychelles and the United Arab Emirates (35).

Of course the magazine's listing, although realistic for its time, may not reflect an accurate taxonomy at this writing since some offshore centers may have encountered adjustments of circumstances since the 1980s. However, as suggested, British colonies or former colonies are well represented in the ranks of offshore financial centers. "The British legal system is particularly well-suited to offshore business" (34). Speaking of the Caribbean, *Offshore Investment* suggested that offshore finance offers strategic benefits to the United States, Great Britain and the Netherlands (34). It also significantly improves political stability in the region (34). It seems clear that their ongoing existence signals the fact that offshore financial centers have value to economic and business interests beyond their boundaries. Their ongoing proliferation suggests that potential host jurisdictions can see potential benefits for themselves.

Writing as early as 1976, Harry Johnson recognized that changes were taking place in international finance that undoubtedly had a role in generating a climate that spawned the phenomenon that has become the offshore financial center of today (Johnson, 1976, 261). He observed that "the major international financial center developed from a strong base as a national financial center in a large and powerful country with the natural market support of the citizens of that country" (261). He went on to explain that those citizens turned to their financial center "for financial services they needed in other countries and the advantage of knowing intimately the nature of the customers involved" (261).

He felt that regional financial centers such as Singapore, Hong Kong and Panama acquired their mission primarily from a combination of geographical proximity to the countries housing the operations of their customers and "the safety and ease of operation of subsidiaries, branches and agencies of foreign banks whose head offices lie in international financial centers" (261).

Johnson was suggesting a derived importance for what he termed regional financial centers. Those centers were not generating customers because of their national size or international power and the competence of their own national banks in the sphere of the international financial business. Johnson seems to have been correct in suggesting that the regional centers are largely hosts to foreign financial institutions that find them convenient. The financial centers were hardly "magnets of financial power in their own right, attracting foreign financial enterprises to establish subsidiaries in order to obtain a piece of the action" (261–262).

The logic of the Johnson assessment appears to have survived impeachment over the intervening years. No one would suggest that offshore financial centers have replicated the international financial centers alluded to by Johnson. In addition, there do appear to be regional considerations that must be assessed in any attempt to understand the contemporary role of offshore financial centers (Johns and Le Marchant, 1993). Those centers have acquired their roles not as smaller versions of New York or London or Tokyo but rather because they are fulfilling international needs that have not been satisfied by the global financial capitols. In fulfilling those needs they have hardly eclipsed the capitols in question. More accurately, they have become facilitative centers in the global economy. Cast in that role, their functions may be regional or extra regional.

If offshore centers are hosts to foreign financial institutions rather than magnets of financial power in their own right (Johnson, 1976), it seems reasonable to ask why foreign financial institutions appear to congregate in certain locations and not in others. Johnson's article concerned Panama, a nation which appears to have been eclipsed as a major offshore center since his investigation. In his article he described Panama as holding two advantages. One was the nation's geographical location, although he qualified that advantage by observing that Panama was "obviously deficient in many of the business and personal living amenities that are taken for granted by people engaged in international financial business" (262).

Johnson attributed the other advantage to two aspects of Panamanian policy. One was the fact that the nation's currency had an absolutely fixed exchange rate with respect to the United States dollar, which was maintained automatically by Panamanian monetary arrangements. The other policy consideration was "that Panama has welcomed foreign financial enterprises with liberal banking laws and a generally laissez-faire attitude" (262).

Some insights concerning what combination of factors may be at play can be gleaned from the real or imagined advantages set forward by existing or would-be offshore financial centers. Cayman Web World has listed what it perceives to be the advantages of the Cayman Islands as an offshore financial center (1996–1997). That jurisdiction is certainly recognized in most financial circles for its involvement in international financial pursuits. By the end of 1994 the Cayman Islands boasted 560 banks and trust companies, representing over 60 countries (1996–1997). Over 31,500 companies were registered there, and the Caymans were also one of the top centers for offshore insurance, with in excess of 350 companies registered (1996–1997).

In making its case for why the Cayman Islands should be considered by those needing offshore financial services, Cayman Web World is, of course, supplying an answer to the question raised by the work of Harry Johnson back in 1976. According to Cayman Web World, the advantages of the Cayman Islands are wide ranging. The islands provide the stability of a well and progressively governed colony of Britain (1996–1997). At this juncture it seems advisable to keep in mind the number of actual or emerging offshore financial centers that have ongoing or historical links to Great Britain. Most of those share legal traditions and even business practices that may make them better understood by prospective international players.

Beyond the link to Britain the Caymans are said to exhibit an established pattern of social harmony, no racial tensions and a comparatively low crime rate (1996–1997). Clearly, a lack of those characteristics would discourage the development of offshore business operations and indeed may discourage operations in locations exhibiting problems. In recent years the decline of Lebanon and Panama as significant offshore centers pays witness to the importance of the considerations alluded to here.

The Cayman Islands are said to have excellent, state-of-the-art telecommunications, efficient air linkages and reliable shipping linkages well able to provide regular freight supply (1996–1997). Of course, any jurisdiction aspiring to success as an offshore financial center requires an excellent transportation and communications infrastructure linking it to the external world. The absence of such linkages are among the major impediments that may prevent the success of aspiring centers.

The Caymans are also the beneficiaries of their proximity to the United States, coupled with good daily connections worldwide (1996–1997). Of course, proximity to a major international financial center has been recognized as an advantage if not a necessity for offshore financial centers; witness the views of Harry Johnson (1976) and more recently Johns and Le Marchant (1993).

Going beyond its reference to the transportation and communications infrastructure, Cayman Web World touts the Cayman Islands as having "a highly developed infrastructure, including ports, airfields, roads, utilities and medical and educational services" (1996–1997). Jurisdictions that are deficient in such facilities experience obvious disadvantages in any competition with jurisdictions that are better supplied.

Cayman Web World has reported that the Cayman Islands possess "a pool of lawyers, accountants and other professionals highly qualified and experienced in the administration of financial services, applying their skills through institutions of repute observing government-set standards of probity" (1996–1997). In the case of such business services, jurisdictions that are deficient in their supply can hardly expect success as offshore financial centers.

Other advantages attributed to the jurisdiction in question include an experienced construction industry able to respond quickly to both business and residential needs and an advanced land registry system, with titles guaranteed by government, which allows for quick and efficient property transactions (1996–1997). Foreign ownership of real estate is unrestricted and efficient processing and registry systems for banks, companies, trust and insurance companies are in place (1996–1997).

Although some flexibility is permitted, banks and trust companies are closely monitored to insure the maintenance of standards. Officials in the posts of deputy inspector of financial services, deputy inspector of insurance and registrar of companies monitor activities in their areas of concern, while allowing greater flexibility in matters such as liquidity ratios and capital formation. Business has ready access to an established financial center, well linked to Euro currency markets (1996–1997).

The Cayman Islands are free of direct taxation, which provides "the ability to accumulate profits free of tax and, for branches or subsidiaries of parent companies elsewhere, the ability to repatriate profits at most advantageous times" (1996–1997). There are no exchange controls, thus permitting the movement of capital in and out, as well as the holding of accounts in any major currency (1996–1997).

Confidentiality between clients and professionals is supported by severe penalties, except in cases involving the government's accepted duty to help in the international investigation of drug-related and other serious crimes (1996–1997). The economy boasts an efficient private sector, able to provide courier service, database access, and facsimile transmission (1996–1997). Beyond such matters there is a fixed exchange rate with respect to the United States dollar, while other world currencies float with the dollar.

Of course, the matters enumerated here as having been put forward by Cayman Web World represent a rather helpful shopping list of the elements that attract clients to offshore banking centers. Presumably, they are the matters that most prospective clients will compare in choosing a specific location for their operations.

Many of the points highlighted by the promotional material concerning the Cayman Islands might well be found in lists of the attributes of various offshore financial centers. They may also be found on the needs lists of many businesses and individuals in search of an offshore center suitable to facilitate their international operations. To be successful any aspiring offshore center must be able to demonstrate social and political stability, and a willingness to insure a legal framework and business environment supportive of international operations. It must provide a tax climate friendly to business and a financial sector that business can feel secure in utilizing.

This calls for a financial service sector that operates with international standards of expertise, professionalism and integrity. Foreign clients, both corporate and private, must be confident of privacy and safety in their dealings. They require state-of-the-art transportation and communications infrastructures. Their business operations in centers of their own choosing must enjoy effective linkages with the centers of power in the global economy and, of course, with various locations significant for their business success.

Foreign corporate players will be most favorably disposed to settings with the various characteristics already mentioned that also have the facilities to host foreign business travelers safely and comfortably. Those players will also value the availability of a skilled labor force from which they can hire effective employees.

Various jurisdictions have emerged throughout the world that appear capable of performing needed services in low-risk business environments. Harry Johnson (1976) was quite correct in suggesting that such jurisdictions are different from international financial centers such as New York or London, since they are not major power concentrations. In more modern terminology the centers in question are facilitators of activity in the global economy.

Among the ranks of real or would-be offshore financial centers there is an obvious hierarchy based upon their ability to compete in providing for the needs of a global clientele. The less-able particular centers may be in the provision of such needs, the less successful they can be expected to be as actual offshore centers. It may be that less successful or perhaps failing centers may be more prone to hosting questionable international activities. However, even those activities will require a certain service base to support their success.

Offshore financial centers as a focus for questionable activities is an idea that is often overworked. Writing in 1996, Edmund Bendelow conceded that "if one were to survey the major scandals which have struck the financial world in the last few years, there was indeed an element of offshore contact in most of them" (1996, 1). However, he pointed out that the scandals in question had a common thread: "they involved cross jurisdictional transactions but the criminal or improper behavior took place onshore" (2).

Bendelow claimed that due to scandals that have occurred it is more essential now than ever before that the onshore professional advisors have a greater understanding of the offshore world. He believed this to be so because the world in question is so large and important to multinational financial transactions. He quoted Walter Diamond to the effect that half of the world's financial transactions take place offshore and stated that the number of offshore centers, worldwide, is approaching 60 (2). He observed that recent estimates of wealth held offshore are at the U.S.$5 trillion level. That wealth, he suggested, tends to gravitate to where it can maximize its return. Thus huge amounts of funds have legitimately been transferred to offshore locations over the last 30 years (2).

Bendelow sees the greatest challenge facing offshore centers for the foreseeable future as being how to regulate their own internal operations so as to be able to continue their relationships to the onshore world in a mutually acceptable manner. In that context he sees the main areas of concern involving such things as the laundering of drug money and the gains from other crime, fraudulent and other wrongful but non-criminal transfers and tax evasion (2).

For continuing and successful onshore/offshore relations those issues must be controlled, and Bendelow sees sovereignty as a serious issue (2). What may be the response of offshore centers to requests for information? Bendelow sees a continuum of likely responses ranging "from no assistance permitted to total and unconditional assistance in every shape or form" (3). In tax cases where one country attempts to assert its rules in the courts of another country, no assistance is probable on grounds of protecting sovereignty. At the other extreme most countries will cooperate "in such matters as the suppression of the drug trade" (5). Bendelow sees all other matters falling between those extremes.

He sees good cooperation between onshore and offshore British jurisdictions with respect to all non-tax-related inquires on serious matters. Similarly he sees good cooperation between most European tax havens and onshore authorities on anti–drug money laundering activity. He sees fair cooperation between onshore and offshore authorities if what is being investigated would be considered a crime in both jurisdictions (3–4). He points out that many larger offshore European jurisdictions are signing bilateral treaties with major onshore jurisdictions to facilitate assistance relating to transborder crimes in specific circumstances (4).

Bendelow points out that ultimately every major European tax haven either has or will have policies intended to assist their major onshore trading partners to suppress crime. He sees such cooperation as being in the interests of the tax havens themselves, "No serious offshore jurisdiction will continue to develop and flourish if it can only do so by condoning criminal behavior" (4).

Thus it appears as though the benefits that are presumed to accrue to the hosting of offshore business and financial activity are the best support that real and would-be offshore centers have for expunging existent criminal elements and discouraging their replacements. Bendelow appears to have been correct in suggesting that offshore centers still "jealously guard their sovereignty" (4). Presumably, a desire to maintain sovereignty may cause clashes between jurisdictions (4). However, it seems as though both onshore and offshore interests desire the continued existence of offshore financial and business centers.

Because many such centers appear to be positioned in rather small emerging nations, it would appear that such jurisdictions see themselves with something to gain from offshore finance. Indeed, it appears as though various emerging nations and small colonial jurisdictions are placing their hopes for material betterment at least in part upon offshore activities.

For offshore activities to thrive in specific locations it is not enough for their hosts to welcome them. Participants in the global economy must see such locations as effective settings for their international activities. Beyond the attractiveness of such locations to potential corporate and individual clients, the wealthier nations of the world must recognize the utility of their continued existence.

In his discussion of Panama, Harry Johnson raised an appropriate question (1976, 263). His question concerned "how far the development of a regional financial center largely financed by foreign capital and staffed or at least directed by foreigners has a spillover effect in promoting economic development and increasing the welfare of the citizens of the host country" (263). The years since Johnson published his article have hardly diminished the significance of such a question. It may not be reviewed frequently with respect to current realities in Panama, but it still appears rather basic as it concerns the current positioning of ongoing offshore activities in the global economy.

Johnson suggested various concerns in answering his own question. "To the extent that the capital and the skilled people would not be in the country otherwise . . . and . . . their presence does not simply replace domestic capital and skills that would otherwise exist," host governments realize a net gain in taxable capacity (263). Of course, in many real world situations the individuals envisaged by Johnson and their activities have been granted tax exemptions or reductions. In such cases gains from taxation and what can be done with them have become moot. Johnson recognized this and suggested that in such cases advantages have to be looked for in the participation of citizens in the activities under discussion (264).

Another benefit to the jurisdictions hosting offshore activities was the provision of employment to the total population (264). Johnson spoke of various opportunities for unskilled workers, but he also recognized the potential for more sophisticated pursuits. He suggested that a financial sector aimed at more than local markets can make a valuable contribution to development by offering a market for what skilled people can do and devoting resources to the improvement of the knowledge and ability of those who are hired (264). He felt that such opportunities would require a strengthening of the educational system so as to turn out graduates capable of performing jobs in financial institutions (264–265). He realized as well that a certain amount of social and political pressure might be needed to encourage foreign financial institutions to hire local residents and provide them with further training (265).

Johnson felt that host nations could also benefit through possible effects on the welfare of their citizens as actual or potential capitalists. He saw the potential for capital gains for landowners supplying land for office and apartment construction. Such gains could be reinvested in other pursuits, thus contributing to employment and growth. The financial sector might also provide citizens with safer and higher yielding outlets for savings, thus contributing to capital accumulation (265). The financial sector might also make financing available to local entrepreneurs on better terms than possible alternatives (265). Johnson also saw the financial sector as a stimulus to business tourism, with consequent benefits to the economy (266).

Even when particular jurisdictions do enjoy benefits of the sort referred to by Johnson, they are hardly free from the risk of altered fortunes. Offshore financial activities may lack continuing reliability as a developmental base (McKee, 1988, 80). "By the successful establishment of an offshore banking center, a Third World nation may place itself at risk from events in the world economy or from the actions of more powerful nations" (80).

Although this appears to have remained true, it seems as though powerful nations may well have something to gain from offshore financial centers to the extent that such centers tend to facilitate the operations of the global economy. Of course, the mere existence of expanding cadres of individual and corporate clients for the services offered in offshore financial centers speaks to the ongoing strength of the demand side of the market for offshore services. Those services are facilitators of economic linkages on a global scale.

Among the facilitators of the activities of individuals and corporations in the international economy are cadres of business services that have become internationalized in their own right. Many such services are finding it expedient to establish outlets for their offerings in offshore financial centers. In so doing they increase the importance of such centers in the global economy. Among the services in question are those offered by the major international accounting firms.

Various major accounting firms and the services offered by them will be highlighted in discussions of specific jurisdictions. However, at this juncture example firms and their offerings will be reviewed as a means of foreshadowing what is to come. One such organization is NEXIA International, "a network of independent accounting firms in more than 70 countries on six continents worldwide" (Clifton Gunderson L.L.C., 1998b). As explained by that firm, "Through our international relationships, you can utilize the resources of one of the world's largest accounting organizations while maintaining local relationships and reliability. We make the connection for you and then act as international liaison" (1998b).

That quotation appears to go to the heart of what major accounting firms or organizations are capable of doing on the international scene. What the largest firms can accomplish with international cooperation through branch offices and local subsidiaries can also be addressed by international networks or organizations of cooperating local and regional firms. Clearly, accounting firms have become major facilitators in the global economy.

Clifton Gunderson L.L.C., through its affiliation with NEXIA International, provides a whole menu of management advisory services, tax services and audit and accounting services to international clients (1998b). Their corporate finance group has been serving client needs in various areas such as target searching, analyzing purchase prices, performing due diligence, and various other financial services in the area of international transactions (1998b). In the consulting field they aim towards assisting companies in meeting quality goals by helping them to understand and improve processes (1998b). "Process improvement increases profitability through the improvement of productivity, product and service quality, and customer and employee satisfaction" (1998b).

The firm is also active in offering assistance on international tax matters and can help with international accounting and auditing issues. "Because accounting standards differ from one country to another, companies with international operations need a CPA firm experienced in various international requirements" (1998b). All in all, the firm claims to offer a comprehensive range of international consulting services.

Grant Thornton International is another major accounting firm on the world scene. It claims to be "one of the world's leading organizations of independent national firms providing audit, accounting, tax and specialist business advice to young entrepreneurial companies" (1998). Their "member firms employ over 18,500 people in 550 offices, in 87 countries around the world dedicated to the needs of growth-oriented business" (1998).

In describing what they do the firm appears to be quite confident: "Our portfolio of core accounting, audit, tax and consultancy services is enriched with our knowledge of economic conditions, regulatory requirements and an insight into different local business cultures and practices" (1998). With even more emphasis they have stated, "We are a vital partner when our clients enter new and unfamiliar markets" (1998). Such statements point to what the current authors expect of major accounting firms in the international sphere.

Yet another prominent accounting firm is Moore Stephens International, which is a network of over 100 accounting and consulting firms with more than 250 offices in 65 countries (Moore Stephens International, 1998). "A wide range of professional services has been developed by member firms over the 85 years since Moore Stephens was first founded to assist clients in meeting their cross-border commercial objectives" (1998). Such offerings are "complemented by local services in each country" (1998).

Part II

Offshore Financial Centers and the Major Accounting Firms in Regional Contexts

Chapter 4

The Firms in Selected Caribbean and North Atlantic Centers

In terms of the hosting of offshore financial centers, the Caribbean basin region could almost be considered an impacted area. No doubt its positioning vis-à-vis the two continents of the Western Hemisphere has something to do with that, as does a user-friendly time zone relationship to the New York financial center. Beyond those concerns is the fact that many of the jurisdictions in question are present or former British colonies and thus share language, laws and customs that may seem attractive to the English-speaking world.

The jurisdictions in question are relatively small in terms of population and exhibit a wide range of characteristics and degrees of involvement in offshore activities. Panama, which was once a relatively important banking center, has declined in importance in recent years due in part to machinations revolving around political events. Aruba and the Netherlands Antilles have also experienced declines in importance due to changes in tax arrangements with the United States (McKee, Garner and AbuAmara McKee, 1998).

Among English-speaking jurisdictions, the Bahamas and the Cayman Islands stand out as major loci for international banking activities. Bermuda is well known as a center for captive insurance. Antigua and Barbuda, and Barbados are making serious strides in expanding offshore activities. The jurisdictions enumerated in this paragraph are hardly all inclusive of real and would-be offshore financial centers in the Western Hemisphere. They will be highlighted here in hopes of reaching a better understanding of the actual role of major accounting firms in such jurisdictions.

ANTIGUA AND BARBUDA

Antigua and Barbuda is a small twin-island state situated in the Lee-ward Islands of the Caribbean. Although independent since 1981, the country operates under English Common Law. This legal tradition, coupled with other institutions dating from its days as a British colony, has contributed to the foundation that has made offshore finance an attainable option in the nation's search for economic development. Other supports for such a development strategy include good transportation and communications linkages, a literate labor force and a willingness on the part of the government to create an environment conducive to international business operations.

The nation's population stands at just under 70,000 and its workforce is employed primarily in tourism and commercial pursuits. "First rate professional services are widely available, including banking, law, accounting, and management resources" (Netforce Group Plc, 1998, 1).

While international banking has been in place for many years, offshore banking dates from 1983. The government has cooperated with the private sector in improving the offshore company and banking environment by introducing new foreign residency, trust and partnership legislation (2). "The prevailing offshore legislation provides for speedy formation of international business corporations (IBCs) at very competitive charges and with minimal compliance procedures" (2). Such formations can be dealt with by a locally registered trust company, or by an accountant or attorney.

The International Business Corporations Act of 1982 provides for "the full exemption of all direct taxes in respect of any international trading, investment or commercial activity including withholding taxes and stamp duties" (2). There is no minimum capital specification, and shares can have a nominal or no par value and can be issued in registered or bearer form (2). The charter of an IBC can be transferred to a foreign jurisdiction or vice versa and a trust company, lawyer or accountant for the corporation can serve as the only member of the board of directors (2).

The act establishes criminal penalties for disclosing the business affairs of clients in regard to banking or trust matters, with the exception of cases where evidence exists involving alleged criminal offenses triable in Antigua (2). IBCs are each required to have a registered office and an agent resident in the country (2).

KPMG is one of the major international accounting firms active in Antigua. In an overview the firm describes Antigua as an attractive offshore jurisdiction (KPMG Peat Marwick Antigua, 1997a, 1), claiming that it has put into place various features making it ideal for permanent residence in performing international business transactions. Antigua is tax free for permanent residents and companies incorporated under the International Business Corporation Act (1).

Among features offered by Antigua, KPMG lists a permanent resident scheme, confidentiality of information and minimum requirements for corporate reports. There are international business companies, exempt insurance companies, offshore banks and international trust companies. Other advantages include exemption from exchange controls, tax exemption from all forms of taxation on profits or gains and from withholding taxes on dividends, interest, management fees and royalties (1).

The firm enumerates the types of advantages they see for potential users of Antigua as an offshore center. Among such advantages are an excellent infrastructure, which includes state-of-the-art telecommunications, modern international transportation facilities boasting daily flights to major international business centers in the United States, Canada and the United Kingdom, and a time zone convenient to both North America and Europe (2). Also mentioned were a highly literate English-speaking population, political and economic stability, reasonably priced office facilities and world-standard accommodation facilities (2). The firm also alluded to an excellent professional community, an up-to-date corporate legal framework and competent judicial system and a choice of major international chartered accounting firms (2).

KPMG offers an extensive menu of corporate services in Antigua. Its corporate services practice offers professional services relating to the establishment, maintenance, administration and cessation of business entities in Antigua (1997b, 1). Services related to the establishment of business are extensive. The firm can assist in various ways on matters of incorporation and registration. It can also appoint directors and a secretary to the company and arrange the first meeting of directors to complete all formalities of formation. Beyond that the firm can provide registered shareholders and can issue certificates, transfers and declarations of trust for registered shareholders. It can arrange directors and shareholders meetings, file for obtaining the appropriate license, appoint bankers and open bank accounts and maintain statutory registers and records (1).

With respect to maintenance, the firm can maintain a registered office, maintain corporate records required by the laws of Antigua and provide corporate secretarial, advisory and compliance services (2). It can apply for the renewal of annual licenses and coordinate annual shareholder meetings and periodic meetings of directors (2). In general it can assist in assuring that client firms remain in good standing and in compliance with relevant statutory provisions in Antigua (2).

In the area of administration the firm can make arrangements for the provision of relocation support and for recruiting and orienting staff as well as for the provision of a business or mailing address (2). Beyond that it can arrange for the maintenance of day-to-day accounting records, for preparing and dispatching invoices and for the management and maintenance of bank accounts (2).

Arrangements can also be made for the banking of funds received as well as for the payment of the company's creditors and for the maintenance of company correspondence, faxes and telephone calls connected to company business (2). KPMG can also make arrangements for the preparation of periodic statements of cash movements, assets and liabilities and for monitoring the receipt of dividend, investment, rental and other types of income. Other arrangements that can be made include the provision of single office or shared office facilities and services, cessation as well as liquidation, emigration, or deregistration of companies or other entities (2).

In supplying traditional auditing and accounting services the firm employs professionals with extensive knowledge of national, regional and international financial markets and expertise in risk analysis (KPMG, 1997c, 1). Beyond auditing the firm also provides additional value-added services. As an example it can identify key matters impacting the reliability of financial information generated and can also assess the adequacy of computerized information systems. It can help with suitable accounting and internal control measures and can provide specialized assistance in accounting, finance and tax areas (1). It can offer advice on organizational and market issues and information technology and can also perform investigations (1).

The firm can conduct audits and reviews related to various business operations and can perform compliance reviews. It can assist in the development of internal audit departments and can train management and employees in matters relating to finance and accounting. Beyond those areas of service it can assist in the preparation of "share offers, prospectuses, and company information for the placement of shares" (1).

KPMG also offers extensive tax-related services in Antigua. The firm provides advisory services targeted to client needs, "taking into consideration both local and foreign tax regimes, and indicating the likely taxation consequences of proposed transactions" (1997d, 2). The firm also conducts reviews of client's structures from the point of view of taxation and geared to changes in legislation (2).

Price Waterhouse is another major accounting firm active in Antigua. In that jurisdiction the firm deals in services that include auditing, accounting, tax, management consulting and corporate secretarial and trustee services (Price Waterhouse, 1991a, 100). As noted elsewhere, the firm boasts a client roster that draws from businesses of all sizes and forms as well as from government agencies, nonprofit organizations and individuals (McKee, Garner and AbuAmara McKee, 1998, 36). The firm claims "notable experience in providing services to the hospitality, manufacturing, agricultural, banking, insurance, construction and service industries, whether as onshore business or offshore investments" (Price Waterhouse, 1991a, 100–101).

In addition to basic auditing and accounting services, "the firm offers assistance with respect to the design and/or review of internal control systems, including reviews of computerized systems" (McKee, Garner and AbuAmara McKee, 1998, 36). The firm deals with various tax-related matters as well as issues concerning mergers and acquisitions, and project evaluation. It can also conduct feasibility studies, which may embrace financial planning and budgeting. Among other forms of assistance offered by Price Waterhouse are executive recruitment services and various services concerned with information technology (see McKee, Garner and AbuAmara McKee, 1998, 36).

Within the context of the present discussion it seems pertinent to note that Price Waterhouse can assist with corporate administration in support of offshore companies, "including the assumption of the duties of a local agent and dealing with staff supervision, reinvoicing and banking needs" (36). This of course speaks to how deeply involved such a firm can become in offshore business matters. Indeed, the firm can advise on all aspects of offshore business (36).

THE BAHAMAS

Among the offshore financial centers of the Western Hemisphere, the Bahamas is the closest geographically to the mainland of the United States. Lying southeast of Florida, the nation is composed of some 700 islands, fewer than 30 of which are inhabited. Internet Bahamas Limited sees that location as offering easy access to the consumer markets of North, Central and South America (1998, 1).

Although the nation is recognized in most circles as an important offshore business and financial center, its financial sector is second in importance to tourism in terms of its significance to the economy. The government has expressed an interest in economic diversification through developing agriculture and industry, but little growth is anticipated in such undertakings (*Bahamas: Economic Trends and Outlook*, 1998, 1). The reasons given include "government inertia, domestic resistance to outside investment perceived as potentially competitive with local business, high labor costs, and competition from other countries in the region" (1).

In 1994 the country hosted 3.4 million visitors, which was more than 13 times its permanent population (1). "Tourism and related services account for over 60 percent of GDP supplying the Bahamian job market, directly and indirectly, with two thirds of the jobs in the Bahamas" (1).

Financial services accounted for approximately 11 percent of GDP (2).

In 1993 the country boasted 415 licensed banks and trust companies as well as five retail banks (1). In 1990 the International Business Companies Act was passed with the intent to enhance the nation's status as a leading financial center (2). It served to facilitate the incorporation of offshore companies and cut associated costs. "By mid-1994 24,200 IBCs—shell corporations . . . had been formed" (2). In 1991 the nation legalized the formation of asset protection trusts, vehicles designed to protect the assets of wealthy persons from domestic courts in their home countries (2).

Internet Bahamas Limited lists various investment factors related to a climate for business (1998, 2). Prominent among such factors is the tax-free status accorded to income. All resident corporations, partnerships, individuals and trusts are free from taxes on corporate earnings, capital gains, personal income, sales, inheritance and dividends (2). Another attraction for investors is economic and monetary stability.

The Bahamian dollar is pegged one to one to the United States dollar. Beyond the features alluded to above the government provides investment incentives such as relief from customs duties on approved raw materials, equipment and building supplies, and exemptions from business licenses and real property taxes for as many as 20 years (2). In the area of exchange control there are no restrictions on current account transactions, nor are there restrictions on the repatriation of profits (3).

Price Waterhouse is among the major accounting firms active in the Bahamas, where it "offers traditional accounting and auditing services as well as management and financial consulting services both domestically and internationally" (McKee, Garner and AbuAmara McKee, 1998, 35). The firm also serves smaller clients, nonprofit organizations, individuals and government agencies (Price Waterhouse, 1992a, 119).

Through its audits Price Waterhouse reviews "the adequacy of the client's system of international accounting controls and the effectiveness of its accounting procedures and presents suggestions to strengthen these systems and procedures" (120).

The firm offers a wide range of business services. It offers assistance in developing corporate plans and strategies and in choosing computer systems. It can also assist with financial restructuring and with mergers and acquisitions. It can provide investment and trade advisory services and advisory services to government, including help with privatization (120–121). It can conduct organization and personnel management studies and can assist with the recruitment of managerial and staff personnel. Beyond recruitment the firm can perform evaluation and compensation studies and can help with employee development and training.

Price Waterhouse also provides corporate services such as "arranging for the incorporation of companies or other entities, including trusts; providing registered office, registered agent and trustee services and dealing with the necessary ongoing administration and accounting for entities" (121). Beyond such matters it assists firms in establishing operations in the Bahamas or in using that country as a base for foreign operations (121).

Deloitte & Touche is another major accounting firm active in the Bahamas. It claims to have eight resident partners and provides accounting services to both foreign and domestic clients, employing international accounting standards (Deloitte Touche Tohmatsu International, 1994, 63). Beyond such matters the firm offers various consulting services as well as company management and representative office maintenance. "The firm has special expertise in the administration of foreign-owned businesses, liquidations and receiverships, and mergers and acquisitions" (63).

BARBADOS

Barbados is another Caribbean jurisdiction that has been making progress in the hosting of offshore financial activities. In a recent article Owen Arthur, the nation's prime minister, asserted that "throughout the decade of the nineties a truly considerable effort has been undertaken by both the private and public sectors to transform the production relationships of the Barbados economy" (1997, 85). Describing this effort at structural adjustment, he saw Phase One as including liberalization, deregulation and measures to boost productivity and competitiveness at its center.

The first phase of the restructuring process also included a phased removal of restrictions on financial markets, the dismantling of price controls and import licensing, comprehensive tax reforms, trade liberalization and privatization (85). Other programs were instituted to boost competitiveness and emphasize productivity as a tool for economic progress (85). According to Arthur, the overall intent was the adoption of "an open, outward looking export oriented approach to the management of . . . economic affairs" (85).

In emphasizing the intent of the new measures Arthur was both clear and definite: "one of the major challenges of economic management is to continue to define the package of policies to enhance their efficiency and effectiveness in the context of rapidly changing domestic and global economic and financial circumstances" (86). In the same vein Arthur suggested that the first phase of structural adjustment was designed to create conditions with which an economy that was too overregulated, too inward looking, too unresponsive to technological change, too resistant to the best practices in institutional and corporate organization and too state led could be made into a dynamic, open and outward-oriented, modern, competitive economy, able to survive and prosper because of its response to stimuli and its acceptance of drastic, far-reaching changes across the board (87).

KPMG is very active in Barbados. Among the areas on its menu of facilitative offerings are assurance and accounting services, consulting services, corporate and financial services and tax services. "Established in 1973, KPMG Barbados is today owned and managed by seven partners and employs 90 persons. Local business operations have expanded to include branch offices in Castries, St. Lucia and St. John's, Antigua" (KPMG, 1997a, 1). The firm operates through KPMG Peat Marwick, which is responsible for assurance, accounting, tax and corporate services; and Peat Marwick Associates Ltd., which operates as KPMG Peat Marwick Consulting Group and provides general financial and consulting services (2).

In the area of assurance and accounting services KPMG Peat Marwick "is committed to responding comprehensively, positively, and in a timely manner to the myriad changes taking place in the assurance profession in Barbados and globally" (KPMG, 1997b). The firm employs qualified professionals, with extensive knowledge of national, regional and international markets, together with expertise relating to risk analysis.

With respect to value-added services, the firm can identify key factors impacting the reliability of financial information generated. It can assess the adequacy of computerized information systems and can provide specialized assistance in accounting, finance and tax areas (1997b). In addition, the firm stands ready to review, recommend and implement suitable administrative, accounting and international control measures, and can conduct audits and reviews related to the acquisition, liquidation, sale, merger and valuation of businesses (1997b). It can perform special investigations and compliance reviews and can assist in the development of internal audit departments. The firm can advise on organizational and market issues as well as on information technology (1997b). The firm is also willing to train management and employees in financial and accounting matters and can help in preparing share offers, prospectuses and company information for the placement of shares (1997b).

"KPMG's Consulting Group provides services to assist clients in formulating and implementing strategies which impact positively upon their corporate performance" (KPMG, 1997c, 1). The firm can assist in improving efficiency with respect to meeting customer demand through enhancing internal systems and processes with a view to achieving lower costs, better quality and reduced cycle time (1). It can also help in the application of technologies to maximize operational and financial efficiency.

In the realm of strategic financial management the firm provides financial advisory services and financial management. It deals with strategy as well as with privatization and with economic impacts and policy advice (1). In the area of performance improvement the firm deals with resource and operations management, change management and human resource management (1–2). With respect to enabling technologies, the firm can assist with information technology, strategy and architecture that involves aligning technology and business goals and also systems selection and implementation. Enabling technologies also include technology and information risk management and emerging technologies, which include groupware, data warehousing and business intelligence (2).

KPMG's corporate and financial services include establishment, maintenance, administration and cessation (KPMG, 1997d). Since extensive detailing of such offerings has been provided earlier in this chapter with respect to similar activities in Antigua, details will not be repeated at this juncture.

"The Tax Practice at KPMG Peat Marwick involves, but is not limited to, providing clients with professional services relating to tax compliance, tax planning, tax consulting and tax support services" (KPMG, 1997e, 1). In the compliance area the firm prepares both corporate and individual returns, reviews assessment notices and prepares value-added tax returns. Among tax consulting services offered by the firm are the implementation of tax information systems, the conducting of special projects and the assessment of alternative proposals. Beyond such matters the firm assists with evaluating or developing proposals to achieve desired ends and also with the development and preparation of position papers. It can also advise on courses of action and help with tax opinions (1).

In the tax planning area the firm can "provide services as well as information relating to local and foreign legislative changes which impact upon corporate and estate tax planning, and personal tax and financial planning" (1). The intent is to help with corporate objectives and minimize an enterprise's total tax burden. The firm can insure the client's awareness of the tax impact on cross-border transactions. It can also assist in the avoidance of double taxation, help to minimize the impact of government restrictions, and help clients to maintain their flexibility in meeting changes in tax and other government regulations (1). Tax support services include assistance with appeals and objections, litigation support, guidance during tax audits and tax training for employees (1).

Deloitte & Touche is another major accounting firm operating in Barbados, where it has been active in the nation's offshore financial sector (McKee, Garner and AbuAmara McKee, 1998, 36). Indeed, the firm professes to have been "a leader in attracting overseas investors who have formed international business companies, exempt insurance firms, offshore banks and foreign sales corporations" (Deloitte Touche Tohmatsu

International, 1996a). The firm stands ready to help its clients with incorporation, the generation of corporate directors, fiduciary administration and operating support (1996a).

Price Waterhouse is also actively involved in Barbados where they offer a wide menu of services. Areas covered include auditing, accounting, tax management consulting and corporate secretarial and trustee services (1994, 120). "Its clients include businesses of all forms and sizes, government agencies, nonprofit organizations, and individuals, and it is organized so that decisions affecting clients are made by partners, who have full professional authority" (120). The firm claims notable experience with respect to providing services within the hospitality, manufacturing, banking, insurance, construction and service industries (120–121). It provides such services to both onshore businesses and offshore investments (121).

A specific breakdown of services offered by the firm covers statutory and nonstatutory audits, special reports and valuations as well as accounting. Beyond those areas the firm is willing to assist with the design or review of internal control systems, including reviews of computerized systems (121). Price Waterhouse can also assist with personal and corporate income tax compliance and can offer advice on and reviews of direct and indirect taxes and tax planning (121).

The firm also offers advice and assistance with respect to mergers and acquisitions and can assist with project evaluation and management. It can perform feasibility studies, including financial planning and budgeting and it also offers information technology consulting. This last offering includes system design, selection and implementation, software sales and support, local area network installation and support and data security reviews (121).

Price Waterhouse offers "corporate administration in support of offshore companies, including acting as local agent and dealing with staff supervision, reinvoicing and banking needs" (121). The firm can assist with executive recruitment and offers advice on all aspects of offshore business in Barbados. It assists with insolvency and deals in trustee and trust administration services. It can arrange the incorporations of companies and offer corporate secretarial services and general business advisory services (121).

BERMUDA

Bermuda is yet another jurisdiction in the Western Hemisphere that has become very active as a locus for offshore business activities. Lying in the western Atlantic some 580 miles east of North Carolina, it is a self-governing colony of the United Kingdom. Its legal system is based upon English Common Law. English is its official language, and its currency, the Bermuda dollar, is at par with the United States dollar. The latter currency is predominant in the international business sector (Molyneux and Storie, 1998, 5).

According to Keith and Lois Forbes, the international business industry has exceeded tourism as Bermuda's biggest revenue earner (Forbes' Bermuda on Line, 1995–1996, 1). That industry, or subsector of the economy, includes such activities as captive insurance, reinsurance investment, shipping and other international companies (1). Beyond those activities the international business sector includes aircraft and ship registration and leasing, collective investment plans, foreign sales corporations, international arbitration, trusts, professional services for international business, as well as intellectual property and software (1).

All of the activities referred to above have come to be considered as the financial services industry. This is the collective name for the "establishment or incorporation or registration and servicing in Bermuda of a large number of business-partnerships and bodies corporate—not owned or operated by Bermudians, falling within the exempted companies category," as well as "the regulation and other servicing, on a comprehensive local and international scale, of their partnership and corporate requirements, as well as those of their principals, by a number of highly specialized Bermudian based businesses" (2).

The Forbeses supply a substantial listing of factors making Bermuda attractive to the international business community. Included are such things as proximity to the United States and links to the United Kingdom. With respect to the United Kingdom, they emphasize a link to the Bank of England and participation in European Union business. They point out that Bermuda is a designated territory under the United Kingdom's Financial Services Act. This they feel "ensures the very highest standards of financial management and responsibility" (2). They see the linkages listed here as helping Bermuda-based companies to enter into the European Union.

The authors see their jurisdiction as a bridge between North America and Europe. By this they mean that Bermuda is ideal for United States corporations with investments in Europe that can be managed from Bermuda (2). They also see advantages for European companies with massive investments in North America. Indeed, they see Bermuda as geopolitically significant for Asian or Middle-East companies with major investments in North America and Europe (2). Of course, such advantages, where they exist, are presumably among those that have made offshore financial centers popular.

The authors present Bermuda as a place to be enjoyed. Specifically, they refer to excellent communications and telecommunications as well as relationships with accountants, bankers and law firms (2). Beyond such matters they speak of an environment supportive of an excellent quality of life (3). In terms of business dealings, corporate personnel can get "practically any type of work done in Bermuda for affiliated or subsidiary or parent companies in the USA, Canada, Europe, or any other overseas jurisdiction" (3).

Other advantages include confidentiality, freedom from unnecessary regulations, political stability and integrity (3). The economy boasts a well-qualified infrastructure of imported and local professionals as well as a well-educated, stable, business-oriented workforce (3). Professional and trade associations cooperate in ensuring that employers and employees are responsive to the needs of industry (3).

Evidence that the advantages alluded to by the Forbeses are real can be seen in the fact that Bermuda hosts many multinational business organizations, including 84 of the top *Fortune* 100 and a similar representation of British, European, Far Eastern and Hong Kong equivalents (4). "Parents, subsidiaries or affiliates of prominent Bermuda-registered companies can now be found in every major city in the USA, Canada, Britain, Europe, Middle East and Far East" (4). By the end of 1995 there were 8,600 international companies registered in Bermuda. Bermuda is the world's largest market for captive insurance companies, hosting about 65 percent of some 3,700 captives worldwide (4).

Among major accounting firms operating in Bermuda is Ernst & Young. Ernst & Young Bermuda offers services in the areas of auditing and management consulting and information services. Beyond those areas the firm also offers actuarial services, tax services, fund administration and corporate recovery and insolvency (Ernst & Young Bermuda, 1997).

In the auditing area, in addition to traditional accounting services, the firm conducts careful analyses of client businesses with an eye to identifying areas of potential risk. The intent of the firm is to communicate more effectively with management and to develop client service objectives that will enhance the benefits to be gained from audits (1997).

Management consulting and information services offered by the firm cover a wide range of concerns. Included are business process reengineering and capacity planning consulting for short-term performance resolution as well as for long-term system resource planning (1997). The firm can also assist in the planning of computer utilization and information technology planning for firms needing assistance with their technology infrastructure (1997).

Actuarial services include loss reserve analysis and rate analysis. Beyond those concerns the firm can conduct feasibility studies and provide insurance and reinsurance company appraisals. It can supply financial modeling and reporting and can conduct strategic and feasibility studies (1997). It can assist with product development and risk management, and can provide second opinions and conduct dynamic financial analysis. It also renders loss reserve opinions and can help with mergers and acquisitions (1997).

"Ernst & Young maintains a full-service tax practice which offers a range of tax-related and business advisory services" (1997). The firm provides tax services to their audit clients as well as to businesses and other entities that are not audit clients. It also offers its tax services to individuals (1997).

Through Fund Administration Services (Bermuda) Ltd., an incorporated company owned by the partners of Ernst & Young, fund accounting and administration services are offered to investment funds domiciled in Bermuda as well as in various other offshore jurisdictions (1997). Among services provided are calculating and distributing NAVs worldwide, as well as calculating and disbursing incentive and management fees and other operating expenses (1997). Other services include maintaining offshore bank accounts and offshore general ledgers, handling subscriptions and redemptions and communicating with existing and potential investors (1997). The firm can also provide directors and act as share registrar and transfer agent. It can prepare financial statements, distribute offering documents and work with multi-currency accounting (1997). It can also provide liaisons with offshore bankers, lawyers and accountants (1997).

"Ernst & Young offers comprehensive corporate recovery and insolvency services" (1997). The firm's partners have acted as liquidators to various insurance and reinsurance companies. The firm has dealt with other receiverships and liquidation assignments involving restaurants and finance companies (1997).

KPMG is another major accounting firm active in Bermuda. That firm sees itself as "the global leader in international public accounting and consulting firms" with "an unrivaled network of offices worldwide" (KPMG, 1997g). It was the first international accounting firm to set up an office in Bermuda and now has nine partners and a staff of over 100 in that jurisdiction (1997g).

The firm provides auditing services in accord with generally accepted accounting principles and statutory accounting regulations (1997g). It deals with standards in vogue in Canada, the United States and the United Kingdom as well as with International Standards. Beyond such service expertise the firm advises on governmental filings and prospectuses and performs internal accounting controls evaluations (1997g). It assists with internal audit functions and performs audits with respect to acquisitions, mergers and stock exchange listings (1997g). It can also provide forensic accounting services and litigation support.

The firm can advise on accounting and financial management as well as matters pertaining to taxation. Its tax services include specialized expertise for the captive insurance industry, a very important component of the international business service sector of the Bermudan economy. That expertise pertains to all aspects of United States taxation. The firm also provides United States tax consulting services to United States investors in corporations, partnerships and trusts in Bermuda and can also provide United States tax services to expatriates (1997g).

KPMG also offers management and actuarial services in Bermuda. "We provide essential support to our international clients in the form of day-to-day administration services and local representation" (1997g). Among actuarial service offerings are loss reserve analysis and certification, pricing of new and existing products, captive feasibility studies and capital adequacy reviews. The firm can also provide profit analysis for both reinsurance and captive exposures (1997g).

The firm is also involved in information technology and EDP consulting. Their services deal with office automation, accounting, communication or network services. In the case of new projects they "can provide full support from the initial planning phase, through evaluation to final implementation and confidence testing" (1997g). They are committed to supplying objective, knowledgeable advice over a wide range of hardware and software products (1997g).

The firm can also offer assistance with corporate recovery, liquidations and receiverships. They are prepared to help with executive selection and can also assist with acquisitions and mergers, disposals and valuations.

THE CAYMAN ISLANDS

The Cayman Islands are yet another Caribbean jurisdiction recognized worldwide as a major offshore financial center. The reasons for the attractiveness of the jurisdiction have been highlighted in detail earlier in the current volume (Chapter 3) and need not be redetailed here. Beyond offshore activities tourism represents the other main source of economic strength for the islands (Columbus Group Plc, 1998). The islands support little agriculture and thus must import the bulk of their food requirements.

The Cayman Islands are located about 180 miles northwest of Jamaica, with the main island, Grand Cayman, situated about 450 miles south of Florida. The population has been estimated at 33,600 (1998). As was suggested earlier, the Cayman Islands connection to Great Britain, together with the use of English Common Law and state-of-the-art transportation and communications linkages, has given the economy an attractive base with which to generate offshore business activity (Chapter 3).

Among major accounting firms operating in the Cayman Islands is Deloitte & Touche. With four partners and a staff of 40, the firm boasts as clients overseas individuals and corporations as well as key local businesses in such pursuits as banking, insurance, the construction of investment funds, real estate, tourism and transportation (Deloitte Touche Tohmatsu International, 1995).

Its range of services includes, of course, the accounting area within which it deals with data processing as well as normal accounting pursuits. The firm "provides compilations of financial statements and makes other presentations and offers advice on the choice and applicability of accounting principles and methods" (McKee, Garner and AbuAmara McKee, 1998, 37). Of course, the firm performs audits and can review agreed-upon procedures with respect to the financial statements of clients (37).

In the management consulting area the firm offers assistance with information technology, notably in the selection, procurement and implementation of appropriate computer packages. It deals in forensics and litigation and can provide expert witness services. Deloitte & Touche Cayman Islands offers corporate and trust services through its fully licensed trust company, RHB Trust Co. Ltd. (Deloitte Touche Tohmatsu International, 1995). The firm can assist with the formation and administration of companies, trusts and offshore investment funds. Beyond such pursuits the firm offers company secretarial work, oversees compliance with local legal requirements and assistance with maintaining statutory records and providing local trustees and directors (1995). "Deloitte & Touche is further diversifying its practice—with particular attention to management consulting and corporate recovery—to better serve both blue-chip multinational and new locally generated businesses" (1995).

KPMG Peat Marwick is another major international accounting firm with operations in the Cayman Islands, where its "office specializes in providing auditing and accounting services, in particular to the offshore banking and insurance industries" (KPMG Peat Marwick, 1991, 27). As noted elsewhere, "The firm . . . has a separate corporate management department that is aimed at assisting offshore companies" (McKee, Garner and AbuAmara McKee, 1998, 38).

The firm can arrange for incorporation and can establish the registered office of the company and can also set up and maintain required corporate records and registers (38). It can also provide officers for the companies, such as a company secretary or other authorized signatories to implement the operational, banking or investment instructions of clients (KPMG Peat Marwick, 1991, 27). The firm is also prepared to supply proxy holders for directors and shareholders for holding annual meetings as required by law.

The firm can provide nominee shareholders and directors, assuming that there is no conflict with professional independence requirements, SEC or other regulations in the latter case (27). Of course, the firm can provide a full range of traditional accounting services. Other services offered include "the registration of ships and yachts in the Cayman Islands; U.S. international tax practice, both personal and corporate; and U.S. personal financial planning" (McKee, Garner and AbuAmara McKee, 1998, 38).

A FINAL OVERVIEW

The jurisdictions that have been discussed in this chapter are relatively small and must rely upon international linkages for their material welfare. All are either former or present British colonies and all have inherited British legal and/or governmental institutions and, of course, the use of the English language. They have all made transitions from earlier economic and strategic foundations and have elected international financial operations as major elements of their economies.

The operations of the major accounting firms in those jurisdictions, especially as they pertain to international concerns, are in some measure an indication of economic success and further potential since the firms are known to choose their locations in order to best serve their diverse business clientele. No attempt is made here to generalize what has been found to various other real or would-be financial centers in the Western Hemisphere. Instead, the authors are content to present their findings for what they are worth in providing an addition to the understanding of the jurisdictions that have been highlighted and, of course, of the contribution of various accounting firms that they host.

Chapter 5

The Firms in Selected
European Centers

In this chapter the emphasis turns to Europe and the Mediterranean. Europe has been prominent in offshore financial circles for some time, highlighted by activities taking place in Switzerland, Liechtenstein and various other continental centers. Such centers will not be the focus of the present investigation since their business climates and the roles of the firms they house are rather well known. Instead, various smaller, perhaps less visible jurisdictions will be highlighted.

Those chosen include the Channel Islands, the Isle of Man, Cyprus, Gibraltar and Malta. In examining those jurisdictions the intent will be to highlight the current role and prospects for major accounting firms in the types of offshore financial centers that are emerging today.

THE CHANNEL ISLANDS

Writing in October of 1990, *Offshore Investment* described Jersey as one of the world's oldest tax havens and Guernsey as a relatively latecomer as a major offshore financial center (1990, 25–26). Lying off the northwest coast of France, those islands are the largest among the Channel Island group that also include Sark and Alderney. Jersey with its area of 45 square miles boasts a population in the 85,000 range, while Guernsey with 24 square miles hosts a population of 60,000. Both Jersey and Guernsey have good air links to the United Kingdom and are linked to France by a local carrier. Walter and Dorothy Diamond report direct flight linkage between Jersey and Paris, Brussels, Amsterdam, Frankfurt and Dusseldorf (1998, 36).

The Baltic Banking Group describes Jersey as one of the world's foremost offshore centers with a long history of security and stability (1998). In supporting that contention they explain that the authorities seek only the cream of offshore business and that Jersey has a "highly sophisticated infrastructure of trust companies, banking services, accountants, lawyers, etc." (1998). The same organization suggests that Guernsey is also highly respected in the world's financial circles (1998).

The economies of both islands are highly dependent upon finance center activities, although tourism, agriculture, horticulture, fishing and light industry do have minor impacts (Diamond and Diamond, 1998, 35).[1] In Jersey the financial sector accounts for 43 percent of income, while in Guernsey it has reached 51 percent (35).

Because of their long standing association with the United Kingdom, both Jersey and Guernsey benefit from some of the basic rules of the European Community (35). The Maastricht Treaty of 1991 made dramatic changes in the fiscal and economic relations between the members of that community but the islands retained their special status. They have been able to remain offshore vis-à-vis Europe and the United Kingdom with respect to taxation, immigration and financial services (35).

"The Channel Islands' relationship with the European Community is a special one, laid down in the third protocol to the Treaty of Accession of the United Kingdom (Roper, 1990, 28). Roper went on to explain that the Islands were within the Common Customs area and the Common Tariff, thus having access to European Community nations for physical exports but without tariff barriers (28). According to Roper, for all purposes other than customs vis-à-vis the European Community the Islands are effectively "third countries" (28).

Richard Rowe, writing about Guernsey, suggested that the jurisdiction had many companies providing a wide range of trustee management, financial and corporate planning and secretarial and administrative services (1990, 34). Companies supplying such services included international accountants, banks and other organizations as well as independent specialist corporate administrators (34). Rowe recognized that international accountants and banks have the benefit of global connections but are frequently constrained by territorial presence, especially in the face of certain trading and confidential considerations (34).

Expanding his point, Rowe pointed to the inflexibility of large organizations in the face of internal rules, suggesting the advantage of independent corporate and trust management companies who "are often able to offer an unbiased, highly personalized and confidential service to their personal and corporate clients" (34–35).

Trust managers can aid in incorporating both resident and non-resident companies both within Guernsey and elsewhere (35). Beyond that they can arrange registered offices, nominate share holders and directors and can assist in ensuring that both domestic and foreign rules and laws are followed. They can also offer management, financial, secretarial and accounting services to firms or their branches in Guernsey. They can also deal with matters related to trusts, including the appointment of trustees and investment and administration (35). Of course, the type of services alluded to by Rowe can often be provided by major accounting firms operating in various jurisdictions. Such firms operating in or through Guernsey and Jersey have the benefit of the stability that those jurisdictions enjoy through their association with the United Kingdom, coupled with their ability to act independently in all domestic and fiscal matters.

Deloitte & Touche are among the major accounting firms active in the Channel Islands. That firm has nearly 100 professional staff in Jersey, where it operates a fully resourced office capable of providing comprehensive tax, forensic and audit services. In their words, "By drawing on worldwide resources, we can advise on the following: preparation of business plans; advice on management buy-outs and other transactions; due diligence for acquisitions, both locally and internationally; advice and assistance for companies planning UK stock market flotations" (Deloitte & Touche, 1999, 2).

The firm provides companies of all sizes with what they consider to be a cost-effective audit service. "In addition to meeting the statutory requirements, our audit work makes a practical contribution to our clients' business success" (3). The firm encourages their audit teams to work for a wide range of clients, thus broadening their experience and helping them to offer "a highly commercial, risk-focused service" (3).

The firm is also quite active in tax work and provides companies with a full range of services, including compliance and help with international tax planning. They also provide comprehensive personal tax advice to high-net-worth individuals (3). In the area of forensic accounting the firm undertakes investigations and valuations. Their investigative activity includes the tracing of funds through international bank networks, while valuations include matrimonial, professional negligence and general commercial disputes (5). Beyond such services the firm also undertakes expert witness assignments (5). It reports that the authorities in Jersey often ask them to act for them in both criminal and civil cases (5).

"Wallbrook is the name used by Deloitte & Touche for companies in their ownership which provide corporate and trustee services" (6). Wallbrook offers a range of offshore services to meet the majority of financial situations, "with solutions that can be designed to suit individual client requirements" (6). Their group services include trust companies, corporate services companies, asset holding companies and executorships (6).

The firm offers company services to a wide range of business sectors, which include investment, investment management, general trading, consultancy, property, shipping and oil (8). The firm provides active management service for clients wishing to use Jersey as a base for investment. In such circumstances they work with investment professionals such as stockbrokers and market makers to ensure that investment objectives are met (8).

For property companies the firm can act in the purchase of land and property. It can handle financial negotiations and can appoint solicitors, agents and rent collectors. Indeed they stand ready to take charge in all areas of property administration, which include insurance arrangements, the payment of bills and local taxes, building maintenance and bookkeeping (9). For trading companies the firm stands ready to negotiate with group companies for the importation of goods (9). It can assist with import and export documentation and with the preparation of letters of credit (9). Beyond such matters the firm can act as a liaison with banks "for instance to ensure the timely transfer of funds worldwide" (9). The firm also stands ready to advise on trusts. It can help with trust structure and can undertake the related management and executor services. The firm has developed a wide range of trust instruments to meet differing needs and circumstances.

Another major accounting firm active in the Channel Islands is Ernst & Young, with offices in both Guernsey and Jersey. In Guernsey the firm provides accountancy services but also offers other forms of assistance such as business consultancy, statutory and secretarial services, tax planning and developing compliance and business plans (1998a, 1). The firm stands ready to assist businesses of all sizes on such matters (1).

In the audit area the firm aims at providing "a (financial statement) audit," covering "broader business risk issues, while also delivering insights and ideas that create advantages" (1). Areas frequently covered by the firm's audit department include reporting on financial statements, the evaluation of accounting, reporting and operational controls, ad hoc reporting and business valuations (1).

With respect to tax matters the firm is well versed in a wide range of issues and in particular "specializes in multinational tax planning and ensuring the smooth operation of offshore tax structures" (2). More specifically the firm deals with corporate tax planning, expatriate tax and location and organizational planning for group finance companies (2). It assists with maximizing tax treaty benefits, as well as with minimizing indirect taxes, including VAT and customs duties (2). It can help with structuring international groups and can offer compliance assistance, not to mention assistance in tax planning through trusts (2).

The corporate and trust division of the firm in Guernsey is the Monument Trust Company Limited. That firm deals with asset protection planning and corporate tax planning as well as personal financial planning. It also deals with property acquisition and yacht registration.

Ernst & Young in Jersey claims to be one of the island's leading professional service firms (1998a). In that setting it has combined an accountancy practice with a substantial trust company and tax consultancy. With a staff of 285 the firm deals in trust and company administration, local and international tax assistance, and audit and business consultancy work. It also offers an investment fund available to clients (1998a).

THE ISLE OF MAN

The Isle of Man is a self-governing dependent territory of Great Britain, lying in the Irish Sea. According to the Baltic Banking Group (1998), the Isle of Man is one of the few offshore areas that is part of the European Union for customs and VAT matters. "Although the Island itself is not an EU member, it is associated with the UK for VAT and customs purposes and a Isle of Man company can therefore be an ideal offshore vehicle for trading with the EU" (1998).

The First American Legal Corporation describes the island as perhaps the most politically stable of all offshore jurisdictions (1998). The island is self-governing with respect to internal administration and social and fiscal policies, while the United Kingdom handles external matters such as defense and foreign representation (1998). The legal system is based upon English Common Law, and the island is considered a low-tax jurisdiction.

The financial services sector is the largest subsector of the economy. The banking industry has been said to be dominated by branches and subsidiaries of the main British clearing banks, although many other banks are present as well (1998). According to the Diamonds, the Isle of Man boasts 45 banks, of which 12 have overseas parents. In addition to the banks, there are 58 deposit-taking and financial advisory firms and 48 trust companies (25). Bank deposits total in excess of two billion English pounds, and bank secrecy is guarded by common-law rules. A unique feature of the island's banking industry is the offer of deposit protection for 75 percent of the first 20,000 pounds (1998).

Beyond banking the island boasts a growing insurance sector with 15 life assurance companies (Isle of Man, 1998). That sector claims to have an increasing number of innovative and flexible products released onto the market for expatriates (1998). "There is a vast choice of schemes, policies and services available . . . including insurance protection, regular savings schemes, capital investments, pensions, stand alone investment funds, asset management, offshore personalized portfolio bonds and trusts" (1998).

The Diamonds acknowledge the importance of financial activities on the Isle but point to an industrial sector, which they also consider to be significant (1998, 23). The latter comprises woolen mills, together with other light industry, including precision engineering, food processing, plastics, laser optics and electronics (23). Products manufactured locally include printed circuits, thermometers, taxi meters, life jackets, briar pipes and leather motorcycle suits (23).

The island also offers ship registration services. According to the Baltic Banking Group, ships that are majority owned by companies or persons resident in the European Union and certain British dependent territories may apply for registration (1998). The island is not considered a flag of convenience, indeed its ship register is part of the British register. Fees are competitive and designed merely to cover costs. No annual tonnage taxes are levied (1998).

The Isle of Man boasts the first free-trade zone to be established in the British Isles (Diamond and Diamond, 1998, 37). Situated at Freeport, it dates from legislation passed in 1982 and 1983 (37). Activities to be permitted included warehousing, export processing, transshipment, assembly, sampling, packaging and labeling (37). The zone is still under development. The first company to operate there was DeBeers Consolidated Mines, which is building an industrial diamond processing plant (37).

One rather large accounting firm operating on the Isle of Man is Moore Stephens International. Although not in the top size group of firms, Moore Stephens International consists of a network of more than 100 independent accounting and consulting firms with over 250 offices in 65 countries. The firm offers a wide range of services through its offices on the Isle of Man and "can call upon a detailed understanding of financial matters, whatever they are—wherever they are" (1998a). The Isle of Man offices specialize in personal and corporate tax planning, trust administration, audit, accounting, captive insurance consulting, IT and management advisory services (1998a).

In the area of trust and company administration the firm offers wide ranging services to both local and international clients. It can assist clients in establishing suitable corporate structures and can deal with all statutory requirements, not to mention creating and servicing fully detailed accounting records. The firm also sets up and administers trusts.

The firm offers comprehensive audit and accounting services. It can give advice concerning the most tax-efficient structure as well as the accounting procedures, business administration, financial planning, cash flow and VAT (Moore Stephens, 1998c). With respect to information technology, it can advise on and put together computerized financial and management accounting systems (1998c). The firm can assist in the selection of the most appropriate hardware and software packages and can also project manage installations. Beyond such matters it offers customized database design (1998c).

The firm offers audit and consultancy services. Its audit approach places emphasis upon realistic planning throughout the audit assignment and offers sensible communications with the accounting staff in a manner designed to minimize disruption and inconvenience (1998c). The firm can also assess financial controls and procedures (1998c). Their audit plan "focuses attention on the key areas of the financial statements, minimizing the time and costs involved in fieldwork and providing constructive and prompt advice on those parts of the operation which have most impact on the successful running of the audit" (1998c).

They gain their audit evidence through analytical review, compliance testing, substantive testing and overall review (1998c). These procedures may point to problem areas and lead the firm to recommend further reviews (1998c). On the island the firm's entire professional staff are qualified members of the Institute of Chartered Accountants in England and Wales or "recognized bodies of similar standing, or are students undergoing approved training courses" (1998c).

Another major international association of chartered accountants active in the Isle of Man is Pannell Kerr Forster International Association. "PKF Worldwide is among the top business advisory organizations, measured by turnover and quality" (1995–1998). Formed in 1969 with four member firms, the association boasted more than 400 offices in 115 countries and a turnover of about $U.S.740 million in 1998 (1995–1998). The firms in the Association are legally independent of one another but offer services of qualified and uniform standards, adhered to by all PKF member firms.

Among principal professional service offerings are audit, accounting and tax assistance. Beyond those matters assistance is offered in the areas of corporate restructuring and corporate recovery and insolvency. Advice can be provided concerning mergers, acquisitions, public listings and management buyouts (1995–1998). In the area of management consultancy, services available include all aspects of financial consulting, human resources and information technology (1995–1998).

Pannell Kerr Forster Management Consultants is the management consulting arm of the organization. Since its emergence in 1970, it has been providing a wide range of services to both public and private sector clients (Pannell Kerr Forster, 1996–1998a). "The firm is entirely independent of any political, manufacturing or contracting interests" and can supply "objective consulting services . . . in all aspects of project planning and marketing, general economic development, organizational services, the use of technology and financial control" (1996–1998a).

By its own account the organization has developed skills and experience encompassing the broad spectrum of management consultancy services. Its assignments cover large public projects as well as assistance to small private companies. Many of their assignments are conducted in cooperation with other specialists such as consulting engineers, architects, planners, agricultural consultants and others (1996–1998a).

Such an interfunctional exposure illustrates how deeply the facilitative activities of such a firm can penetrate an economy. Economic and business sectors in which the organization can assist include healthcare, central government, local government, large engagements in developing countries, education, financial models for major projects, information technology and systems, franchising and private finance initiative (1996–1998a).

In the area of healthcare Pannell Kerr Forster provides advice to both public and private health sector organizations (1996–1998b). They offer strategic planning feasibility studies, development of business cases, financial management, IT and information systems, project appraisal, cost improvement, organization review and performance management (1996–1998b).

They offer assistance to central government and government agencies, including "advice in establishing procedures and structures necessary to adapt to a more commercial role and affecting change, including advice on resource accounting and budgeting . . . and the private finance initiative" (1996–1998b).

They also offer support to local authorities in implementing legislation, especially the compulsory tendering regulations recently extended to professional services (1996–1998b). Although this type of service appears to pertain to circumstances in the United Kingdom, the organization may well be able to extend similar services elsewhere throughout its network. Such assistance certainly speaks to yet another dimension for positive inputs from the organization. "Assistance includes corporate strategies to implement the regulations effectively, client side support in specifying and tending the services and contractor support, in planning and bidding for the services" (1996–1998b).

Another way in which the Pannell Kerr Forster organization is of assistance through its global network is through engagements in developing countries. In that regard it provides advice to public and private sector bodies, designed to address the financial and strategic problems and the lack of managerial skills often faced in such locations (1996–1998b).

The organization can give advice to universities on information technology and issues to do with information systems (1996–1998b). Issues included are financial, physical resources, personnel and payroll and research and consultancy (1996–1998b). The organization can also help with development and costing methodologies to do with teaching and learning in higher education. In addition, it can provide "value for money studies to grant maintained and private secondary schools" (1996–1998b).

In the realm of financial modeling Pannell Kerr Forster reviews complex project forecasting and financing models in order to ensure accuracy and reliability and can develop models to reflect underlying contracts or business activity. With respect to financial, strategic and operational consultancy, the organization can assist with all aspects affecting performance, profitability improvement, product profitability analysis, cost reduction, financial feasibility studies and fund raising (1996–1998b). A recruitment service, including psychometric testing, is available, involving all senior and middle-range posts in both private and public sectors (1996–1998b).

Pannell Kerr Forster is also involved in information technology and computer consultancy. This area involves the "development of management information and IT strategies, efficiency reviews, project planning and control, computer applications, implementation programs, office automation, voice and data communications, computer audit and security" (1996–1998b).

Of course, the range of services offered by Pannell Kerr Forster through its network may be of assistance in a setting like the Isle of Man. Some services may act as facilitators in the domestic economy of that jurisdiction, while others may facilitate business and economic linkages involving activities in the Isle of Man and external constituencies. Space does not permit a detailed review of services offered by every major international accounting firm operating in the Isle of Man. Given the jurisdiction's advantageous location vis-à-vis the United Kingdom, not to mention Europe, it is hardly surprising that it hosts various major accounting firms. Examples include Price Waterhouse Coopers, Ernst & Young, Deloitte Touche Tohmatsu and Horwath.

CYPRUS

Cyprus, an island nation with a population approaching three-quarters of a million, is well known for its offshore financial activities. The nation has been divided since the Turkish invasion of 1974 but nonetheless has done rather well economically and has been described by Rodney Wilson as a high-income service economy (1992, 4). Wilson saw fruitful comparisons between the nation and various small island economies, many of which are offshore financial centers. Some of the small island economies cited by Wilson are reviewed in the present volume. Examples include Bermuda, the Cayman Islands, the Channel Islands, the Isle of Man and Malta.

As reported by the Library of Congress, the Turkish invasion disrupted various farming, manufacturing and commercial arrangements (1991). Since the island has been partitioned, the Greek Cypriots have appeared to have been the more successful. As early as 1980, the Republic of Cyprus had developed a tourist industry that boasted in excess of a million visitors annually (1991). Trade and manufacturing activities were expanding, and the country had become a regional finance and service center, filling the regional vacuum left by events involving Beirut (1991). Whether such gains will be sustained in the face of a reemergent Beirut remains to be seen.

The expansion of the Cypriot economy has not been without changes in emphasis. Manufacturing activities have become relatively more important, while the primary sector has lost ground by comparison. "Manufacturing depends upon exports, most to the Middle East and the European Community. . . . However rising labor costs and relatively low quality products stood in the way of future industrial growth" (1991). As early as the late 1970s, the service sector had eclipsed other activities to become the most significant component of the Greek Cypriot economy (1991).

In 1988 services accounted for just over half of GDP (1991). Although tourism was the leading component of the sector's expansion, "the other branches of the services—transportation, storage, telecommunications, finance, insurance, real estate and business services—also experienced steady growth and improvement" (1991). According to the Library of Congress, offshore enterprises represented another dynamic portion of the service sector, attracted to Cyprus due to generous tax concessions and the island's position vis-à-vis Europe and the Middle East (1991).

The advantages of selecting Cyprus for offshore activities were highlighted in a recent report (Cyprus, 1998). "The island's excellent infrastructure, English legal system, high quality of life and low cost of living combined with its well educated labor force, good industrial relations and generous tax incentives, create an ideal business climate" (1998). Cyprus boasts a very good communications, commercial and professional infrastructure. In addition, a modern companies act based upon legislation in the United Kingdom is in place. Cyprus has established international banking arrangements and an operational double taxation treaty network. Offshore companies on the island enjoy low rates of taxation as well as strict regulations governing secrecy and the release of information (1998).

In his assessment of Cyprus and its potential as an offshore business center, Wilson was correct in suggesting that much offshore business can go the way of telecommunications as an alternative to actual physical contact (1992, 80). Although acknowledging that the country has excellent telecommunications, he suggested that most aspiring offshore centers have such facilities, thus telecommunications in and of themselves are hardly a distinct advantage (1992, 81). "Indeed the telecommunications infrastructure has improved remarkably in most of the Middle East in recent years" (81).

Nonetheless, Wilson was favorably disposed towards the potential of Cyprus as an offshore financial center and cited the island's obvious positioning advantage in dealing with the Middle East (82). Wilson attributed interest in Cyprus on the part of offshore companies to two potential origins. First of all, he referred to Western businesses with heavy Middle Eastern interests that might benefit from Cyprus as a regional headquarters, service base or coordinating center (82–83). Second, "there are companies in the Middle East which can benefit from carrying out certain activities with a regional or international orientation from a less regulated or more secure base outside their home country" (83).

According to Wilson, Western enterprises have a regional base designed to monitor and manage ordering as well as to arrange the shipment of goods and deal with invoicing and payment (83). He suggested that financial management functions may be considerable and may benefit from a regional base through client knowledge and faster market intelligence (83).

Walter and Dorothy Diamond are also positively inclined towards Cyprus as a setting for offshore business (1998, 7). Among benefits cited by them as accruing to foreign companies are low operating costs, efficient local clerical workers, excellent communications, convenience of location and legislation based upon English Common Law. However, the Diamonds agree that the dispute involving Greece and Turkey has deterred some investors (7).

In spite of any negative overspill from the political situation, the Diamonds report that offshore companies are expanding their numbers by 30 percent per year (7). Three-quarters of the firms in question represent trading, contracting, investments, consulting and management services (7). According to the Diamonds, the government sees Cyprus as a setting for various companies offering business and financial services (7–8). Others have suggested that "clear policies adopted in connection with offshore banking and financial services as well as modern legislation ... on international trusts give Cyprus major advantages and total flexibility as an international business and financial center" (Eracleous & Eracleous, 1998a, 3). Those authors described the financial services industry as thriving and offering strong advantages, such as fiscal and other incentives and adequate legislation, to its members (3). They identified Cyprus as a dependable regional and international center.

Tax incentives aimed at offshore companies and their staffs are among factors supporting the business environment (3). Double tax agreements are in place between Cyprus and 26 countries, and the nation, generally speaking, enjoys friendly international relations (3). As mentioned earlier, Cyprus possesses a quality infrastructure and quality professional services. It also boasts good educational facilities, which include university-level instruction. Cyprus is not seen to be a tax haven, but it is considered to be a low-tax jurisdiction (3).

The Diamonds have reported Cyprus to be a major link in Eastern and Western trade (1998, 8). They point out that architects and engineers are being invited to base their headquarters in Cyprus for projects involving the Middle East generally and more especially the Gulf region (8). According to them hundreds of firms have moved to Cyprus from Beirut, but some are retracing their steps in the face of a more stable situation in Lebanon (8). Arab firms account for about 30 percent of offshore companies in Cyprus, which of course speaks to the importance of Middle Eastern linkages in that jurisdiction (8).

The island has been described as ideal for the establishment of shipping companies (Eracleous & Eracleous, 1998a, 6). A large number of shipping firms are registered in Cyprus, their vessels totaling in excess of 2,600, with tonnage estimated to be above two million (6). Indeed the country ranks as fourth in the world with respect to ship registrations (3). According to the Diamonds, the island's main ports, Limassol and Larnaca, have become major container transshipment centers in the eastern Mediterranean (1998, Cyprus, 35). More than 4,500 ships owned by 100 shipping firms visit the island over the course of the year (3).

According to Bavishi, major accounting firms have been quite active in Cyprus (1991, Appendix B, 33). According to him, Arthur Andersen was the only member of the Big Six not represented. The other five firms boasted 46 partners in Cyprus. Beyond those major players various other rather large firms were also active on the island.

Prior to its merger with Price Waterhouse, Coopers & Lybrand professed to be the largest organization of management consultants and chartered accountants in the country (1998a). The firm had a staff of 400 functioning through six offices (1998a). Of course, it was offering traditional audit, accounting and tax services, and beyond those it was equipped to assist with VAT services and also payroll and related services. It also provided services geared to offshore clients, including all of the assistance needed for the setting up and management of offshore entities (1998b). In that regard the firm stood prepared to assist with offshore company administration services, the establishment and operation of company bank accounts and accounting and financial reporting services. Coopers & Lybrand also stood prepared to offer financial advice on all matters pertaining to business and to help obtain residence and work permits and locate accommodations for both individual and office use. The firm was also able to help with executive search and recruitment activity, not to mention nominee and trustee services (1998b).

The firm is very active in financial and management consulting (1998c). In that capacity it assists with business strategy and planning as well as with financial planning and control. It deals with the reorganization of businesses and process reengineering as well as with investment appraisal and the preparation of feasibility studies. It handles mergers and acquisitions and company flotations and can assist with family businesses and management succession. It can also help with the preparation of information memoranda on industry sectors or businesses.

In the area of information technology the firm can assist in developing strategy and can deal with project management, information systems security and effectiveness as well as systems delivery and integration (1998d). In the related area of computer software services the firm has established a fully owned subsidiary, Cycom, to assist clients with computerization efforts (1998e).

The firm stands ready to assist with project management consulting (1998f). It suggests that "project management reduces risk by helping to maximize return on investment, ensuring that the project achieves desired goals and that those goals correspond to the business objective" (1998f). The firm focuses on the introduction and implementation of goal-directed project management and on training in project management. It deals in interim project management and project audits.

In the area of business recovery services the firm carries out diagnostic investigations of borrowers in financial distress on behalf of lenders (1998g). It stands ready to advise and assist in the implementation of corporate turnaround strategies and can provide independent monitoring of the borrowers' performance and compliance with the lenders' conditions. It can also carry out formal receivership work (1998g).

In the area of human resources consulting the firm is quite active as well (1998h). Its core services include assessing the effectiveness of organizational and management structure and developing and implementing performance appraisal systems (1998h). It conducts salary surveys and develops reward and recognition schemes and offers advice and help with the establishment of medical and other employee benefit schemes. It also stands ready to assess training and development needs within organizations (1998h).

The other party to the merger referred to above, Price Waterhouse, was also active in Cyprus, where it had previously merged with the local practices of T.C. Christofides and C. Tsielepis. Beyond that in 1982 "an associated firm was established with N. Ionides . . . providing services in tax, bookkeeping and other non audit services as its prime objective" (1991b, 159).

In Cyprus Price Waterhouse offered services in audit and accounting, taxation and management consulting (159). In the accounting sphere the firm stood ready to perform independent audits of client organizations and their operations. "We view the independent audit as a means to ensure that management is provided with reliable financial and management information through the operation of appropriate controls and procedures" (159). In addition to satisfying the audit requirements prescribed in Cyprus, the firm saw their audits as constructive, cost-effective management aids (159).

In tax matters the firm could serve the needs of both corporate and individual clients. Its tax service "works closely with the audit practice, providing integrated service to those businesses requiring both capabilities" (159). In the area of management consultancy, services included the design and implementation of accounting systems, feasibility studies, computerization, assistance with setting up businesses and human resources.

Eracleous & Eracleous is a local accounting firm that is active in providing a selection of business-related services. It is active in the area of offshore finance and can help with the formation and management of offshore companies, individuals with international trusts, tax planning, auditing and accounting (1998a and b).

With respect to the formation of offshore companies the firm functions in Jersey, the Virgin Islands, the Bahamas, Panama and the Isle of Man, in addition to Cyprus (Eracleous & Eracleous, 1998e). They can provide "shelf" ready-made offshore companies and can act as nominee directors, trustee shareholders, company secretary, registered office and trustees (1998e). They deal in translation notarization and legalization of company documents and in opening bank accounts and the formation of international trusts (1998e). They can advise on migration matters and on customs- and excise-related matters (1998e).

In the realm of company management the firm can offer full management, the handling of bank accounts, orders, payroll and bookkeeping. It is also active in management consulting and can assist with tax planning, double tax treaties, business plans and feasibility studies (1998e). It also deals with shipping, ship management and the registration of vessels and yachts (1998e).

By way of summary it seems clear that Cyprus is strategically located in the Mediterranean and has the opportunity for being a significant player in the region, if not in the world. The island is well linked by transportation and communications, which strengthens its position as an offshore center. Its ongoing ethnic difficulties have not destroyed its potential as a link between Europe, the Middle East and North Africa.

The island's government appears to be well aware of the advantages alluded to above and is encouraging international business and economic interests. Certain international service activities are experiencing substantial success, notably tourism and financial endeavors. Major accounting firms have assumed important roles in facilitating international services, not to mention other forms of business and economic activity in Cyprus. Their actual importance appears obvious from their service offerings that have been discussed above. Certainly they have major contributions to make to the ongoing success of Cyprus as an offshore financial center.

GIBRALTAR

Gibraltar is a dependent territory of the United Kingdom, located in southwestern Europe on the southern coast of Spain. Its location has been of strategic importance throughout history since it overlooks the entrance to the Mediterranean from the North Atlantic. It occupies a very small amount of land and its natural resources are negligible.

As of July 1995, its population was estimated as approaching 32,000 (Gibraltar, 1998). The territory "benefits from an extensive shipping trade and offshore banking" (1998). The banking sector contributes 15 percent of GDP, while tourism, shipping service fees and duties on consumer goods generate revenue as well. The public sector accounts for more than 70 percent of the economy (1998).

The economic base of the territory shows some diversity. Included among business sectors are such things as tourism, banking and finance, construction and commerce. Support facilities for large British naval and air bases are also significant. Beyond such enterprises are transit trade, a supply depot in the port, and light manufacturing of tobacco and roasted coffee as well as mineral waters, candy and canned fish (1998).

The territory has undergone a substantial investment program in infrastructure in order to insure that international standards are met. "There is now a wide selection of office space, warehouses, light industrial areas and residential accommodations available" (Deloitte & Touche, 1998a).

According to Walter and Dorothy Diamond (21), the revenues of the territory are derived mainly from financial services, supplies for visiting ships, entrepot trade, tourism, transshipment and a government-sponsored lottery. The Diamonds explain that port facilities are being expanded to service larger vessels as well as to attract more merchant shipping. A naval dockyard that closed in the mid-1980s has been replaced by a business in commercial ship repair (21). The Diamonds suggest that the shipyard will be a prominent part of a new Europort, consisting of a business and financial center containing a luxury hotel planned for construction on the Mediterranean side of the territory (21).

Nearly all goods moving through Gibraltar enjoy exemption from customs duties and thus the territory functions as a freeport for goods not destined for its domestic market (21). To enjoy such an exemption proof must be provided that the goods in question are in transit. Such goods can be stored in a reserved area of the harbor (Government Stores) or they can be imported under bond for eventual reexport (21).

The transshipment capabilities of the territory are in the process of being expanded. "Drawback procedures also make possible a refund of total or partial duties paid for certain duty-liable goods such as automobiles when subsequently reexported from Gibraltar and clothing materials used in the local manufacture of garments for export" (37). The Diamonds point out that beyond warehousing the Government Stores are used for assembly, blending and a limited amount of processing (37).

Gibraltar has been gearing up as an offshore financial center. According to the Diamonds, the territory's status as a center was especially enhanced by Company Rules defining the parent/subsidiary relationship. Such directions dating from 1991 and 1992 are quite attractive to certain international business interests. As the Diamonds explain, "Companies formed under legislation that took effect on January 1, 1992 . . . as holding companies of 5% or more interest in other firms are exempt from tax on European Community based subsidiaries in which they hold 25% or greater voting interest" (2). They go on to explain that such companies are subject to the full 35 percent corporate tax on income derived elsewhere.

The Diamonds explain that European Union subsidiaries are exempt from taxes on dividends to their parent companies (2–3). "By reducing withholding taxes on EU shareholder dividends to 1% the Gibraltar holding company offers non-EU investors a tax-advantage vehicle for European investments" (3). Such arrangements are useful in EU countries with the exceptions of France and Spain (3).

Bavishi has reported the presence of major international accounting firms in Gibraltar (1991, Appendix B, 29). All told, major accounting firms were reported as having 17 partners in that jurisdiction, 10 of whom were associated with the Big Six. Coopers & Lybrand and Ernst & Young each had three partners, while KPMG and Price Waterhouse boasted two each (29). Other firms represented in Gibraltar included Nexia International, Grant Thornton International and Moores Rowland International (29).

Deloitte Touche Tohmatsu International, although a relatively recent addition to the business community in Gibraltar (1991), has become one of the leading accounting and auditing firms in the territory (Deloitte & Touche, 1998b). By the firm's own assessment all services provided are guided by common global principles that influence the way in which they perform their tasks (1998c). Services are provided in the fields of audit and accountancy, tax, consulting and reconstruction and insolvency.

In the auditing and accountancy area the firm is prepared to assist clients to achieve business objectives, to strengthen management and to improve profitability (1998c). Services offered include auditing and review, computer auditing, internal audit services and full accounting services, as well as the preparation and analysis of management accounts. Beyond such practices the firm provides due diligence reviews, financial forecasts and projections and financial consulting. It can also assist with internal control systems and procedures and can provide litigation support. With respect to the service cadres included above, the firm boasts a business advisory division that deals exclusively with smaller companies (1998c).

In the realm of taxation the firm's services "are designed to assist clients to take full advantage of tax legislation in support of their business objective" (1998c). They suggest that the tax legislation of the territory encourages the tax efficient use of Gibraltar by non-residents and they stand ready with specialized advice in that area (1998c). Included in the tax services offered are such things as the use of the territory in international structures, local tax advice and expatriate tax advice. The firm can also assist with personal tax and financial planning as well as with international tax matters.

With respect to consultancy the firm states that its "consulting services cover the full scope of business management-operations improvement, financial management, strategy and planning, and information technology" (1998c). Among their service offerings are such things as financial consulting, business planning, organization and methods as well as assistance with regard to management information systems and information technology. Beyond such areas the firm stands ready to assist with cost management and treasury and cash flow management (1998c). Confidence in what they hope to accomplish can be seen in their own pronouncements. "Not only do we find effective solutions to our clients' business needs, we turn ideas into action, helping our clients successfully implement the solutions we propose" (1998c).

The firm also stands ready to assist in matters of reconstruction and insolvency. In that regard it points to the possibility of major corporate collapses and economic uncertainty, suggesting the need for creditors to be well informed when making decisions with respect to debt recovery (1998c). The firm stands ready with expertise in those areas.

Through its subsidiary, Deloitte & Touche Trust & Corporate Services Limited, the firm stands ready to provide offshore services (1998d). Indeed, the firm's subsidiary specializes in a full range of company secretarial, trust services and other general administration (1998d). Specific offshore service offerings include the incorporation of Gibraltar-registered companies and the registration of branches of foreign firms registered in the territory. Also included are "company secretarial services including provision of registered office, company secretary, nominee shareholders and directors" and the incorporation of companies worldwide (1998d).

The firm assists with applications for exempt or qualifying status as well as with the opening and administration of bank accounts and invoicing and accounting services. Other offerings include payroll services, trusts setup and administration and trustee services. The firm can assist in forming asset protection trusts and Gibraltar foundations, as well as with the registration of high-net-worth individuals (1998d).

MALTA

Malta is a small nation comprising three islands in the Mediterranean, 60 miles south of Sicily. With a population in the 348,000 range its economy is chiefly dependent upon tourism, government-controlled dry docks and shipyard and light industry (Diamond and Diamond, 1998, 20–21). Tourism boasts 900,000 visitors annually and accounts for one-third of GNP (20). Malta hosts 170 foreign and 230 domestic manufacturers, producing textiles, footwear, processed foods, chemical products, metal goods and printed materials for export markets (20). Additional industrial expansion faces obstacles in the form of serious shortages of water and electricity (20).

The nation was a British Crown Colony from 1800 to 1964 and is still a member of the British Commonwealth. Its civil law is based largely on the Napoleonic Code, while its criminal law has Italian roots (33). Despite such legal institutions the court system derives from English principles and British legislation is the model for Maltese company and tax law.

Although Malta has in the neighborhood of 2,200 registered offshore companies, including in excess of 200 so-called international companies evenly divided between trading and non-trading, it is phasing out offshore companies over a period of nine years (1). The aim is for the nation to become a financial center for both domestic and foreign companies with an "onshore" designation. Many existing companies are Russian or Eastern European.

Malta has developed an export processing zone at Marsaxlokh on its eastern coast. "A container terminal already in operation will be supplemented by a duty free warehouse and an oil products terminal for storage, blending and bunkering" (35). Activities permitted in the zone include such things as warehousing, transshipment, assembly, processing, packing, repacking and ship chandlering (35). Tenants are free of exchange controls and exempt from import duties, stamp taxes, inheritance and gift taxes and other taxes based upon a 15-year governmental guarantee (35). Foreigners employed in the zone pay income taxes at a reduced rate. Tenants of the zone pay a 5 percent income tax and are required to keep audited accounts. License fees and annual renewals are also levied (35). Malta is one of a small number of offshore trading centers with lengthy lists of double taxation treaties that permit holding companies to apply the benefits (36).

There were 27 partners in major accounting firms resident in Malta in 1991 (Bavishi, 1991, Appendix B, 31). Price Waterhouse and Coopers & Lybrand each accounted for five partners, while Deloitte Ross Tohmatsu had six (31). Other large international accounting firms represented in Malta included Dunwoody Robson McGladery & Pullen, Hodgson Landau Brands International, Moores Rowland International, Nexia International and Summit International Associates, Inc.

Price Waterhouse, which recently merged with Coopers & Lybrand, was represented in Malta since 1977 by its correspondent firm, Naudi, Giorgio, Leone Ganado & Co. (NGLG). NGLG has been providing a full range of professional services to national and international clients (Price Waterhouse, 1991c, 190). The firm boasts a staff of 60 with five partners (190).

The firm provides a wide range of services to local, national and international organizations (191). Clients are drawn from banking, manufacturing, tourism, property, shipping and insurance (191). "A significant portion of the practice is devoted to serving the special needs of foreign multinational companies doing business in Malta, including those operating in the oil and gas industry" (191). Among services provided are audit and business advisory, tax, management consulting and offshore services (191).

In the field of auditing the firm can perform statutory audits and examinations of company forms. Audits are carried out in accordance with International Auditing Guidelines or any other standards such as those employed in the United States or the United Kingdom. "As an important part of these regular audit services, we issue reports to management with recommendations to improve internal controls and administrative efficiency" (191). According to the firm, its audits put considerable emphasis on understanding the concerns of management in all areas of their business and are not just limited to the financial function (191). A range of special services such as acquisition, accounting assistance and special investigations are also provided (191).

The area of taxation services includes routine compliance work as well as support for clients during negotiations with tax authorities and assistance with strategic tax and business planning. The tax services offered by the firm cover the entire gamut of taxes applicable to international business, including internal tax and "Maltese company tax with specialist exemption in double taxation treaties" (192).

The firm offers a variety of services in the area of management consulting. Included are help in connection with setting up a business in Malta and the filing of applications and follow up with the Malta Development Corporation (192). Assistance can also be provided in the recruitment of appropriate locally hired staff and the design and

implementation of accounting systems as well as systems design, evaluation, conversion and upgrading (192).

Because of the nation's efforts to become an international and business
center, Price Waterhouse "equipped itself in this specialization" (192).
Offshore service offerings include advice concerning corporate and financial structures. The firm also acted as nominees for locally registered
offshore companies and assisted with the registration of ships and offshore trusts.

A FINAL OVERVIEW

As was the case in the Caribbean, the jurisdictions discussed in this
chapter are rather small and dependent upon forces beyond their boundaries for their economic well being. They are also linked historically to
Great Britain, and all have inherited various legal and/or governmental
institutions from that nation. In varying degrees they are all desirous of
encouraging offshore financial activities as major components of their
economies.

The major accounting firms have been quite active in the jurisdictions
in question and are providing significant menus of business and financial
services to both domestic and international clients through their local
offices. It seems quite clear from the involvement of those firms that the
jurisdictions in question are functioning in some respects as offshore financial centers. Such involvements are especially significant in light of
events shaping a more unified future for the European continent.

NOTE

1. In the edition of their work, *Tax Havens of the World* (1998), the Diamonds
supply detailed information on in excess of 60 jurisdictions. The jurisdictions
covered are listed in alphabetical order and pagination is internal to each jurisdiction. In the present volume references to the work in question are to the
jurisdiction being discussed and page references are to that jurisdiction.

Chapter 6

The Firms in Offshore Centers in the Persian Gulf, the Indian Ocean and the Far East

This chapter deals with an at large selection of jurisdictions from the areas of the world not covered in previous chapters. It begins in the Persian Gulf with coverage of Bahrain and the United Arab Emirates. Those jurisdictions were thought to be of special significance because of their role in the Arab world. Following that analysis, the focus switches to the Indian Ocean and a review of the situation in Mauritius and Seychelles. Although neither of those jurisdictions are equal in prominence as offshore financial centers to various other locations that have been featured in this volume, they are included because of their potential for influence in the region they occupy. The third section of the chapter deals with two centers from the Asia/Pacific area—Singapore and Vanuatu.

THE PERSIAN GULF

In the last quarter of the twentieth century Bahrain has emerged as a rather significant financial center in the Middle East. According to the Diamonds, the nation's rulers have lightened offshore regulations and, beginning in 1975, have instituted a program intended to encourage Bahrain's emergence as a Middle Eastern financial tax haven (1998, 1). According to those authors, the licensing of 50 large banks to become offshore banking units and 21 to serve as investment banks has permitted the nation to replace Beirut as the Arab money capital. Whether Bahrain will be able to sustain such a prominence in the face of a reemerging Beirut remains to be seen.

Bahrain is an archipalagic nation of 33 islands, situated 15 miles from the coast of Saudi Arabia, near the southern shore of the Persian Gulf.

Major cities include Manama and Muharraq. Jeffrey Nugent and Theodore Thomas have described the skyline of Manama as recently experiencing "the addition of high-rise, luxury hotels, commercial buildings and parking structures in the heavily congested commercial center" (1985, 5).

Nugent and Thomas describe the nation as "attempting to discern a way to blend the rich traditions of the Arab and Islamic cultures indigenous to the gulf with the values of urban industrialized Western societies" (5). The nation boasts a 16-mile causeway that facilitates road traffic between it and Saudi Arabia (Diamond and Diamond, 1998, 7). Nugent and Thomas describe a nation, modern in appearance with heavy automobile traffic, modern roads, a busy international airport, dry-dock and ship repair yard and other industrial endeavors including an aluminum smelter, a major oil refinery and a variety of light and heavy industries (1995, 3–5).

According to the Diamonds, manufacturing has become the most significant contributor to gross national product (21 percent) as oil reserves have declined (1998, 6). They identified oil as contributing 17.7 percent and banking and insurance 16 percent (6). Coopers & Lybrand International have described Bahrain as the commercial hub of the Gulf, having modified its framework to support both investments and business ventures (1996, 3).

"The nation's population is approaching 600 thousand and is increasing at a rate of roughly 2.5 per cent per year" (McKee, Garner and AbuAmara McKee, 1999, 69). Roughly one-third of the population is composed of non-citizens. According to Coopers & Lybrand International, Bahraini women are eager to work, and educational standards are more advanced than those found in neighboring jurisdictions (1996, 7). Islam is practiced by 85 percent of the population, although other religions are permitted.

"A long tradition of association with other cultures, a stable government and a strong sense of national identity have made Bahrain a pleasant place to live" (1996, 7). Despite this assessment, the Diamonds do see some political uncertainties in the nation. They refer to heightened activity among subversive elements and difficulties relating to Iran (1998, 4). Shiite Muslims have staged street demonstrations favoring a ban on alcohol and night clubs, and other disruptive activities have been attributed to Shiite Muslim guerrillas (4).

The nation enjoys strong international transportation linkages. Its international airport is among the most active in the Middle East, boasting 35 airlines servicing 70 destinations (7). Passenger traffic is in excess of four million persons per year (7). The Diamonds describe Mina Subrum as having a deep water harbor with 16 berths capable of servicing large tankers and ocean freighters, a container terminal with two roll-on, roll-off berths and two shallow water berths (8). According to Coopers & Lybrand International, the nation "is ideally located at the center of trade routes for VLCCs which spend more time loading and unloading in the Gulf than in any other waters" (1996, 13).

"The nation has been the entrepot for the region and is also a distribution center" (McKee, Garner and AbuAmara McKee, 1999, 69). Although oil still dominates the trade account, the government has actively encouraged non-oil exports (Coopers & Lybrand International, 1996, 13). Bahrain has been termed "one of the most diverse economies of the Gulf region," boasting the Gulf's largest concentrations of manufacturing firms and the largest community of international bank branches (Arab World Online, 1997a, 1).

Coopers & Lybrand International have identified aluminium as the nation's oldest industry save for oil and gas (1996, 19). "Following an expansion in the period of 1990–1992, Aluminium Bahrain is now capable of producing 460,000 tons per year" (McKee, Garner and AbuAmara McKee, 1999, 70). The Diamonds have identified major projects affiliated with the smelter to include a cable factory, an aluminum sheet plant, and an atomizer that pulverizes hot aluminum for use in processing paints, inks and explosives (1998, 6). The Diamonds describe further diversification as including a $300 million iron pelletizing plant, a $350 million petrochemical venture with Kuwait and Saudi Arabia, a tire plant and factory facilities for light industry (6).

Bahrain has recently been described as "the Middle East's pre-eminent financial hub" as well as "a key player in world financial and banking services" (Arab Net, 1997, 1). Indeed, Arab Net describes Bahrain as "an international and regional interbank money market centered on its offshore banking sector" (1). According to the Diamonds, Bahrain does face major competition from Cyprus and the United Arab Emirates (1998, 8). In spite of such competition the offshore banks in Bahrain handle assets of $70 billion, and the daily foreign exchange turnover of the nation's financial institutions is close to $4 billion (1). The total earnings from offshore banks exceed $50 million (8).

Bahrain "hosts international law firms, insurance companies, certified public accountants and various consultants in a rather sophisticated service sector" (McKee, Garner and AbuAmara McKee, 1999, 70). Arab Net suggests that the presence of such activities has "stimulated the evolution of other related financial establishments including the Bahrain Stock Market, the money exchange sector, the real estate and construction business and other commercial enterprises" (1997, 1).

Since Bahrain has moved in the direction of hosting offshore financial services, it is hardly surprising to find that it enjoys the services of various major international accounting firms. Bavishi identified Bahrain as having 18 partners, 14 of whom were affiliated with the Big Six (1991).

One of the big six that was very active in the country was Coopers & Lybrand, which of course has since merged with Price Waterhouse.

"Operating as Coopers & Lybrand/Jawad & Habib & Co. the firm offers a wide menu of services" (McKee, Garner and AbuAmara McKee, 1999, 76). Its service menu includes management consulting, information technology services and human resources consulting. Also included are financial services, business assurance, business recovery and insolvency, litigation support services and company formation.

The firm declares its workforce to be well informed on both local and Gulf-wide issues and thus prepared to contribute value to its clients organizations. Bahrain has also been interested in developing its tourism industry and the firm offers services in that area as well. It stands ready to assist with business strategy appraisal and formulation. "It conducts market surveys, feasibility studies, operation reviews and economic, social and environmental impact studies" (McKee, Garner and AbuAmara McKee, 1999, 77). It can also assist with marketing strategy and planning, project finance, concept design and evaluation, as well as project management. Beyond such matters the firm stands ready to help with management selection and contract negotiation.

With respect to information technology the firm is willing to assess the effectiveness of real or proposed information systems as well as to establish plans for the future direction of information systems. It is also able to assist in system delivery and with the quality management of software and with system security through the identification and countering of threats to confidentiality. It offers contingency planning with respect to disaster recovery.

The firm also offers assistance with human resource management and management improvement. It deals with executive search, recruitment and management and is willing to assist firms in the identification of the appropriate management organization structure and personnel needs.

Financial services are an important component of Bahrain's economy and the firm is quite active in that area. It can assist with corporate strategy as well as with organizational change and can also help with human resource training. It assists with financial management, management information and the controlling of risks. It also offers assistance with treasury and cash management, corporate finance, financial audits, taxation and regulation.

In the area of business assurance services the firm's intent is to strengthen business control, thereby increasing the value of organizations. In that regard service offerings include accounting, statutory audits and other audit-related services that range from internal to environmental. Beyond such matters the firm deals with computer assurance services, risk management, forensic accounting and corporate training. In the area of business recovery and insolvency the firm sees its role as support for financial stakeholders with respect to risk management. Presumably the merger of Coopers & Lybrand and Price Waterhouse can only strengthen the merged firm's ability to maintain and enhance the service menu that was in place.

KPMG Fakhro is the local KPMG affiliate in Bahrain. Various traditional accounting services, such as audits, reviews and compilations, accounting and bookkeeping and business share valuation are offered through its general practice department. The firm also deals with offer documents, investment memoranda and procedure manuals. It provides accounting advice and control reviews as well as risk assessment reviews. It offers forensic accounting support and liquidation advice and can perform feasibility studies. It can also supply Saudi tax advice and can provide investment placement and debt restructuring and/or scheduling advice. It conducts insolvency investigations and helps with arbitration, legal custodianship and liquidation.

The firm stands ready through its shares department, to administer public issues as well as to offer registrar and transfer agent services. Through its legal department the firm deals with company formations and flotations. It assists with the registration of trademarks and with the translation of legal documents and liquidations. It helps with drafting and reviewing contracts of legal documentation and also with the preparation of business law compilations.

In the management consulting arena the firm's services are divided into three subcategories—financial management, human resources and information technology. Financial management includes strategic business planning and strategic cost management. The firm also conducts feasibility studies, market appraisals and reviews of efficiency and effectiveness. It assists with executive searches and selections as well as with remuneration studies and psychometric testing. With respect to information technology its services include strategy and system selection and implementation. It also deals with system diagnostics and reviews and systems disaster planning.

The United Arab Emirates share a relatively unique position with Bahrain among offshore financial centers, since they offer significant linkages between the Arab world and the international economy. They represent "an independent federation of seven emirates comprising (broadly from southwest to northeast) Abu Dhabi, Dubai, Sharjah, Ajman, Umm Al-Quwain, Rus Al-Khaimah and Fujeirah" (Deloitte Touche Tohmatsu International, 1996a, 1). They comprise an area of 32,000 square miles in the eastern Arabian peninsula between Saudi Arabia and Oman.

Prior to independence in 1971 the Emirates were known as the Trucial States and were bound by treaties with the United Kingdom (1). According to the Diamonds, the nation is far stronger economically and politically than had been anticipated at its independence (1998, 4). It entered its third decade with oil and gas revenues of $17 billion, a gross domestic product of $40 billion, and one of the world's highest per capita incomes (4). The nation boasts the world's third largest oil reserves and produces two million barrels per day, making it the seventh biggest producer (4).

The individual Emirates are well connected to each other and to neighboring countries by newly laid road networks (Deloitte Touche Tohmatsu International, 1996a, 2). "Modern telephone, telex and telecopier systems connect the United Arab Emirates with most of the world," and "major international couriers are well represented and provide service at competitive rates" (2).

It seems clear that the Emirates enjoy transportation and communications linkages to support competitive offshore financial services. However, the Emirates are pursuing broader developmental goals. In an effort to reduce the petroleum dependency of the oil-producing emirates, both federal and Emirate governments are encouraging investment in fields considered beneficial to the nation (3).

According to the Diamonds, large natural gas reserves have been discovered in Abu Dhabi and are being processed at a $500 million liquefaction plant on Das Island (1998, 5). Although an oil refinery has been completed and another is in the planning stage, the nation has diversified from fuels by setting up manufacturing operations that include a steel mill, steel fabrication complex and cable plant (5). The ongoing successful expansion of non-petroleum sectors of the economy has been attributed directly to government policy (Deloitte Touche Tohmatsu International, 1996a). The industrial sector includes textiles and clothing, footwear, electrical appliances, power station transformers, auto parts and furniture as well as stationery and paper products, air conditioning and refrigeration equipment, plastic containers, surgical gloves and ophthalmic lenses (1996a, 7 and McKee, Garner and AbuAmara McKee, 1999).

The governments of the various Emirates are actively attempting to attract investments of expertise and capital (Ernst & Young, 1990, 3). Beyond a good transportation and communications infrastructure the emirates enjoy "a virtual absence of taxation" as well as "a well-structured financial sector with no exchange control regulations" (3). Free-trade zones have been put in place and financial reporting requirements at both federal and local levels are minimal (3). Other advantages from investing in the nation include the availability of cheap energy, access to inexpensive regional labor markets, the absence of duties on imported raw materials and the export of finished products as well as closeness to regional markets (Deloitte Touche Tohmatsu International, 1996a).

According to Ernst & Young, important sectors of the economy beyond its energy components include "utilities, communications, construction, banking and financial services, manufacturing projects and tourism" (1990, 4).

The country offers incentives to foreign investors able to provide needed technical expertise and willing to work in collaboration with citizens (Deloitte Touche Tohmatsu International, 1996a, 7). The investors are given various concessions beyond which no direct incentives "such as capital grants, subsidized loans, preferential contract schemes or import quotas or loans that protect domestic industry are available" (7).

The Diamonds explain that all of the Emirates welcome foreign investment for development projects while emphasizing local participation in ventures (1998, 3). As an example, they point to Sharjah as particularly eager to attract manufacturing, warehousing and consumer goods projects. To encourage such projects Sharjah has established industrial estates in the city and an export processing free-trade zone near its airport (3). Among incentives offered are free consulting services, aid in capitalization, donations of land, low land-leasing rates and reduced rates for power and water (3). The Emirate is trying to become an offshore banking center as well as serving as a company headquarters for the Middle East and Gulf regions (3).

Although federally sponsored general incentives to foreign investors are hardly extensive, free-trade zones have been developed and the tax climate is attractive. According to Ernst & Young, "Foreign companies establishing businesses in the free trade zones are offered special concessions, including an exemption from the requirement of having local ownership or a local sponsor" (1990, 9).

The Emirate of Dubai has been a trading center and entrepot within the Middle East for some time (see McKee, Garner and AbuAmara McKee, 1999). The Emirate hosts a free-trade zone, Jabel Ali, 21 miles from Dubai City (Diamond and Diamond, 1998, 17). The Jabel Ali zone complex is one of the world's largest man-made ports, providing excellent facilities for trade, manufacturing and services (Ernst & Young, 1990, 5). According to Deloitte Touche Tohmatsu International, Dubai hosts 950 international operations (1996a, 8). The zone employs some 5,000, most of whom are foreigners (Diamond and Diamond, 1998, 17).

The Diamonds point out that Dubai has ample support services, including local labor, health and medical facilities and inexpensive energy, not to mention the inputs of the zone operators to expedite documentation and minimize red tape (1998, 17). The harbor comprises "sixty-seven berths, over fifteen kilometers of quay, and a container terminal with the most up-to-date handling equipment that is capable of handling any class of ship" (Deloitte Touche Tohmatsu International, 1996a, 8).

According to Bavishi, the United Arab Emirates has 43 partners in major accounting firms, including 28 from the Big Six (1991). Prominent among the major firms servicing the country is Ernst & Young. That firm's involvement in the Middle East dates from 1923 and comprises 15 offices in 11 countries, with a total professional staff in excess of 800 (Ernst & Young, 1997a).

Ernst & Young views its main business in the Middle East as the auditing of financial statements (1997b). Nonetheless, they claim to have "one of the largest management consulting practices in the world" (1997c). Among consulting services offered are business planning and control, as well as financial planning and control and performance improvement (1997c). The firm also offers assistance with business process reengineering, organizational change management and organization and management development as well as human resource management. It works with information and computer systems, mergers and acquisitions and privatization and off-set services.

It offers a wide range of accounting and financial services (1997d). It can advise on the choice and implementation of accounting systems and can review systems presently operational to insure their relevance and control (1997d). It helps with fraud prevention and offers risk assessments and detection services. It also helps with tax matters, whether this involves giving advice or the actual preparation of returns (1997e and f). It can also assist in preparing management and financial accounts (1997d).

Ernst & Young also involves itself in business community training and indeed runs fully equipped training centers in various offices in the Middle East (1997g). It has put together specific training programs for a variety of organizations (1997a).

Another major accounting firm active in the United Arab Emirates is RSM International. By its own assessment it is the tenth largest full service accounting and consulting organization in the world (1998a). It is represented by 76 member firms and 12 correspondent firms in 77 countries (1998a). In addition to the United Arab Emirates, the firm is represented in Mauritius.

The firm sees itself as able to offer significant personalized assistance to its corporate clients. "Our approach to developing solutions to your needs is anchored in an adequate understanding of the business and industry sector(s) in which you operate" (1998a). This, they feel, permits them to design solutions to fit the unique characteristics of their business clients (1998a). They are clearly aware of the needs of international operations. "Our approach is based on the 'long-term view'—a view corporate management must take if their international goals are to be achieved" (1998a). They claim that their team will be aware of the local and international issues affecting their clients' industry and organization (1998a).

RSM International provides a full range of audit and accounting services. In addition, they offer specialized services such as due diligence work, royalty payments, audits and inventory observation assistance in the traditional accounting services area (1998a). Their clients run the gamut from startup companies to very large, multinational organizations, many of which are publicly traded (1998a).

Audit and accounting services range from bookkeeping and the preparation of financial statements to audits of historical financial statements (1998a). Other accounting service offerings include audit and other attestation services, prospective financial statements (forecasts and projections), exempt offerings assistance, performance of agreed upon procedures and outsourcing services (1998a).

In the area of taxation the firm is experienced in providing extensive services to multinational firms and can provide export-related tax services (1998a). The service menu includes areas such as asset planning, accounting methods and periods—tax engagements and business valuation and transfer considerations. It also includes common paymaster/payroll agent services, divorce and separation tax planning and estate and gift planning engagements. The firm can also deal with multistate tax issues, personal financial planning and trusts and estate income tax returns (1998a).

RSM International is heavily involved in consulting activity. Its areas of focus include international business development, international information technology, international cash and financial management and global human resources (1998c). In the business planning area the firm's services include annual/business planning, family/business succession planning and strategic planning (1998c).

In the area of management information systems the firm offers data processing controls reviews, disaster recovery planning, financial accounting systems evaluation and improvement design and long-range information systems planning (1998c). It also assists with management information requirements evaluation, systems (application) development and modification with respect to both microcomputers and midrange computers. It also offers systems installation, implementation and support and systems selection for the above ranges of computers. It can also help with telecommunications systems selection (1998c).

The firm boasts diverse offerings in the field of financial management consulting, including assistance with bankruptcy and reorganization, business valuations, cash management and contribution/profitability analysis studies (1998c). Beyond such matters it offers due diligence reviews, financial feasibility studies and financial projection and modeling. It offers financing assistance, profit enhancement programs, profit planning and rate models.

The firm also offers temporary comptrollership assistance, corporate roundtable consulting, employee benefits consulting and employee climate and attitude surveys (1998c). It can assist with employee incentive compensation planning, human resources diagnostic reviews and human resources information systems. The firm offers management assessment and counseling and management compensation planning as well as management/supervisory training and development programs and organization planning and evaluation (1998c). It also offers outplacement services and performance evaluation and appraisal programs, and it can assist with personnel policy manuals and employee handbooks as well as with personnel selection and executive search. The firm also stands ready to assist with wage and salary administration programs (1998c).

In the sphere of marketing consulting the firm offers site location analysis and selection. Its operations consulting services menu includes high-spot operational reviews, operational reviews and also help with production and inventory control systems, design and development selection, production and inventory control system implementation and reviews and productivity improvement consulting (1998c).

THE INDIAN OCEAN

Mauritius is a small island nation lying in the Indian Ocean some 500 miles east of Madagascar. It embraces 720 square miles of territory and boasts a population of 1.1 million people. The country gained its independence from Great Britain in 1968 and has embraced a republican form of government, while maintaining membership in the British Commonwealth. English is the official language, although most of the population is also fluent in French. The legal system draws upon both English and French law.

A Library of Congress study sees Mauritius as having become relatively prosperous and diverse in terms of its economy (1994a). According to that study, Mauritius has emerged from an early post-independence situation of high unemployment and reliance upon sugar exports. "The 1970's were marked by a strong government commitment to diversify the economy and provide more high-paying jobs" (1994a). The period from 1971 to 1977 saw the creation of about 64,000 jobs (1994a).

The nation's economy gained some strength from the creation of export processing zones (EPZs), although criticisms have been leveled at labor practices associated with them (1994a). "By the 1980's . . . the economy experienced steady growth, declining inflation, high employment, and increased domestic savings" (1994a). The EPZs surpassed sugar as the principal export earning sector and, in fact, employed more workers than the sugar industry and the government combined (1994a). The government planned further economic diversification for the 1990s including the development of the nation as a center of offshore banking and financial services (1994a).

According to S. Moonesamy, "Mauritius provides an ideal environment for banks, insurance and reinsurance companies, captive insurance managers, trading companies, ship owners or managers, fund managers and professionals to conduct their international business" (1996). Various types of offshore activity can be conducted in the country, including banking, insurance and funds management (1996). Other offshore activities include international financial services, operational headquarters and international consultancy services.

Beyond those activities offshore business opportunities include shipping and ship management, aircraft financing and leasing, international licensing and franchising and international trading. Other activities include international data processing and information technology services, offshore pension funds, international assets management and international employment services (1996).

In 1992 Mauritius passed the Freeport Act, which provided for the establishment of freeport zones. The Act established a Freeport Authority with the objectives of controlling and managing the freeport zone, promoting and encouraging external trade and providing infrastructure and storage facilities in the freeport. The authority was also intended to advise the minister of finance on the development of free zones (Anon, 1998). The authority has the power to issue operating licenses in freeport zones as well as to allocate space in the zones. It can levy rents, charges and/or dues on licensees and can contract with individuals for services or facilities in keeping with its prerogatives (1998).

The freeport zones are located in Port Louis and at the international airport. Such zones are considered as exterior to Mauritius and are enclosed and guarded with access and egress confined to authorized entry and exit points, thus preventing the evasion of customs duties, import levies and sales taxes (1998). Among activities authorized for the zones are warehousing and storage, breaking bulk and sorting, grading, cleaning and mixing. Also included are labeling, packing and repacking, minor processing, simple assembly and any other activity prescribed by the minister of finance on the advice of the Freeport Authority (1998).

Liberal incentive packages have been established for firms seeking cost-effective storage, assembly and redistribution locations, including such things as exemptions from the company tax and also customs and import duties and sales taxes on all finished goods, machinery, equipment and materials imported into the freeport zone (1998).

Preferential rates are provided for warehousing and storage and reduced port charges are prescribed for all goods destined for reexport. No foreign exchange controls are imposed, enterprises can be totally foreign owned and there exists the possibility of selling a percentage of total turnover on the local market. Access to offshore banking facilities is also available (1998).

There are other advantages to be had by companies operating from the freeport. These stem from the nation's membership in the Indian Ocean Commission, the Preferential Trade Agreement, the Cross Border Initiative and the Lome Convention. The port and airport infrastructures are high in quality, as are telecommunications linkages (1998).

As early as 1991, Bavishi identified Mauritius as hosting 26 partners in the leading international accounting firms, 22 of whom were affiliated with the Big Six. Those included six each from Coopers & Lybrand Deloitte Ross Tohmatsu International and KPMG. The remaining four were associated with Price Waterhouse. Other major firms represented were BDO Binder with two partners and Pannell Kerr Forster with the same number (Appendix B, 6).

Prominent among accounting firms in Mauritius is the recently formed Price Waterhouse Coopers, the successor to two previously independent international accounting firms. Robert Bigaignon, the new firm's country leader, describes the objectives of the new firm: "The merger offers to all our clients in Mauritius and in the region access to substantially greater resources worldwide" (Price Waterhouse Coopers, July 1, 1998). He sees the merger as "providing enormous scope and scale in critically important emerging markets, as well as faster deployment of new products and services through more efficient management of a larger investment pool" and suggests that the firm's "ability to increase investment in technology and knowledge management ensures clients access to leading edge solutions" (July 1, 1998).

The new firm began operations with a client base of some 1,000 companies. Its intention is to provide a full range of business advisory services to leading national and local companies as well as to public institutions (July 1, 1998). Services to be provided include audit, accounting and tax advice as well as management, information technology and human resource consulting. The firm is also providing financial advisory services, which include assistance with mergers and acquisitions, business recovery, project finance and litigation support. Other services offered by the firm include business process outsourcing services, public relations, market research and economic research services (July 1, 1998). The firm in Mauritius also services Madagascar, the Seychelles and other Indian Ocean islands as well as portions of Eastern Africa (July 1, 1998).

The Seychelles Islands are another Indian Ocean jurisdiction that has become active in offshore financial activities. Lying north of Madagascar, the nation gained its independence from Great Britain in 1976. It is a member of the British Commonwealth and derives more than 60 percent of its foreign exchange earnings from tourism (Seychelles, 1998).

The nation is adequately equipped with transportation and communications infrastructures. Its airport can handle wide-bodied aircraft and its port, Port Victoria, can handle 20- and 40-foot containers as well as break-bulk. The nation also deals in ship chandelling and bunkering.

With a population in the 72,000 range the economy is neither strong nor diverse. Manufacturing exists on a limited scale. "As of 1991 only 2,563 persons were employed in a total of eighty-eight enterprises, twelve of them parastatals" (Library of Congress, 1994b). Most manufacturing firms are rather small, with a number being import substitution industries (1994b). However, "to encourage foreign interest in the manufacturing sector the government has developed a new investment code guaranteeing full repatriation of profits and capital, protection against nationalization, free import of capital goods, and other incentives" (1994b). Despite these initiatives the government reserves the right to require that it share an interest in large-scale industrial ventures (1994b).

As has been suggested, tourism is very important to the nation's economy. "About 15 percent of the formal workforce is directly employed in tourism and employment in construction, banking, transportation, and other activities is closely tied to the tourist industry" (1994b). Despite the importance of tourism, the government has no intention of encouraging the industry beyond what seems acceptable, given the size of the nation.

"While the Government is examining its options to disengage further in direct economic activity, it is also very keen to create an enabling environment for businesses, both domestic and those dealing both in the offshore world and international arena" (Seychelles, 1998). In 1994 the Investment Promotion Act was passed as an encouragement to inward investment. It provided fiscal incentives to businesses geared to the domestic sector and also to those aimed at export markets. The act established generous tax breaks for guaranteed periods for projects ranging from tourism, agriculture and manufacturing through to services.

The Seychelles report on the New Business Center listed various attractive elements in the new investment policies, among which were allowing for 100 percent foreign ownership and, as mentioned earlier, 100 percent repatriation of capital and profits. In addition, the new policies called for no foreign exchange controls, withholding tax on dividends, personal income tax, wealth tax, gift tax, property tax, capital gains tax or death duties (1998). Accelerated depreciation was permitted, as was the unlimited carry forward of losses arising out of depreciation. Work permits were made available for expatriates and reasonable rates were provided for corporate taxation, social security and incidental benefits (1998).

Offshore business was stimulated by the enactment of a suite of legislation in December of 1994 that covered the registration of offshore companies, offshore trusts and licensing for international trade zone companies. Since that time additional legislation has been introduced covering the licensing of offshore banks, offshore insurance companies and the setting up of a securities industry (1998).

Promotional materials from Seychelles observes that "the laws prevailing in the Caribbean, notably the Bahamas and the British Virgin Islands, are very similar to those adopted by Seychelles" (1998). As an example it suggests "the IBC Act of the Bahamas would have similarities with that of the Seychelles, whilst the International Trusts Act of Seychelles is an amalgamation of various laws prevailing in the Caribbean" (1998).

The nation has created a freeport and export processing zone as a means of attracting economic activity. Such ventures should be potentially productive, since the nation has one of the deepest seaports in the region and is strategically situated with respect to major shipping routes. Its port is efficient and cost-effective and it boasts efficient communications linkages. The institutional environment appears to be user friendly and efficient. The legislation dealing with the international trade zone provides for zero taxes and license fees that are fixed for life. It is a "One-Stop Shop Approach for redistribution, manufacturing, light assembly or export services" (1998). It also grants eligibility to sell in the domestic sector and permits firms to hire 100 percent foreign labor (1998).

The nation is promoting itself as a serious financial and business hub. "Its IBC laws, trust laws, international trade zone laws are among the most modern in the world" (1998). Satellite communications, an established banking sector, together with professional management service companies add support to the offshore aspirations of the nation (1998). In Seychelles the major accounting firms had four partners in 1991, three from BDO Binder and one from KPMG (Bavishi, 1991, Appendix B, 19).

THE FAR EAST

Singapore has been described recently as a small prosperous state situated astride one of the world's busiest sea lanes (State of Hawaii, 1999, 1). It suffers from resource limitations and a small domestic market and "more than any other country relies on foreign investment and external demand to power its economic expansion" (1). The same report suggested Singapore's strengths to be in real estate development, logistics, and planning and management (1).

According to the Hawaiian government report, the port of Singapore is the world's largest in terms of shipping tonnage. Indeed, the country acts as a trading and distribution hub for Southeast Asia and is a major transshipment link between the region and the world at large (1).

The nation's government is seeking "the development of Singapore as an international financial center and regionalization of local operations to counter inherent internal limits to growth." The British Club has seen the nation as having taken a pragmatic, carefully planned approach to economic development, "building upon its traditional strengths in entrepot trade and shipping, while gradually diversifying into banking and financial services and other high-value-added sectors" (1999).

Speaking of the nation's success as a port, the British Club points to 700 ships in port at any time, representing more than 600 shipping lines, linking more than 800 international ports (1999). "A key factor that has made Singapore a strategic hub in the Asia Pacific region is its efficient highly reliable, state-of-the-art communications infrastructure" (British Club, 1999). The Hawaiian government report identifies Changi Airport as Southeast Asia's major hub airport, boasting links to 108 cities by more than 2,100 flights by 58 airlines each week (5). Singapore's goal is to become "the leading air hub in the entire Asia-Pacific region by the end of the century" (5). Whether or not such an ambitious goal has been realized remains to be seen, but the airport "is capable of handling 24 million passengers a year" (5).

The Hawaiian report saw financial and business services and manufacturing as the most significant economic sectors, accounting for 31 and 27 percent of GDP, respectively (5). "After almost a decade of continuous growth, the Singapore economy slid into technical recession in 1998, affected by events in Asia" (The British Club, 1999, 1).

In his analysis of Singapore as an international financial center, Donald R. Lessard suggested that this jurisdiction has transformed itself from a home-based banking center in the 1960s to a regional financial center (1993, 201). He saw the country as desiring to become an international financial center as well as a regional or perhaps international capital center (200). In defining the last mentioned designation he suggested that such a center "not only engages in the financing of businesses, but also in the management and control of operations, including not only the creation of entrepreneurial capital, but also strategic roles in corporate growth and restructuring through joint ventures, alliances, internal expansion, and mergers and acquisitions" (200).

Chungsoo Kim and Kihong Kim have suggested that services have been estimated at 70 percent of GDP and 70 percent of the total workforce in Singapore (1990, 184). Those authors explained that Singapore compensates for a chronic deficit in merchandise trade through a surplus in service trade (184). Certainly, Singapore has relied upon its financial sector as a growth stimulus (McKee and Garner, 1996, 84). The Kims ranked Singapore as third in Asia as an international financial center behind Tokyo and Hong Kong (184).

Lessard saw the nation's emergence as a regional financial center as taking place gradually in the post-independence period from 1967 into the mid 1980s (1993, 201). He saw the insecurity of that period as the catalyst that pushed the government into promoting the financial sector and orienting domestic financial institutions in an outward looking direction (201). He noted that the government in the late 1960s encouraged reputable international financial institutions to establish their regional operations there (201).

As Lessard has suggested, "Financing of crossborder trade and investment within the Asian-Pacific region and between that region and the rest of the world, attracted foreign non-financial corporations into the region" (203). Large foreign banks followed their customers and set up branch networks there (203). Lessard was quite correct in suggesting that "a foreign bank that is well established in a national/regional environment in Singapore/Asia, could provide useful information, contracts, advice and financial services to its domestic clients who may be considering the possibility of entering the Asian markets" (203). Of course, various business service groups by locating in Singapore might well attract both domestic and foreign business clients wishing to conduct business in the region. As early as the mid 1980s, seven areas of growth for the financial sector were identified by the Economic Review Committee. Included were risk management, fund management, capital markets, untested securities market, financial and commodities futures, financing of third country trading and reinsurance (203).

Bavishi reported all of the then Big Six accounting firms active in Singapore in 1991. He noted the existence of 160 partners, all but 30 of whom were associated with the Big Six. Smaller firms represented included BDO, Dunwoody Robson, McGlaney and Pullen, Horwath International, Moores Rowland International, Summit International Associates Inc. and TGI (Bavishi, 1991, Appendix B, 19).

In a relatively recent publication a Price Waterhouse operating manual for Singapore was used to illustrate how extensive the operations of an accounting firm can be (McKee and Garner, 1996, 86). Of course, that firm has since merged and now functions internationally as Price Waterhouse Coopers. Nonetheless, the Price Waterhouse publication referred to speaks volumes concerning services offered.

According to the manual, Price Waterhouse in Singapore was serving "a large number of major local and international organizations as well as many smaller clients, public sector entities, non profit organizations, and individuals" (1990, 162). The firm at that time was providing comprehensive training to strengthen the expertise of its staff and was supporting its operations with both technical and library resources (163).

Beyond traditional service offerings in auditing, accountancy and taxation the firm was providing assistance in management consultancy, corporate reconstruction and insolvency. Assistance was also provided with respect to mergers and acquisitions and business advisory and corporate secretarial services. Other services offered included share and business valuations and stock exchange listings (163). The firm was serving an extensive clientele, including "financial institutions, insurance companies and both multinational and local businesses in the industrial, commercial and service sectors" (163). Any firm capable of delivering such a range of services would be in a position to supply major inputs to the nation's economy and beyond.

Price Waterhouse Management Consultants Pte Ltd., a firm that was wholly owned by the partners of the accounting firm, was offering various services. "Full-time consultants with directly relevant experience in industry are able to provide a broad range of consulting skills to senior management" (164). The firm was a part of the international network of Price Waterhouse and was able "to supplement the skills of its own consultants" with services involving general management and information technology, together with finance, manufacturing, marketing, human resources and personnel recruiting (164).

In situations involving potential insolvency the firm attempted to preserve businesses and create opportunities (164). If liquidation or receivership became necessary, the firm attempted to help in maximizing the realizations of creditors. This was recognized as evidence of a strong facilitative role with respect to supporting a healthy business climate (McKee and Garner, 1996, 87).

As stated by Price Waterhouse, "Our insolvency personnel possess a wide range of business skills and they believe in making a positive contribution to the economy by reconstructing and nursing back to viability businesses that are in financial difficulty" (1990, 164). The firm was providing assistance with business reviews and corporate reorganizations as well as with judicial management, delinquent debts and receivership of debenture holders.

The firm also stood willing to participate directly in the acquisition activities of its clients. In that area of operation services offered ranged from identifying businesses suitable for acquisition to help in integrating such acquisitions. The firm was offering advice in accounting and taxes as well as "any other matters which may arise during negotiation or completion of an acquisition" (165). The acquisition services offered by the firm were international in scope and designed to supply advice irrespective of the positioning or nature of the business being considered (165).

The firm stood willing to coordinate a full range of business advisory services for firms of varying size. In Singapore it was actually assisting in the setting up of businesses. In that regard it helped firms in the acquisition of operating facilities and also in staff recruitment. The firm was also assisting clients in familiarization with local statutory and regulatory requirements as well as in the privatization and flotation of companies.

Through its corporate secretarial service offerings the firm played a significant role in linking Singapore to the global economy. Those services included providing for the incorporation or registration of business endeavors and obtaining approvals for opening representative offices (165). The firm was also capable of obtaining reports on credit status, not to mention information concerning directors, shareholders and company financial positions (166). The firm could also assist with issues relating to expatriate employees (166).

Moores Rowland International is another major accounting firm active in Singapore. By its own assessment that organization is "one of the top 10 networks of independent accounting practices in the world" (1998a). It "brings together the capabilities of 140 independent accounting firms in 82 countries" (1998a). MRI boasts members in every region of the world dedicated to making it easier and more profitable for their clients to engage in international trade.

Among services offered are assistance with business organization in foreign countries and tax structures. Beyond such matters it can assist with due diligence and assurance engagements as well as with the acquisition of foreign subsidiaries. It can also assist with legal and banking contracts in foreign locations as well as with international business information and advice on information technology. In addition, it provides foreign market assessments and export strategies (1998a). Clearly, such services provided in Singapore help to enhance the role of that jurisdiction as an offshore financial and business center.

Certainly, advances in transportation and communications over the past 25 years have made most parts of the world more accessible and have signaled the emergence of a truly global economy. In theory at least one would expect that smaller jurisdictions should have much more positive prospects in this new international environment. However, the extent of such positive prospects for specific economies depends strongly upon how those jurisdictions are linked to the global economy. Indeed, where linkages are weak or nonexistent, material advancement may be largely unattainable. In another context, speaking of the Pacific theater, it has been suggested that "in spite of improvements in transportation and communications, many of the islands of the Pacific may be limited with respect to material betterment for want of appropriate external linkages" (McKee and Garner, 1996, 104).

Writing in 1985, Te'o Fairbairn divided the islands of the Pacific into growth economies, limited-growth economies and no-growth economies (46–54). Vanuatu was included in the most favorable cohort. Fairbairn saw the jurisdictions in that cohort as having already made progress through planning and "a considerable input of private foreign investment" (46).

Ingo Walter once suggested that "countries with very small open economies have often embraced the financial secrecy business as a way of promoting economic development" (1990, 188). He has identified various island economies in the Pacific as tax havens, including the Cook Islands,

Guam, Maldives, Nauru, Vanuatu and Tonga (187). Of course, any jurisdiction wishing to adopt offshore finance as a developmental vehicle will have to convince international financial interests of the advantages it has to offer (McKee and Garner, 1996, 107). "The onus will always be on the potential host country to convince the international financial community of its potential stability, as well as the soundness of its legal system, and other institutions related to conducting business" (McKee, 1988, 90).

Of course, small jurisdictions able to supply facilitative services to the international business community may be in a better position than those who cannot. Prominent among the various business service providers in the global economy have been the major international accounting firms. Jurisdictions hosting such firms may well enjoy certain developmental advantages.

In Vanuatu, Bavishi identified nine partners in major international accounting firms. Included were two from Coopers & Lybrand and one each from KPMG and Price Waterhouse (1991, Appendix B, 10). Other firms represented were Moores Rowland International with two partners and Pannell Kerr Forster with three (10).

The firm of Moores Rowland has identified Vanuatu as the South Pacific's premier tax haven (1998b, 1). The firm sees the nation's status as a tax haven as having had a major influence upon commercial activities and describes Vanuatu as an extremely active financial center (1). Extensive business and financial facilities are available in Vanuatu, a circumstance to which the firm attributes the nation's tax haven status (1).

"The absence of . . . taxes, duties and controls, coupled with state of the art communications and highly-developed professional services, make Vanuatu an ideal center for foreign investors to base their surplus funds for investment or to base off-shore companies forming part of a wider international or financial network" (1). Indeed, the firm sees the Vanuatu government as committed to making the country the Pacific's foremost tax haven.

The country is comprised of a chain of approximately 80 islands situated about 1,750 kilometers northeast of Sydney, Australia. Ten islands account for 90 percent of the total land area (2). The nation's financial center is located in Port Vela, the nation's capital, on Elate Island (2). The city hosts 20,000 of the nation's population of 140,000.

The Republic of Vanuatu is a parliamentary democracy, having gained its independence from Great Britain and France in 1980. It is a full member of the British Commonwealth, the French League of Nations and the United Nations as well as various international organizations. The legal system is based upon English law.

Moores Rowland describes the country as having a dualistic economy, comprising a smallholder subsistence agricultural sector and a small monetized sector, the latter being based upon established plantations, ranches and associated trading, manufacturing, banking and shipping services, together with the tourist industry. Copra is the most important cash-producing rural activity. "Nearly all domestic exports are primary goods, the principal ones being coconut products, beef, cocoa, coffee and timber" (1997d, 2).

With the advent of commercial laws in the early 1970s, an offshore finance and financial center emerged, together with "a rapid expansion in the number of support organizations and professionals in Port Vila" (2). The financial center produces significant government revenue through business license fees, insurance, banking and trust company licenses, annual company registration fees, stamp duties and other small fees (2). The center also generates foreign exchange through capital transfers, professional fees and interest (20).

Moores Rowland's Vanuatu team of professionals are the group's South Pacific specialists (1998b, 1). The firm is a founding member of the Vanuatu Financial Center Association (1). It "provides accounting, auditing, management and consulting services to government, offshore clients, local business, and individuals from around the world" (1). They provide wholesale company incorporation services to finance, legal and tax guidance professionals (1).

The firm sees itself as a central figure in the offshore financial centers of the Pacific (1). It offers a complete range of professional accounting services and incorporates international and local companies as well as insurance companies and banks (1). It serves as a registered agent and maintains a registered office address in the country of incorporation (1). It deals in all aspects of company and trust management, including bookkeeping, the establishment and management of bank accounts, arranging for corporate credit cards, corporate management and advice on corporate taxation. It has subsidiary and associate entities dealing with trustee services, real estate sales and management, communications services, banking and legal services (1).

The service menu offered by Moores Rowland includes company incorporation services, trust settlement services and registered agent and registered office (1998b, 1). It can provide nominee directors, officers and shareholders (1). In the realm of communications it provides a complete range of mail forwarding, including forwarding of incoming faxes, mail forwarding by post or courier and telephone answering and message forwarding (1). Corporate services include maintaining all statutory records, which includes the preparation of minutes and the preparation and filing of license fees (1). On request they will "prepare any required resolutions or other day to day corporate secretarial services and assist with opening letters of credit, preparation of contractual documents, control and manage bank accounts, collect income for clients, arrange for legalization of documents" (1).

Accounting services available from the firm include bookkeeping, payroll accounting, annual accounts, management accounts and auditing (1). Offshore banking services are offered via the Pacific Bank Limited. Included are such services as back-to-back financing, back-to-back deposits and trusteeships. Other offerings include offshore bank accounts in any currency, credit card services, mutual funds and portfolio management (1).

With respect to trustee/nominee services the firm deals with discretionary trusts, unit trusts, nominee accounts, declarations of trust and powers of attorney (1–2). Through Vanuatu Real Estate Consultants and Transpacific Property Consultants Ltd. the firm can handle commercial sales, residential sales, resorts and islands, businesses, valuations and management and project development (2).

The Price Waterhouse presence in Vanuatu was alluded to elsewhere (McKee and Garner, 1996, 113). "The Vanuatu practice is a part of the Price Waterhouse Australian Firm and operates from an office in the capital of Port Vila. Clients over a wide area of Vanuatu are served from this office" (Price Waterhouse, 1992b, 63). The firm in Vanuatu dates from 1972 when it was established "to provide professional auditing, accounting, management consulting, and financial services to both local and international clients" (63). Through links with its offices throughout the world the firm indicated its ability "to provide distinctive comprehensive service on an integrated basis to global clients based in Vanuatu" (64). It would appear that major accounting firms have significant potential for influencing business development and linkages in Vanuatu.

Part III

Institutional Parameters for Accounting Practice

Chapter 7

Accounting and Business Environments in the Caribbean and the North Atlantic

The institutional, business and legal environments in which the accounting firms carry out their missions are the subjects of the next three chapters. This chapter concerns five jurisdictions that host offshore centers located in the Caribbean and North Atlantic: Antigua and Barbuda, the Bahamas, Barbados, Bermuda and the Cayman Islands. Each has developed laws, regulations and institutions that have as their goal the fostering of offshore center operations as an important part of their economies. The arrangements differ from country to country, although there are many similarities. The accounting and business environments of each are reviewed with a particular eye to the effects upon accountants and the accounting firms.

ANTIGUA AND BARBUDA

Antigua and Barbuda is a member of the British Commonwealth of Nations, the United Nations, the Organization of American States, the Organization of Eastern Caribbean States, the Caribbean Common Market, the International Monetary Fund and the World Bank. The island state's governance system is similar to and based on the British legal and parliamentary system. The capital city is St. John's on Antigua (Price Waterhouse, 1991a, 3).

The currency unit, the Eastern Caribbean dollar (E.C.$), is divisible into 100 cents, with a fixed exchange rate of E.C.$2.7 to the U.S. dollar (1991a, 11). The economy is largely open and based on free enterprise principles. Although sugar cultivation was the country's primary product before the 1960s, tourism is now economic leader accounting for approximately 60 percent of GDP. Population has doubled over the past three decades during a period when agriculture declined from 40 to 12 percent of GDP. Antigua has good international transportation and communication links. The country is in the same time zone as the United States and Canadian Atlantic coast.

Public utilities, airport and seaport are government owned and operated. The government's Central Marketing Authority controls import and distribution systems for basic foodstuffs. The government, the islands' largest landowner, follows a policy of selling land for tourist and residential development projects. Despite the large government sector, government policies seem to indicate that government's economic intervention will give way to more private sector opportunities in the future. The country's businesses are increasingly in the private sector. Local industry has enjoyed protection against imports that would compete with local products. The government's policy currently appears to be moving toward freer trade. Antigua and Barbuda do not have a stock exchange.

A small and growing offshore center in Antigua and Barbuda dates from the passage of the International Business Companies Act in 1982. With this law, the legal system and forms of business were structured to accommodate both domestic and offshore sectors. The country became a tax haven. An international business company (IBC) is exempted from all local taxes so long as it does not carry on business in or with the domestic sector of the economy. Aspects of the international offshore center and its operations are discussed below after the sections on the domestic sector.

For business within the country, licenses for wholesaling, retailing, banking, insurance must be obtained from the Ministry of Finance. Professionals, including lawyers, architects and accountants, must register and pay an annual license fee to the ministry. Importing and exporting goods is not controlled, but appropriate licenses are required (16).

Foreign investors may own businesses in the country without ownership participation by nationals. Prior approvals must be obtained and approval depends upon the business type and form. Land may not be owned or leased on a long-term basis by non-citizens. The Non-Citizens Land Holding Regulations Act provides for license issuance to own or lease land on a case-by-case basis (16).

Appropriate private foreign investments are welcomed by the government with tax holidays, duty-free imports and other investment incentives common. Investments and profit may generally be repatriated. Qualified new businesses may receive exemptions from exchange controls (20).

The Companies Act provides for business in Antigua and Barbuda to be carried on by sole proprietors, partnerships, joint ventures, local incorporated companies and foreign company branches (41).

The Registrar of Companies section of the Attorney General's Office regulates company affairs as required by the Companies Act. Businesses must register in accordance with the Business Registration Act, providing the business name and the names of the individuals who own the business.

Sole proprietorships are usually reserved for citizens. A non-citizen must have approval of the ministry to operate as a sole proprietor. A foreign investor who wishes to operate as a proprietorship must also obtain a work permit. These are issued in cases where the proposed business is in a specialized area and where there are expected benefits to the country (46).

If a foreigner is accepted as a partner or as a joint venture participant, approval must be obtained from the Ministry of Economic Development. Permission from the ministry is also required to operate a branch of a foreign company.

Branches of companies incorporated outside of Antigua and Barbuda must provide information to the registrar of companies upon formation and thereafter. Parent company charter or articles of incorporation setting forth bylaws and information on directors of the parent company must be provided. The branch must designate at least one resident person to receive legal notices and processes on behalf of the company. Financial statements of the parent company must be filed each year.

Private or public companies may be formed in Antigua and Barbuda. A private company must not solicit for subscriptions for share or debentures and must have at least two but no more than 50 shareholders, whereas a public company may have shareholders without limit so long as there are a minimum of five shareholders. Shares may be issued as bearer securities or registered. A stated value is required since no par stock is not permitted. Treasury stock transactions are not allowed (42). Incorporators may provide company bylaws or, by default, bylaws are promulgated in Table A of the Companies Act.

If company shares are to be of the bearer variety, they must be fully paid before issuance. Different classes of share voting rights are permitted. Preferred stock may be issued. Payment of dividends or buy back of shares from contributed capital is not permitted without court approval. Shareholder liability is limited to shares paid up or subscribed. Annual shareholder meetings must be held.

A file kept in the courthouse can be viewed by the public for each company that has been awarded a certificate of incorporation. The file contains details of share capital, list of directors and secured debt. This file also contains company annual returns (43).

Shareholders must hold a meeting each year at which they consider the directors' report and a report on company accounts, approve dividend declaration and hold necessary elections to the board of directors.

Directors may include non-citizens. Appointment of auditors is provided for in Table A of the Companies Act, but company accounts are not required by the Companies Act to be audited. Legislation requires audited statements for banks and similar institutions but for no other businesses (44–46). A requirement for annual audit of financial statements is included in the bylaws of many companies, however, and it is usual for companies to have annual audits.

The Inland Revenue Service also does not require audited statements or audited tax reports but may be concerned when they are not provided. Books of account adequate for proper income reporting are required by the Income Tax Act. As a general practice, before lending to a business, banks do require audited financial statements (56).

As noted above, a government license to practice public accounting is required. Development of an accounting professional association is underway but is in the formative stages. Most practicing public accountants are members of overseas professional associations and follow the requirements and rules of those groups.

Antigua and Barbuda has not developed generally accepted national accounting principles, generally accepted auditing standards, or disclosure requirements. International Auditing Guidelines of the International Federation of Accountants and International Accounting Standards of the International Accounting Standards Committee are generally used as reference by practicing accountants (57).

The International Business Companies Act of 1982 provides qualifying businesses with an automatic 50-year guarantee of tax-free status for operations offshore. The legislation also applies to offshore banks, trust companies and insurance companies, in addition to international business companies (3). The act provides for complete tax exemption, complete exchange control, exemptions and freedom to operate bank accounts anywhere. Such companies have no minimum capital requirement. There is no requirement for statutory audits. Shares may be issued as bearer, and in such cases the owner need not be registered.

While all of these provisions are applicable to the IBC, those in banking, trust companies and insurance companies have additional requirements. An IBC may obtain a license to do business as an offshore bank. In this case minimum capital required is U.S.$1 million. Confidentiality for all business transactions is a legal requirement. For an IBC trust company minimum capital is U.S.$500,000. Quarterly returns are required. Trust accumulations are not limited. IBCs in the insurance business have a reserve requirement of at least U.S.$250,000. Banks, trusts and insurance IBCs must file annual audited financial statements.

Two resident citizens who file articles of incorporation may form an Antigua IBC. One of the two must be an attorney. An IBC may only carry on international trade or business outside of Antigua. The incorporation fee is U.S.$250 with $250 per year renewal fee. The IBC is required to have only one shareholder who may be the only director. If solvent, an IBC may purchase and cancel its own shares. Directors and shareholders must have an annual meeting in Antigua and Barbuda. Other meetings may be held outside of the country. Proxy voting is allowed. Shareholder and board of directors meeting minutes are required to be kept on file at the IBC registered office in Antigua.

THE BAHAMAS

The economy of the Bahamas has both domestic and offshore sectors. The legal system and the forms of business permitted work to accommodate both of these sectors. Offshore business and financial activities are substantial according to Deloitte Touche Tohmatsu International (Deloitte Touche Tohmatsu International, 1996c, 5). Bank confidentiality laws prohibit disclosure of information to foreign governments except after approval by the Bahamian Supreme Court (9).

The banking system, government securities and exchange controls and the money supply are all regulated by the Central Bank of the Bahamas. Currency transactions are categorized as "resident" if made in the domestic economy and "non-resident" otherwise. There is no stock exchange in the Bahamas. However, trust companies broker the shares of public companies (29).

Direct investments by residents made in any non-Bahamian currency require approval. Direct investments in Bahamian assets by non-residents require approval and registration. Non-residents must have approval to borrow Bahamian dollars but may borrow without restriction in any other currency. Residents must have approval for all borrowings in other than the Bahamian dollar (Price Waterhouse, 1992a, 10). Further, non-residents must have approval of exchange control to convert foreign cash to Bahamian dollars, or to purchase assets within the country. To send cash remittances out of the country, residents must have exchange control approval. Any foreign currency that is received for exports must be exchanged for Bahamian dollars, except where permission is obtained from the Central Bank to keep the foreign currency. No controls are imposed on imports.

The Companies Acts allow for formation of domestic business organizations that operate in similar fashion to companies in other parts of the world. The International Business Companies Act 1989 was passed to segregate and limit the domestic effects of operations of the Bahamian offshore centers. Businesses formed under this act may not conduct business with residents of the Bahamas.

Business entities formed to conduct domestic business under the Companies Acts may take the form of sole proprietorship, joint venture, general or limited partnership, companies limited by share, companies limited by guarantee, private trust, branch or office of a foreign company. Sole proprietorships are generally found in the small organizations in the retail trade. Business licenses must be obtained. There are no government registrations or reporting required when forming a joint venture. Such arrangements are generally made by contract between the parties to the joint venture. Of course, the Bahamian currency exchange controls apply and appropriate fees must be paid (Deloitte Touche Tohmatsu International, 1996c, 33).

Partnerships in the Bahamas may be either a general or limited partnership. A general partnership in which all partners have unlimited liability may be formed without a written partnership agreement for most types of general partnerships. To form a limited partnership at least one partner must assume unlimited liability. A written partnership agreement is required and must be registered. Only unlimited liability partners may manage the business of the partnership. For trading in the Bahamas business licenses are needed (46).

Limited liability companies may be companies limited by shares or companies limited by guarantee. An incorporation application must be filed by at least two people. The name of the company must include "Limited" or "Ltd." An annual report indicating company owners and their proportional share of ownership is required. Financial statements are not required to be a part of this report (43). The board of directors must have at least three members for a public company, two for private companies. An annual audit of financial statements is required for public companies. A private company must also obtain an annual audit, except where shareholders agree not to have an audit (44).

For a company limited by shares the owners' liability is limited to the amount paid in or subscribed for shares. For a company limited by guaranty the extent of owners' liability is a designated maximum amount to be paid in if necessary upon winding up of the company (48).

In the Bahamas mutual funds may take the form of a company, unit trusts or partnerships. A prospectus for the sale of mutual fund shares must be distributed to the public. This prospectus must be filed and approved by the Central Bank. Mutual funds from other countries may operate in the Bahamas by using the trust form (49).

Residents and non-residents may form private revocable or irrevocable trusts. The Bahamian Trustee Act of 1995 governs these arrangements, which are viewed as agreements between private parties. Such trusts do not require registration (47).

Foreign corporations may operate branches or registered offices but must not be in direct competition with a Bahamian business. A trading branch must register in accordance with the Bahamas Companies Act. Business licenses are required, and exchange controls must be observed.

When a branch either holds real estate or engages in litigation, it must register under the Bahamas Companies Act and provide information about the parent company's incorporation, its officers and its directors. Financial statements for neither the branch nor the parent need to be submitted or publicly disclosed. There are no stated requirements for branch accounting, books or records (45).

A special form of the limited liability company is the international business company (IBC). The IBC may be appropriate for holding companies that do business outside the Bahamas, for offshore trading companies doing business outside the Bahamas, for offshore investment companies, for shipping companies or for mutual funds. IBCs are formed and regulated in accordance with the International Business Companies Act of 1989. An IBC may not conduct business with residents of the Bahamas and may not own Bahamian real estate. Nor may an IBC do business as a bank or insurance company or maintain registered offices for other companies. IBCs pay the government initial and annual filing fees but, as noted elsewhere in this volume, IBCs are not subject to Bahamian taxes.

IBC ownership and related information must be kept confidential. Ownership, operation or control may lie within or outside of the Bahamas. The IBC may be private or public. The public IBC issues shares to the public and therefore must have approval of the Central Bank. A foreign company that meets the requirements may register as a Bahamian IBC. The IBC may have limited life and may also take on the characteristics of a partnership (33).

The IBC needs to file only minimal information with the Registry of Companies. Account books and records may be maintained outside of the Bahamas. Neither the issuance nor the audit of IBC financial statements is required. The IBC must, however, maintain a registered office that can act as a legal home and have a resident registered agent who can receive legal notices and the like (37).

The government encourages direct foreign investments in the Bahamas when the investments further national economic growth and prosperity. The Investments Board oversees foreign investments, which must have any required local business licenses and permits. Projects are not permitted to compete directly with Bahamian citizens (3). Ownership participation by Bahamians is required and the percentage of such ownership may vary on a selective basis.

Minimal recordkeeping requirements are prescribed for most business entities. Payroll records, including cash paid to employees, must be kept in detail under the requirements of the National Insurance Act of 1972. Detailed accounting records with audited annual financial statements are required for banks, trust companies, credit unions, insurance companies and unions. Annual reports must be submitted to the appropriate ministries.

The form and content of the financial statements is not set out in the law. But by common practice the balance sheet, statement of profit and loss, and the statement of changes in financial position are included in the definition of financial statements. Appropriate explanatory notes necessary for adequate disclosure are also common practice (55).

The government has not set valuation bases or methods to be used. The Bahamas Institute of Chartered Accountants has recommended that International Accounting Standards be the basis generally accepted for financial statements. This recommendation is followed in general practice, but some subsidiaries and branches of foreign corporations follow their home country accounting practices and standards (55).

Financial statements are expected to represent a "true and fair view" of the company's financial position and the results of its operations. British reporting concepts prevail. Although assets may be valued upward, historical cost is the basis generally used for asset valuation. Should assets be revalued upward the corresponding credit is made to an appraisal increase account. The straight-line basis is the usual method for depreciation of assets (56).

Inventory values are set at cost with the common methods being first-in first-out, actual, average and retail. A loss is booked when the net realizable value of an asset falls below cost on a permanent basis. Leases are normally accounted for in consonance with International Accounting Standards. That is, finance leases, those where ownership risks and rewards are owned by the lessee, are accounted for as though purchased with subsequent depreciation taken into profit and loss accounts. Payments for operating leases are recognized in the accounting period when the cash is paid or received.

Since research and development costs are rare for Bahamian companies, no generally accepted method for the accounting treatment has been set. For construction or other long-term projects, interest costs on borrowings specifically for the project in question may be capitalized as part of the cost of the resulting asset.

The purchase method of accounting for company mergers is the usual treatment. Pooling of interests may, however, be used when the apparent purchaser and the acquired firm are basically equivalent in size and standing. When the purchase method is used, goodwill is determined at acquisition of the subsidiary. Such goodwill may be recognized and kept at the original amount indefinitely, amortized over its estimated useful life or written off to expense in the accounting period in which the merger took place (56).

Consolidated financial statements are prepared where a parent corporation effectively controls 50 percent or more of a subsidiary company.

Those subsidiaries that are not controlled or are not 50 percent or more owned are reported as an investment in affiliates on the parent corporation's financial statements (58).

Bank, trust, and insurance companies need to obtain specific licensing from the Ministry of Finance and Planning and the Registrar of Insurance Companies, respectively. Bank and trust companies must file audited financial statements with the Central Bank and publish a balance sheet and audit report in the *Official Gazette*. Insurance companies must file audited financial statements with the Registrar of Insurance Companies and publish financial summaries in the *Official Gazette* (52–53).

Although statutory auditors are not required by the law, companies organized under the Companies Acts are required to have independently audited financial statements. IBCs, it should be noted, have no requirement for their financial statements to be audited. By the letter of the companies law government ministries can allow any person to act as independent auditor. In practice, however, company directors are responsible for the decision and professional accountants are engaged who are either individual practitioners who are member of the Bahamas Institute of Chartered Accountants or members of reputable accounting firms.

BARBADOS

Barbados has an efficient infrastructure with an effective legal system. The country consists of an area of 166 square miles with Bridgetown, the capital, the only substantial population center. The approximate population is 260,000. The country's very high English literacy rate is estimated at 98 percent of the population.

A British colony until independence in 1966, Barbados is today an independent nation within the British Commonwealth. The country is a member of the United Nations and the Organization of American States. Its parliament of two houses is modeled after the British parliament. The legal system is also patterned after English statutes and common law. Final appeal from the Barbados courts is to the Privy Council in England (Price Waterhouse Coopers, 1999, Chapter One).[1]

The economy is a small and open one with four basic sectors: tourism, agriculture, manufacturing and offshore financial services. Tourism is the top producer. A broad-based and expanding offshore business center includes international business companies, captive insurance companies, offshore banks, foreign sales corporations, shipping companies and trusts. The successes of the offshore center businesses are aided by Canadian and United States tax treaties that have been entered into by Barbados.

Barbados is a member of the Caribbean Common Market (CARICOM) as well as a beneficiary of the Lome Convention with the European Union, the Generalized System of Preferences (GSP) and Caribbean Basin Initiative (CBI) schemes of the United States, and Caribcan, a Canadian incentive program (Chapter 2).

There is an import licensing system, and import duties are levied in the forms of customs duty, stamp tax, consumption tax and various surcharges. These constitute major added costs for imported goods.

Some businesses must have government approval through various licensing systems. Chief among them are utilities, broadcasting, banking, international business and insurance. State ownership has declined in the recent past, and the government is committed to continuing this policy (Chapter 2).

The currency is the Barbados dollar (Bds.$) which is pegged to the United States dollar at a parity of U.S.$1.00 = Bds.$2.00 (Price Waterhouse, 1994, 6). Commercial banks maintain a forward currency market. Exchange controls are in force and administered by the minister of finance and the Central Bank of Barbados (35). Offshore businesses have been exempted from the exchange controls for offshore transactions.

Direct investments in Barbados's domestic economy by foreigners must have approval in advance from the Central Bank. On entry into Barbados foreign investment monies should be registered in order to insure later repatriation. Repatriation of these funds is generally allowed by the Central Bank after all local taxes have been paid (Ernst & Young, 1999c, Section F). Capital gains on foreign investments may be remitted to foreign investors on a rate of return calculated on original foreign money invested. Furthermore, such returns must have the approval of the Central Bank. Purchase of Barbados securities and purchase of real estate for private use with foreign money by non-residents must have prior approval (Price Waterhouse, 1994, 14).

Non-residents must have Central Bank approval to borrow local funds. Non-residents are authorized to have bank accounts, which are titled "external" accounts. Such accounts may receive transfers from other "external" accounts. Remittances overseas require Central Bank approval. Likewise, residents in Barbados need approval to borrow foreign monies. Payments for certain imports must have approval for the overseas payments to be made. Payments in foreign currencies for exports are required to be converted into Barbados dollars (14, 15).

The International Business Company Act enabled the international financial center activities that are well established and growing. There are a number of different types of arrangements that can be made for offshore operations. Some of these are the international business company, offshore banks and trusts, offshore captive insurance companies, foreign sales corporations and flags of convenience shipping companies. As noted above, treaties with Canada, the United States and other countries have made a number of these offshore arrangements viable. Barbados is not a pure tax haven in that taxes are levied. A number of advantages, however, make the offshore company operations attractive: low tax rates, no currency controls except for the domestic sector, low costs, free-trade zones and confidentiality laws. Barbados does require various licensures and fee payments.

Varying regulation, administration and taxation have been established by legislative acts that have been deemed appropriate for the type of business activity carried out by an offshore center entity. Although information is not made public, detailed reporting and filings are required with the appropriate government body.

Audit requirements vary. All offshore banks and insurance companies must have an annual audit and file audited statements. IBCs are required to have an audit when their gross revenue is greater than Bds.$1 million. On the other hand, foreign sales companies are not required to have an audit.

A wide variety of overseas business activities may be carried on by the IBC. Such companies may not, however, conduct any business in the local economy. The IBC may be a Barbados incorporation or may be an overseas company branch which registers to do overseas business as an IBC. CARICOM residents may hold no more than 10 percent of the capital in an IBC. Enclave manufacturing for export only is permitted by an IBC. Records and books of the IBC may be kept in a foreign currency. Annual fees must be paid. The tax rates on IBC profits are from one to two and one-half percent.

To conduct offshore banking operations a license must be issued by the minister of finance. The IBC must be incorporated in Barbados, and it must have at least one director resident within the country. Capitalization must be at least Bds.$1 million for non-residents and Bds.$250,000 for resident shareholders. Such banking IBCs are limited to doing offshore banking from within Barbados. The minister of finance must received quarterly financial reports and audited annual financial statements. The company must accumulate a reserve fund from earnings equal to its company capitalization by reserving at least 25 percent of annual profits (27, 28).

Under the Companies Act authorized forms for organizing and carrying on business within the domestic economy of Barbados are the sole proprietorship, partnerships, branches of foreign corporations and domestic corporations. A foreigner or a citizen may carry on business as a sole proprietor. The foreign individual must of course comply with the immigration statutes. Limited partnerships may be used for up to 20 partners if there is at least one partner who accepts unlimited liability for partnership obligations. Limited partners have their liability limited to their investment. General partnerships are similar to those in other

English Common Law countries. A joint venture can be carried out in either the partnership or corporate form of business organization. Branches of foreign companies, called "external companies," may operate in Barbados. Such branches do not require equity participation by locals or residents. The branches must register with the registrar of companies and pay required fees. They must also file annual reports with the registrar. The invested amounts and resulting earnings are generally able to be repatriated without restriction, but as noted above, approval is needed (Price Waterhouse, 1994, 55).

Incorporation of limited liability companies requires that articles of incorporation be provided and approved by the registrar of companies. Minimum capital is not specified, except for companies seeking to be approved as banks or insurance companies. A stated value is required for shares. Bearer shares are not authorized. There is no requirement for citizens or residents to participate in the equity. The minimum number of shareholders is one. Share transfers are unlimited. A corporate resolution may increase the original stated capital. Stated capital may be decreased by resolution if the corporation meets a solvency test. So long as solvency tests are met, treasury stock transactions are permitted (50, 51).

After the certificate of incorporation is received from the registrar, the board of directors appoints the first auditor and the corporate officers. Subsequently, auditors are appointed by resolution of shareholders at their annual meeting. The secretary of the corporation must be a chartered secretary, an attorney-at-law or a Barbados-chartered accountant (52). Corporate records, minutes, and registers must be maintained at the registered office of the company.

All domestic public companies and private companies with assets or gross revenue above Bds.$1 million are required to have audited financial reports. These companies must make the audited financial reports available to shareholders and must file copies with the registrar of companies. This financial information is also made public if appropriate. Financial statements may not be issued unless they are accompanied by an auditor's report. The Income Tax Act requires that tax reports include the audited financial statements (66). A company may seek approval from the registrar to be relieved from disclosing some required information to the public on the basis that disclosure would be detrimental to the company and its shareholders.

To be eligible to be appointed auditor for a corporation, an accountant must hold a certificate to practice public accounting and must be a member of the Institute of Chartered Accountants of Barbados.

Domestic companies must keep their books of account and related records at the company registered office in Barbados. If the books are kept outside Barbados, adequate reports must be sent to Barbados quarterly (65). Records within Barbados must be adequate to determine the proper and correct amount of taxes payable by the company.

Accounting practices and standards have not been legislated. The Institute of Chartered Accountants of Barbados was charged in the Companies Act with the responsibility of drawing up appropriate professional and accounting standards. The Institute of Chartered Accountants of Barbados was created in an act of parliament in 1974. The institute was founded to regulate professional ethics, discipline, and professional standards (66).

Members of the institute are also members of accounting associations in other countries, in particular Canada and the United Kingdom. The standards for audit in Barbados are the International Auditing Guidelines. International Accounting Standards that the institute found appropriate for use have been selectively approved for use in Barbados. Should the adopted IAS not cover a given situation, practicing accountants commonly employ standards from their home country (67).

Financial statements consist of the balance sheet, income statement, retained earnings statement and statement of changes in financial position with appropriate disclosures in notes to the financial statements. The first-in, first-out method of inventory valuation is commonly used. Last-in, first-out is not an acceptable method. The value of real estate assets is permitted to be written above cost based on independent appraisal. Plant and machinery assets are depreciated on a straight-line or declining-balance basis over asset useful live (Price Waterhouse Coopers, 1999, Chapter 12).

Goodwill arising from the purchase method of accounting for an affiliation of companies may be written off over goodwill useful life or as approved by directors. Consolidated financial statements are prepared for parent and controlled subsidiaries. Those major investments in companies not consolidated are given the equity method treatment. Deferred income taxes are accounted for by the liability method. Should the taxes payable method be used, disclosure must be made of the effects of not using the liability method. Statutory reserves are required only for banks and insurance companies. Adequate disclosure is required so that the financial statements fairly present the results of operations and the financial position of the company (Chapter 12).

Requirements for those companies listed on the Securities Exchange of Barbados are more stringent. Companies listed on the exchange must operate a transfer and registry office in Barbados. Annual and quarterly financial reports must be provided to each shareholder or publicly disclosed. The reports must be comparative with the prior period report provided. An auditor's report must cover each annual financial statement. Foreign investors may purchase shares listed but must have the approval of the Central Bank (44). Cross-trading arrangements have been set up with the Trinidad and the Jamaican stock exchanges (Chapter 6).

BERMUDA

The capital city, Hamilton, houses most of Bermuda's business entities. The Bermuda population, estimated at 60,000, has a high standard of living, with a per capita annual income in excess of U.S.$27,000. The economy is almost entirely in the private sector. There are no income or profits taxes, capital gains taxes or withholding taxes. Import taxes account for about 30 percent of government revenues with the remainder coming from use taxes. The Bermuda dollar (Bd.$) is divided into 100 cents and for most purposes is on par with the U.S. dollar. Bermuda is not a member of any trade bloc (Price Waterhouse Coopers, 1999, Chapter 1).

Tourism is the major industry, closely followed by international business services. These include insurance, reinsurance, corporate, individual and public investment holdings, mutual funds, unit and personal trusts, shipping, trading and management companies (Chapter 1).

The economy is stable and prosperous, with little or no unemployment. Approximately 22 percent of the work force are from outside of Bermuda because sufficient local workers are not available. The cost of living is high. Thus government policies and actions are directed at keeping the costs of locating in Bermuda as low as possible. In 1995 inflation was gauged as 2.5 percent. The government's budget philosophy is to restrict borrowing. A ceiling of not more than 10 percent of GDP has been targeted for direct government borrowing and government guarantees of semipublic and private debt (Chapter 2).

The government is very active in securing foreign investments in entities based in Bermuda but which are not in competition with local businesses. These offshore companies are referred to as exempted undertakings such as exempted companies, permit companies, exempted partnerships and exempted unit trusts. These can be 100 percent owned by non-Bermudians, are not subject to foreign exchange controls in Bermuda and can readily obtain exemption up to March 28, 2016 from any future legislation imposing income taxes in Bermuda (Chapter 3). Major reasons for the offshore operations are the opportunity to hold, accumulate and transfer capital and income without local tax or exchange control. The ability to do business with minimum host government supervision is another major benefit for the offshore company (Chapter 3).

Foreigners are generally restricted to no more than 40 percent of the ownership in domestic entities. Foreign ownership of housing is controlled. Houses in the top market range or specified condominiums only are available to foreigners. Corporations are not permitted to own real estate in Bermuda. These restrictions are designed to protect local Bermudian interests.

Exchange controls are in force for all domestic companies and for residents who work for local companies. Exchange of the Bermuda dollar for residents and local companies is subject to a 0.25 percent tax on the purchase of a foreign currency. Exempted companies and non-residents may trade and maintain bank accounts in any currency. The exchange control or tax does not apply. Exchange controls are not generally applied to trust settlements on behalf of non-residents (Chapter 6).

Consent of the Monetary Authority must ordinarily be received for the issue or transfer of any share or security. For sufficient reasons, such as publicly traded securities, blanket permission for share issues and transfers may be granted.

Bermuda's laws are descended from English Common Law. Forms of business found in Bermuda are therefore quite similar to those in other English-speaking countries. The Bermuda Companies Act of 1981, as amended, governs business organizations. Common forms of business organization authorized in Bermuda include: companies, local or exempted; companies incorporated in another country and granted a permit to do business from within Bermuda; general or limited partnerships, local or exempted; and trusts (Chapter 9).

While business can be conducted using the partnership form, most businesses incorporate as limited liability companies. Companies incorporated outside Bermuda must receive a permit to operate in Bermuda. Such permits are issued only as special situations. The Bermuda government policy is that companies located in Bermuda should be incorporated in Bermuda (Chapter 3).

The limited liability company may chose to operate in the local domestic economy or operate as an exempted company. Local domestic companies are required to have at least 60 percent Bermudian ownership. They may transact business worldwide or in Bermuda only (Chapter 9).

Exempted limited liability companies may have up to 20 percent Bermudian ownership. An exempted company is the most common form used by international businesses to transact business from Bermuda. The exempted company is so called because of its exemption from restrictions on the percentage of share capital that may be held by non-Bermudians. The exempted company may not own or have interests in land in Bermuda, own any interest in a domestic Bermuda company or carry on domestic business of any kind in the domestic Bermuda market. Exempted companies are required to conduct their business transactions in a currency other than Bermuda dollars.

Permit companies are incorporated in jurisdictions other than Bermuda but are granted a permit to transact business from Bermuda. Permits are obtained through a license granted by the Ministry of Finance (Ernst and Young, 1999b, Section D).

Company formation is generally by way of registration under the Companies Act. Formation under a private act of the Bermuda legislature is available and is necessary for companies requiring special provisions. The procedures are similar to those via registration, except that a parliamentary act is required (Price Waterhouse Coopers, 1999, Chapter 9).

To form a company by registration, a proposed company name should be reserved with the registrar of companies, and an advertisement should be placed in a local newspaper announcing the intention to incorporate with the said company name. The principal objectives of the company need to be stated. The incorporators next apply to the minister of finance with appropriate information for permission to register the company. The choice between a local domestic company and an exempted company is made on this application (Chapter 9).

After receiving approval from the minister of finance, the memorandum of association should be filed with the registrar of companies. Upon issuance of the certificate of incorporation, the incorporating group will convene an initial shareholder meeting. At this meeting, shareholder by-laws are approved, the auditors are selected and the board of directors is elected. The first meeting of the board of directors will follow to elect company officers, determine the fiscal year, establish a registered office and deal with other matters necessary to commence the business of the company. Except for the newspaper advertisement and the memorandum of association, information submitted with the application must be held confidential and is not available to the public. The only other documents available for public inspection are the certificate of incorporation, the memorandum of association, the register of shareholders and details of registered charges over the company's assets. Corporate financial statements are not filed with any government unit, nor are they available to the public (Chapter 9).

The authorized share capital of an exempted company must be at least equivalent to Bds.$12,000. This minimum must be fully subscribed but need not be fully paid. Shares may not be in bearer form and are required to have a stated par value. The company must have at least three shareholders. Shareholder liability is limited to the amount of unpaid subscriptions. Transfers of shares of exempted companies are subject to prior approval by the Bermuda Monetary Authority, except in the case of mutual funds and publicly listed companies where general consent is granted.

Different classes of shares with special rights or limitations may be issued. Redeemable preference shares are permitted if authorized by company bylaws. If authorized in the memorandum of association, the company may repurchase and cancel its own shares. Shares may not be reissued. A subsidiary company may purchase shares of its parent, but the parent may not provide financial assistance for such repurchase (Chapter 9).

Soon after the minimum share capital has been subscribed and after a five days notice is provided to shareholders, a statutory meeting is held to elect the board of directors. Thereafter, an annual general meeting of shareholders, which may be held outside Bermuda, is required to receive the financial statements and the reports of directors and auditors. Directors and auditors are also elected at the annual meeting. The meeting can be by means of a telephone conference if permitted in company bylaws. Shareholder meeting minutes must be maintained at the company's Bermuda-registered office. Majority vote decides matters before meetings of either directors or shareholders. Dividends must be paid only out of distributable profits. Distributions or liquidating dividends may be paid from contributed surplus (Chapter 9).

Corporate records and the register of shareholders must be kept in Bermuda. Accounting books and related records may be kept outside Bermuda, so long as records in Bermuda are sufficient such that the directors can determine with reasonable accuracy the financial position of the company each quarter. An annual audit is required unless waived unanimously by all shareholders. The audited financial statements are not required to be available to the public, nor is there a requirement to file with any government authority (Chapter 11).

The accounting profession in Bermuda is governed by the Institute of Chartered Accountants of Bermuda (ICAB), which is formally affiliated with the Canadian Institute of Chartered Accountants (CICA). The accounting and auditing standards of the CICA are generally followed in Bermuda. The pronouncements of the Auditing Standards Committee of the CICA vary little from those in the United Kingdom and the United States. The CICA has not codified standards and procedures to the same extent as those of American Institute of Certified Public Accountants (Chapter 11).

To become a member of the ICAB, applicants must complete appropriate practical experience and pass the uniform examination for admission to the profession used in Canada. Members of ICAB may use the designation "chartered accountant." Qualified accountants may be admitted to ICAB on the basis of their membership in an approved foreign professional accounting body (Chapter 11).

International accounting standards, which are normally supplemented by Canadian generally accepted accounting principles, are recommended by the ICAB. Accounting principles are generally those of the CICA. The *CICA Handbook*, which contains the requirements as to accounting principles and reporting practices formulated by the Accounting Standards

Committee for the CICA, is considered the single most authoritative pronouncement on generally accepted accounting principles and reporting practices in Canada and in Bermuda. These generally accepted accounting principles are used by public and private companies.

The principles are similar to those in the United States. In recent years there have been some differences between the two sets of principles. For example, in the United States all research and development costs should be expensed immediately; in Canada, development expenses that meet certain criteria should be deferred and amortized. Also, in the United States foreign exchange translation differences arising from an enterprise's own transactions or those of an integrated subsidiary are recognized immediately in the income statement. In Canada such translation differences arising from long-term debt are deferred and amortized over the life of the debt (Chapter 12).

The CICA is a member of the International Accounting Standards Committee (IASC). Although there are some differences between the International Accounting Standards and CICA pronouncements, in many respects the IASC and CICA pronouncements correspond closely such that use of one set of standards complies with another set.

As noted above, Canadian generally accepted accounting principles (GAAP) and auditing standards are generally applicable in Bermuda. Bermuda companies are permitted to follow the GAAP of other jurisdictions. This frequently occurs where a parent company desires to use standards from the home country. In these cases ICAB recommends that only internationally accepted accounting standards be used. Full disclosure of the GAAP used needs to be made in the financial statement notes and the auditors' opinion (Ernst & Young, 1999b).

The basic components of annual financial statements of companies are the following: balance sheet, income statement, statement of retained earnings, statement of changes in cash and notes. Management's "Discussion and Analysis of Financial Condition and Results of Operations" must accompany the financial statements (Chapter 12).

A clear and concise description of significant accounting policies must be provided in the notes, particularly when a selection has been made from alternative acceptable accounting principles or when the accounting principles and methods are peculiar to an industry in which the company operates. Small and large companies alike must follow the disclosure requirements (Price Waterhouse Coopers, 1999, Chapter 12).

CAYMAN ISLANDS

In the view of Deloitte Touche Tohmatsu International the Cayman Islands maintains liberal trade regulations that do not limit or significantly affect international businesses (1995, 13). There are no price controls, exchange controls, taxation or reporting requirements for international movement of funds (12, 16). The government revenues are raised by import duties and use taxes and business licensures and fees (Ernst & Young, 1995, 1, 25).

The currency has been fixed at parity with the U. S. dollar such that C.I.$1 equals U.S.$1.20. Any major currency, however, may be used in the Cayman Islands for banking and for other transactions (Deloitte Touche Tohmatus International, 1995, 2, 3).

Based on English statute law and common law, the Companies Law governs business in the Cayman Islands. Businesses intending to operate onshore in the domestic economy are authorized to take the forms of a sole proprietorship, trust, general or limited partnership, branch of a foreign company or an ordinary company. Several types of authorized exempted companies are designed to carry on business offshore but directed from the Caymans.

Each individual who carries on a trade or business is required to take out an annual Trade and Business License for each place of trade or business (Ernst & Young, 1999a). Foreign sole proprietors are permitted in the domestic economy but must have an additional license under the Local Companies (Control) Law of 1976, as revised. The foreign sole proprietor would also need a work permit.

The trust form may be either an ordinary trust, which has no registration requirements but has a maximum duration of 150 years, or an exempted trust, which requires that a trust deed be filed with the registrar of trusts. These files are not public documents but may be inspected by the trustee or anyone authorized by the trust. The advantage of the exempted trust is that it may receive a government guarantee of exemption from future taxes for up to 50 years (34).

A partnership in the Cayman Islands is generally created by a written partnership agreement. General partnerships are governed by the Partnership Law of 1983. A person or corporation may be a partner. Legal liability of partners in a general partnership is unlimited. Partners are jointly and severally liable for partnership obligations. There is no public disclosure required. There are no specific requirements for capital or for accounting books and records, except those written into the partnership agreement.

Limited partnerships may have any number of partners with limited liability but must have at least one general partner who has unlimited liability. This form of partnership must be declared with an appropriate information filing with the registrar of limited partnerships and published by government notice by the general partners. A list of all limited partnerships kept by the registrar is open to the public. The general partners are responsible for partnership management. Limited partners may advise the general partners but may not conduct partnership business.

The Exempted Limited Partnership Law allows a partnership that is exempted from most filing and publication requirements to function as a limited partnership. Exempted partnerships may not conduct business with the Cayman Island public. Formation requires filing a statement that includes appropriate information with the registrar of exempted limited partnerships. Fees are due at initiation and annually thereafter. At least one general partner must be a Cayman Islands resident or a corporation with Cayman registration. A notice of dissolution must be filed by a general partner with the registrar. An exempted limited partnership interest may be assigned to another or redeemed. The accounts of the exempted limited partnership are not required to be audited (Price Waterhouse Coopers, 1999, Chapter 9).

Branches of foreign corporations are permitted to operate by providing the appropriate information and documents to the registrar of companies. Information such foreign companies must file includes the following: a certified copy of the memorandum and articles of incorporation that define the constitution of the company, a list of all directors with addresses and occupations and the identification of the Cayman resident authorized to accept legal notices and the like on behalf of the company. Initial and annual fees are necessary. The foreign branch must publish its places of business in the Cayman Islands (Chapter 9).

The ordinary company may be formed with liability unlimited or limited by shares or guarantee. The incorporators may choose to register as a resident or non-resident company. Resident companies are formed to do business onshore in the domestic economy. The Local Companies (Control) Law of 1995 governs these companies. A company must have at least 60 percent local ownership if it conducts business within the islands (Chapter 9).

Ordinary non-resident companies may not do business in the domestic economy. Their attributes are similar to the exempt company described below. Ordinary companies may not issue no par value, nonnegotiable or bearer shares. The company must maintain a register of shareholders at its registered office in Cayman Islands, and the register must be filed annually with the registrar of companies. A general shareholder meeting is required once per year (Chapter 9).

There are no restrictions on foreign ownership of land. The Land Registry lists ownership, liens and charges for public inspection. All development and planning projects must be approved by the Central Planning Authority (Deloitte Touche Tohmatsu International, 1995, 11).

Companies formed to do business outside the Caymans require no local licensing. They may be formed to carry on any legal purpose by filing with the registrar of companies. These offshore companies may be either ordinary non-resident companies; foreign companies incorporated outside the Caymans, which are required to conduct an annual shareholder meeting; or exempted companies, which are not required to have such annual meeting of shareholders (Ernst & Young, 1995, 7–8).

There are no minimum capital requirements for an exempted company. Shares may be issued as no par value, negotiable or bearer, or with a par value. Dividends may be paid from retained earnings, share premium, contributed surplus or new share issuance, so long as solvency tests are met. Exempted company operation is generally delegated to the board of directors, who are expected to act in good faith and to act in the best interests of the company. The board may have any number of members. At least one board meeting must be held each year. Annual shareholder meetings are not required. A registered office in the Cayman Islands with corporation name displayed outside is required. There must be a registry of shareholders kept at the registered office, but it is not required to be sent to the registrar of companies or to be public information. A register of mortgages and charges is also required to be kept for inspection by creditors and shareholders. Only the address of the company is available for public inspection (Deloitte Touche Tohmatsu International, 1995, 25).

Each Cayman company must keep proper books of account such that a true and fair view of the company's affairs may be drawn up and such that company transactions can be explained. The statutory records required to be kept available for the board of directors' inspection include a register of members, a register of directors and officers, a register of charges and minutes book. Although not required by statute, bylaws usually require that the directors must report on company accounts at an annual general shareholder meeting (Ernst & Young, 1995, 35).

There are no Cayman accounting and auditing standards. The Cayman Islands Society of Professional Accountants provides guidance when needed. The society has indicated that it agrees with the work of the International Accounting Standards Committee as it seeks to have basic international standards that can be used for all financial statements.

The accounting and auditing standards of any country that is a member of the International Accounting Standards Committee may be used. Commonly used are the standards of the U. K. Institute of Chartered Accountants, the Canadian Institute of Chartered Accountants and the American Institute of Certified Public Accountants. Each company must follow the standards and practices of only one country, and they must be applied on a consistent basis unless change is justified (36).

There is no requirement for audit of annual financial statements for all corporations in the Cayman Islands. However, banks, trust companies, corporate management companies, mutual funds and insurance companies do require an annual audit of their financial statements that must be submitted to the appropriate government agency (36).

NOTE

1. The CD-ROM *Doing Business and Investing Worldwide*, published by Price Waterhouse Coopers in 1999, contains information guides to 80 countries. Here references will be to the CD-ROM and not to individual information guides. Chapter references are internal to guides for particular jurisdictions being discussed.

Chapter 8

The Climate for Accounting and Business Services in Selected European Centers

This chapter continues the analysis with a selection of offshore center host jurisdictions situated in Europe and the Mediterranean. The changing conditions found in these jurisdictions reflect the larger changes taking place in the European Community. Institutional, legal and business arrangements in each of the selected areas are being adjusted and changed with the goal of better serving offshore customers in Europe and in the larger global economy. The chapter begins with the Channel Islands, followed by the Isle of Man, Cyprus, Gibraltar and Malta.

CHANNEL ISLANDS

St. Helier, the capital of Jersey with 28,200 residents, and St. Peter Port, the capital of Guernsey with 16,600 residents, are centers of business and commerce on the Channel Islands. Total population of the islands is estimated at approximately 144,800, nearly all in Jersey with 82,000 or Guernsey with 60,000. English is used with some small rural elements speaking in local Norman patois individual to each island (Price Waterhouse Coopers, 1999, Chapter 1).

The islands have never been part of the United Kingdom. Two bailiwicks of Jersey and Guernsey administer their own internal affairs including taxation. The United Kingdom has responsibility for defense and international affairs. The islands are excluded from the European Community for most purposes, except for those dealing with tariff-free trade within the community.

Island laws are based in ancient customary law of the Duchy of Normandy but have evolved such that recent commercial and trust law are substantially influenced by English law. United Kingdom court decisions are cited as authority, should precedent under local law not be available. The Privy Council in London is the appellate court of last authority for the islands. Island authorities recognize the increasing importance of the international financial centers, which the island hosts (Chapter 1).

The Islands maintain a monetary union with the United Kingdom and use the pound sterling as well as local currencies issued by Guernsey and Jersey. The 1993 GNP for Jersey was 1,340 million, or 16,341 pounds sterling per person. Guernsey's 1994 total GNP was 895 million (1994), or 14,917 pounds sterling per person. The banking and finance sector of the economy constitutes over 50 percent of the Jersey and Guernsey economies. Tourism on Jersey is 26 percent of her economy, with 16 percent in tourism for Guernsey. Private investment holdings account for 16 percent of both Jersey and Guernsey economies. Agriculture is 4 percent for both economies, with light industry in Jersey 2 percent and 8 percent in Guernsey (Chapter 1).

Dramatic growth has been experienced over the past quarter century as banking and related fields have expanded particularly in the areas of private trusts and investment management. Island banks total over 130 and have approximately 63 billion pounds in deposits (Chapter 1).

The Channel Island company laws are generally based on English Common Law principles and on English legislation. There are some differences between the provisions of each island in regard to business organizations. Investors may choose from the following acceptable forms of business organization that are commonly permitted in each jurisdiction: sole proprietorship, general or limited partnerships, branches of foreign corporations, companies and various trusts, mutual funds, unit trusts and collective investment schemes (Chapter 9).

A sole proprietor may carry on most kinds of business in the islands. Should the business name be different from the owner's, the business must register under the Registration of Business Names Law in Jersey. Such registration is not required in Guernsey, which relies upon the fraud common law. Accounting books and records are required as necessary to substantiate tax returns (Chapter 9).

Partnerships are formed and may operate according to English Common Law. In a general partnership, partners are joint and severally liable for partnership obligations. A partnership agreement is generally drawn up which sets forth partners rights and obligations. This agreement is private to the partners. In Jersey, if a partnership uses another name other than partners' personal names, the partnership must be registered under the Jersey Registration of Business Names Law (Chapter 9).

Partners may be corporations. Partners are not required to be resident in Jersey. A registered office must be maintained on the island. There is neither requirement for financial statement audits nor filings. Sufficient accounting records must be kept to support tax returns (Chapter 9).

Recent legislation in Jersey now allows limited partnerships under the Limited Partnerships (Jersey) Law of 1994. There must be at least one general partner who retains unlimited liability for partnership obligations and one or more limited partners with liability limited to their investment in the partnership (Chapter 9).

Branches of foreign corporations may be established without registration. For banks, insurance companies and collective investment entities permission must be received from the relevant authority. If the branch does not use the full corporate name of its parent, approval to use its business name is necessary in Jersey (Chapter 9).

There are three principal laws that govern corporations in the Channel Islands: Companies (Jersey) Law of 1991, Companies (Guernsey) Law of 1994, and Companies (Alderney) Law of 1994. Within Jersey and Guernsey only companies limited by shares are incorporated. Alderney law allows companies limited by guarantee.

Private or public companies are permitted in all jurisdictions of the Channel Islands. A public company must issue a prospectus, which must be registered with the registrar, as the vehicle to offer shares for public purchase (Chapter 9).

In Jersey a company may be formed by a firm of advocates or by a firm of accountants. Advanced approval of the proposed name of the Jersey company must be obtained. An application together with all necessary information is made with the registrar of companies.

In Guernsey local advocates, upon the instructions of banks, trust companies, accountancy firms, or clients, may undertake the formation of a company. Registration is made with the Greffe, and all incorporations need approval of the Financial Services Commission. Advanced approval of the company name is not required in Guernsey (Chapter 9).

In both jurisdictions at least two subscribers are required. The true beneficial owners must be disclosed, but such information is not made public. A certificate of incorporation is granted after approval of the registration, under normal circumstances a minimum of five business days. In Jersey an urgent incorporation may take only two hours. Companies must obtain any other permits or licenses necessary under any other laws in order to conduct business in the Channel Islands (Chapter 9).

Upon incorporation the first company directors are appointed by the subscribers. An inaugural shareholder's meeting is held at which the appointment of directors is accepted, a corporate secretary is appointed, the registered office address is approved and shares are issued to subscribers, followed by any appropriate share transfers. A register of company directors, secretary and members must be maintained. The company name must be displayed outside the registered office.

Authorized capital may be denominated in any currency. At least two shares must be issued. In Alderney the requirement is one. No par shares are not authorized in Jersey or Guernsey, but are permitted for Alderney corporations. There are no statutory limits to the amount of the initial authorized capital. Issued shares may not exceed the authorized amount. Different classes of shares may be issued such that some shares have different voting, dividend or other rights. Bearer shares may not be issued, but a trust arrangement can achieve the same end (Chapter 9).

With approval of authorities and the bylaws, capital can be increased by shareholder resolution. Reductions require a special resolution and approval of the court, which must be satisfied that the interests of the creditors are protected. In Guernsey shares may be issued at a discount, subject to the court's approval. Redeemable shares may be issued that are redeemable at the option of the shareholder or the company provided that at least one class of shares is not redeemable. Stock dividends are permitted (Chapter 9).

A public company in Jersey must have at least two directors. A private Jersey company and all Guernsey companies are allowed to have only one director. A company secretary must be appointed by every company. Officers of the company need not be residents in the Channel Islands.

Each company must keep a register of directors and secretaries. In Jersey, for public corporations, this register is open to the public. For a private company the registers are open only to it shareholders, officers and the registrar. In Guernsey all company registers are open to all (Chapter 9).

An annual meeting of corporation shareholders is required. The meeting need not be held in the Channel Islands. A private Jersey company need not have shareholder meetings if agreed to by all shareholders in writing. Shareholders may vote by proxy or in person. At the annual meetings shareholders will consider reports on the accounts, dividend declarations and appointment of directors and auditors. Dividends may only be paid from net accumulated earnings (Chapter 9).

In practice, financial statements are made in conformity with current United Kingdom accounting standards. In Guernsey the financial statements need to be sent to shareholders at least 10 days prior to the shareholders' meeting. The company is required to keep shareholder meeting minutes open to shareholders at its registered office. Each year a report that discloses shareholders and their share capital is required.

Trusts may be established by declaration of trust or by deed of settlement. In Jersey trusts are governed by the Trusts (Jersey) Law of 1984, the Trusts (Amendment) (Jersey) Law of 1989 and the Trusts (Amendment No. 2) (Jersey) Law of 1991. In Guernsey trusts are governed by the Trusts (Guernsey) Law of 1989 and the Trusts (Amendment) (Guernsey) Law of 1990. Each island jurisdiction has enacted investor protection laws designed with mutual funds, unit trusts and collective investment schemes in mind (Chapter 9).

Companies are required under the Companies (Jersey) Law of 1991 and the Companies (Guernsey) Law of 1994 to keep adequate accounting records. Other entities may have such requirements in their founding documents. In any case all entities doing business within the domestic economy will find such records necessary for tax purposes. Companies generally prepare accounts in accordance with United Kingdom generally accepted accounting standards (Chapter 11).

Financial statements must be prepared in accordance with generally accepted accounting principles and must be designed to present a true and fair view of the profit and loss account and the balance sheet (Chapter 12).

An audit is required only for public companies or companies that are in banking, insurance or mutual fund businesses. In Guernsey audits are required for all companies unless exempted by the Companies Ordinance of 1991. Financial statements do not generally need to be published or filed. For banks, collective investment schemes and insurance companies, however, financial statements must be filed with appropriate regulatory bodies. In addition, the accounts of a Jersey public company must be filed with the registrar. For companies owned by residents the tax authorities will require copies of company financial statements. Banks trading in the domestic economy are required to make financial statements open to the public. Audit of private companies is required if stated in the articles or a shareholder resolution (Chapter 11).

By law, audits must be conducted by a members of one of the recognized United Kingdom or Republic of Ireland professional accountancy societies. The Societies of Chartered and Certified Accountants in Jersey and in Guernsey have no licensing or other regulatory powers but do consist only of members who are also members of the United Kingdom or Ireland professional bodies (Chapter 12).

Separate auditing standards and procedures have not been adopted in the Channel Islands. However, as the law requires the audit to be performed by a member of the major United Kingdom or Republic of Ireland accountancy bodies, they are required by those bodies to conform to United Kingdom practice. The United Kingdom procedures are amended in cases where overseas investors, notably from the United States and Canada, require audit reports to conform with standards in home countries or International Accounting Standards (Chapter 11).

Ernst & Young have summarized the responsibilities of accountants laid down in the codes of conduct of the professional accounting institutes. Accountants are expected to perform professional responsibilities with integrity and care, to be independent with respect to the client in fact and appearance, never to be associated with financial information that is false or misleading and to make only proper use of confidential information (Ernst & Young, 1999).

THE ISLE OF MAN

The Isle of Man consists of a 221-square-mile area with an estimated 69,000 total population of English-speaking people. Douglas, the largest town, with a population estimated at 20,000, is the main financial center. The legal and governmental structure has its roots in the eighth century Vikings' Norse System, an influence that is still felt today.

The island has never been part of the United Kingdom but rather is a crown dependency with U.K. control of external relations and defense. Domestic matters, including taxes, are the province of the local government, subject to royal assent. The legislature consists of the Keys, whose members are elected in public referendum, and the Legislative Council, whose members are elected by the Keys from their own membership. The chief minister, who is elected by Keys members, has responsibility for the government. For all practical purposes the judicial system is based on English Common Law and the statutes based on English law (Price Waterhouse Coopers, 1999, Chapter 1).

Per person gross domestic product (GDP) is lower than that of the United Kingdomm with Isle of Man GDP being about 74 percent of the U.K. GDP. However, the Isle of Man quality of life is exceptional, with low unemployment, low crime rates and excellent physical environment (Chapter 1).

Government ownership in the economy is minimal, with private ownership and free enterprise principles followed. The Isle of Man hosts a vigorous center for international offshore financial operations that in 1991–1992 represented approximately 35 percent of GNP. Manufacturing was reported to be about 11 percent of GNP, with tourism 7 percent (Chapter 1).

The Companies Consolidation Act governs business activities in the Isle of Man. Business may be organized as sole proprietorships, joint ventures, general or limited partnerships, trusts, branches of foreign companies, companies with a variety of features and foreign entities. All forms of business organization, whether for domestic or offshore operations, are open on an equal basis to domestic and foreign investors (Chapter 9).

A sole proprietorship is an unincorporated entity in which one individual carries on a trade or business with unlimited liability for the entity's obligations. There are no formal regulations relating to a sole proprietor. Foreign investors are permitted to establish sole proprietorships in the Isle of Man. Such non-citizens need to have work permits issued in accordance with the island's Control of Employment Acts.

The Isle of Man has no regulations specifically dealing with joint ventures. Such ventures may be carried out by two or more existing business entities that join in a project or enterprise. Such undertakings may be carried out with or without establishing a separate entity. The rights and responsibilities of the parties to the affiliation are generally set forth in a contractual agreement (Chapter 9).

A branch of a foreign company does not have legal existence apart from its parent corporation. The foreign company must file appropriate information with the registrar of companies to establish a branch or to hold land within the Isle of Man. Such filing must include copies of the parent's incorporating documents, information about the parent company directors and secretary, and the naming of a resident of the Isle of Man authorized to receive notices and service processes for the branch and the parent company (Chapter 9).

General and limited partnerships are formed between two or more individuals generally by means of a partnership deed. Most businesses, whether in the Isle of Man or offshore, may be carried on by a partnership. Partnerships do not constitute a separate legal personality under Isle of Man law. A partnership, except for those set up for lawyers, accountants and stock exchange members, must have no more than 20 partners, who need not be residents. A corporation may be a partner. In a general partnership all partners have joint and several liability for partnership obligations. Limited partnerships, which require proper registration at the General Registry, must have at least one general partner who manages the firm's business and who retains unlimited liability for partnership obligations. Limited partners are liable only for invested capital. Should a general or limited partnership name not contain names of partners, such name needs to be registered at the General Registry. Filings of the partnership agreement or financial accounts is not required (Chapter 9).

Trusts for non-resident beneficiaries have many advantages in tax planning and are used extensively for activities that do not generate income in the domestic economy of the Isle of Man. Trusts may be used for asset protection or for public investment funds and may be unit trusts or investment trusts. The Prevention of Frauds (Investments) Act of 1968 regulates the operations of unit trusts. Trusts may be efficient ownership forms for royalties, patent right income and the like (Chapter 9).

Isle of Man companies may be either public or private. Companies may be formed to grant shareowners unlimited liability, liability limited by shares or liability limited by guarantee with or without shares. Incorporation procedures require filing of proper articles of incorporation including company bylaws. These can be of standard form. Off-the-shelf companies are permitted. Prior approval of the corporate name, which must include "Limited" when limited liability has been granted, needs to be obtained from the registrar of companies. There must be at least two subscribers for a private company. For a public company a prospectus must be filed with the General Registry.

Companies in general must have an authorized stated capital and must indicate how this will be divided among the individual shares. Different share classes with differing rights may be issued. Shares may be denominated in different currencies and differing stated amounts. No par shares are not permitted. While a minimum of two shares must be subscribed for initial incorporation, thereafter, a corporation may be the sole shareholder. There are no other restrictions on the number shareholders. Shares are free from restriction on transferability. Shares may be issued even though subscriptions have been only partially paid. Treasury stock transactions are permitted (Chapter 9).

The private company limited by shares has been the leading organizational choice. Private companies may not sell shares or other securities to the public. Government regulations and required filings for a private company are less cumbersome with fewer required disclosures. Annual audited financial statements are not required. However, an annual corporate report must be filed with the General Registry.

Private limited companies have liability limited to invested capital, no restrictions on the number of shareholders or the transferability of shares, less detailed disclosure requirements and do not file accounts with the General Registry. Private companies have separate legal existence, but beneficial ownership need not be disclosed unless the owner in question is a resident of the Isle of Man. Bearer shares are permitted (Chapter 9).

Companies may also be formed with liability limited by guarantee with or without share capital. Member's liability consists of the subscribed amounts that will be paid in should the company be insolvent upon dissolution. The Companies Act allows substantial freedom in the specifications of incorporation such that corporate arrangement may be selected to fit diverse needs of the financial community, particularly in the tax planning areas.

Except for those that are financial, insurance or exempt, companies commonly are required to have two or more directors, who must be natural persons. Directors are not required to be residents and may be citizens of any country. No restrictions exist on loans to directors or shareholders. A company secretary, who may be a director, must also be provided to be the officer primarily responsible for compliance with company laws. No residency or nationality restrictions apply to the secretary, except for exempt companies, which must have a resident as secretary. Directors and secretaries may need to hold a work permit. Unless directors have defrauded or acted in fraudulent manner, they have no liability for company obligations (Chapter 9).

Annual shareholder general meetings must be held at which shareholders receive reports on company accounts, director reports and auditor reports. Shareholders declare dividends, which may only be paid from accumulated earnings. Stock dividends are permitted. Shareholders also elect directors, appoint auditors and fix the remuneration of auditors. A private company is exempt from reporting the accounts to a general shareholder meeting on an annual basis. Dormant companies need not appoint auditors (Chapter 9). For companies that specialize in banking, insurance, shipping and public investment funds, the Isle of Man has appropriate regulatory agencies that control the establishment in these specialized areas and monitor company activities once established.

The Isle of Man does not have an accounting professional institute except for local chapters of United Kingdom institutes. Separate accounting principles have not been promulgated. Instead the country has chosen to follow the Statements of Standard Accounting Practice (SSAPs) and the Financial Reporting Standards (FRS) issued by the United Kingdom Accounting Standards Committee and its successor, the Accounting Standards Board. These standards are in effect mandatory for companies. The Accounting Standards Board is supplemented by the Urgent Issues Task Force, which issues UITF statements (Chapter 12).

Detailed requirements for keeping accounting books and related records as well as for preparation of financial statements are laid out in the Companies Act. Boards of directors must present at the annual shareholder meeting a balance sheet and income statement prepared to set forth a true and fair view of company affairs. The content and form are detailed in the Companies Act and generally follow the U.K. approach to reporting and disclosure. A cash flow statement is also required by FRS 1. Consolidated statements must be prepared that include subsidiary companies. An auditor's report covering the financial statements is required. Significant accounting policies must be disclosed in footnote form to the financial statements (Chapter 12).

SSAP 2 set forth the fundamental accounting principles to be applied in keeping accounts and reporting: the going concern concept—the presumption that a company is a going concern; the accrual concept—revenue and expenses are recognized in the period earned or incurred; the consistency concept—accounting policies from one year to the next should be consistent; and the prudence concept—anticipate no gains but provide for all losses in periodic reports (Chapter 11). While tax laws do not affect accounting reporting, many adjustments as laid out in the tax laws must be made to report taxable income.

To support and prepare the financial reports, companies must keep adequate accounting records at their registered office or at another location at the discretion of the directors. The books must be open to inspection by company officers. If the books are kept outside the Isle of Man, accounting information must be sent to an island location such that proper financial reports can be prepared at least each six months. Accounting and related records for all practical purposes must be retained for six years (Chapter 12).

Isle of Man law recognizes members of the United Kingdom Institutes of Chartered Accountants or Chartered Association of Certified Accountants as being qualified for public practice. There are no separate institutes for the Isle of Man. Audits have been required by the Companies Act for many years (Chapter 11). Auditors are obliged to follow the professional responsibilities and conduct laid out by the institute of which they are a member.

CYPRUS

Cyprus lies at the northeastern end of the Mediterranean Sea and has a land area of 3,572 square miles. The Greeks, who originally settled Cyprus, have had the greatest influence on its language, culture and religion. The British, who last controlled Cyprus before independence in 1960, have influenced commerce, law and administration. Many aspects of the society are modeled after British counterparts. Today, the Republic of Cyprus is a member of the United Nations, the World Bank, the International Monetary Fund, the Commonwealth and the Council of Europe, and has entered into a customs union agreement with the European Community (Price Waterhouse Coopers, 1999, Chapter 1).

Population in 1990 was estimated to be 700,000, with Greek Cypriots accounting for about 77 percent and Turkish Cypriots, the second largest group, at 18 percent. About 20 percent of the population live in the capital of Nicosia, the island's main administrative and commercial center. Limassol, Larnaca and Paphos are also population centers.

The Cyprus constitution provides for a presidential system of government. The president is head of state and the Council of Ministers, who initiate legislation and administer the government. The elected House of Representatives has legislative power. The legal system is based on that of the United Kingdom, with the statutes regulating business being based on English law (Chapter 1).

Greek and Turkish are the official languages. English is widely spoken and is commonly used in business, the courts and the government. Most laws are officially translated into English.

The justice system consists of six district courts and six assize courts. Final appeal rests with the supreme court. Recourse to the European Commission from judgment of the supreme court may be available, as Cyprus has accepted the relevant provisions of the European Convention on Human Rights (Chapter 1).

Cyprus has also agreed to the New York Convention on the Recognition and Enforcement of Foreign Arbitration proceedings and has passed an Arbitration Law. Arbiters' awards can be enforced in court, and a foreign award may be enforced in Cyprus by an action in common law (Chapter 1).

Gross national product per capita in 1992 was 5,297 Cypriot pounds. Cyprus follows the principles of free enterprise with the government limited to safeguarding the system, indicative planning (general guidance and advice in planning) and the provision of public utilities. The economy has been growing at an average annual rate of 5.5 percent. Inflation is in the 3 to 4 percent range with nearly full employment.

The official currency, the Cyprus pound, is divided into 100 cents. In 1992 the Cyprus pound was linked to the European Currency Unit (ECU), demonstrating Cyprus's intent to integrate its economy with that of Europe and eventually to join the European Union as a full member (Chapter 1).

In recent years, as agriculture has steadily declined, the manufacturing and services sectors have increased. Tourism has increased, contributing foreign exchange and having beneficial effects upon the domestic economy. The service sector is the largest sector of the economy and includes hotels and restaurants, transport and communications, trade, finance, insurance, real estate, ownership of dwellings, public administration and services (Chapter 2).

The establishment of Cyprus as a regional commercial and financial center has contributed substantially to the growth in the service sector. The ratio of foreign trade to national income has continued to increase, bringing with it an increasing sensitivity in the domestic market to foreign influences.

Cyprus is now an important business and financial center that hosts over 12,000 offshore business entities. A main objective of the government of Cyprus is to make Cyprus an important financial center and within that to attract offshore companies that conduct their activities outside Cyprus but manage them from within (Chapter 2).

The business forms that may be chosen in Cyprus are sole proprietorships, partnerships, branches of foreign companies and companies. Sole proprietorship may be formed by citizens of Cyprus and by foreign investors who comply with the Exchange Control Law and the Aliens and Immigration Law and Regulation. Such businesses are free to carry on business in the names of the owner or under a business name registered under the Partnership and Business Names Law, Cap. 116.

The Partnership and Business Names Law, Cap. 116 governs partnerships in Cyprus and is the same as its English counterpart. A partnership is registered by submitting a return to the registrar in which the name, object and duration of the partnership with the names and addresses of the partners are included. A general partnership must consist of fewer than 20 persons, who may be foreigners or citizens, resident or non-resident. A corporation may be a partner. In a general partnership all partners are jointly and severally liable for partnership obligations. A partnership agreement is drawn up setting forth various rights and obligations of partners (Chapter 9).

Limited partnerships are permitted in which one or more general partners manage the business and retain unlimited liability for partnership obligations and one or more limited partners have liability limited to their investments in the partnership. Limited partnerships are not commonly found in Cyprus (Chapter 9).

Joint ventures in which any two or more individuals or corporations affiliate for a particular project or business are solely a matter between the parties involved. There are no registration or other requirements in the law for joint ventures. A written joint venture contract is recommended but not required.

Companies incorporated outside of Cyprus may establish a place of business within Cyprus. Such foreign company branches are required to register with the registrar of companies by filing certified copies of the parent company's documents of incorporation with other required information. Such filing must be in Greek or in a Greek translation. The parent company must file the annual accounts that are published in the company's home country. These too must be in Greek or a Greek translation (Chapter 9).

Cyprus companies are governed by the Cyprus Companies Law, Cap. 113, which is based on the United Kingdom Companies Act of 1948. Most corporations are limited liability companies that have share capital. They are referred to as companies limited by shares. Shareholder liability consists of only the investment in the company, assuming all subscriptions have been paid in (Chapter 9).

Companies limited by guarantee are usually pursuing nonprofit objects. In this form the shareholders guarantee to pay in an amount of capital should the corporation become insolvent. Companies limited by guarantee are not common.

Corporations may be either private or public. A public company may sell shares or debenture bonds to the public through a prospectus. A minimum of seven shareholders is needed for a public company but there is no ceiling set on the maximum allowable numbers of shareholders. Shares of the public company are freely transferable (Chapter 9).

A private company must have between two and 50 shareholders. Share transfer must be restricted in the company bylaws. Sale of shares or debentures to the public is prohibited. A private company may have one or more directors, whereas a public company must have a minimum of two directors.

A private company may qualify as an exempt private company by meeting the following conditions. A corporation does not hold the position of director of the company. No more that 50 persons hold company debentures. Only the holder of company shares or debentures has interest in them. Another corporation does not hold shares or debentures of the company unless that holder is itself an exempt private company. Should the private company qualify as an exempt company, it does not need to include its financial statements in its annual return. The company may grant loans to its directors. It may also appoint a person who does not have the statutory qualifications to act as auditor (Chapter 9).

Incorporations are carried out through the registrar of companies. Articles of incorporation and bylaws are submitted after first determining that the proposed company name is acceptable to the registrar of companies and whether the desired name is available. A Cyprus company can generally be incorporated within 10 days (Chapter 9).

Company authorized share capital and the division of that capital into shares is set forth in the articles of incorporation. There is no statutory ceiling for the amount of total share capital, but issued capital may not exceed the authorized total. No par shares are not permitted. Different classes of shares may be used, each having different voting, dividend or other rights. Preferred shares, which commonly carry the right to a fixed dividend but do not carry voting rights, may be issued. Shareholders may vote by use of proxies.

A number of legal requirements have provisions that are designed to ensure that the capital remains intact. Dividends may only be paid out of net earnings. Unless following proper liquidating procedures, a dividend may not be paid from capital. A reduction of capital may only occur when approved by the court after it is satisfied that creditor interests are not damaged. Companies may not purchase their own shares or provide financing for others to do so. Subsidiaries are not permitted to own shares in their parent company. Cyprus does not require participation in corporate ownership by Cyprus nationals. Issuance of shares or transfer to foreign nationals will require Exchange Control approval (Chapter 9).

Company directors have duties and powers similar to businessmen carrying on business for their own account. Legal provisions for directors are largely designed to ensure that potential investors and the general public have sufficient and proper information about directors' relationships with the company. A director who holds interests in the company or associated companies needs to disclose these facts to the company. The company is required to record the directors' interests in a register open to inspection by the public (Chapter 9).

Each company must name a corporate secretary who is the officer primarily responsible for compliance with Companies Laws. Neither the directors nor the company secretary must reside in Cyprus.

An annual meeting of shareholders is required at which the company financial statements are presented, directors and auditors are elected, dividends are declared or confirmed and remuneration of the auditors is set. Directors' meetings are held as necessary to carry out company business. Neither shareholder nor director meetings are restricted as to where they may be held (Chapter 9).

Companies incorporated under the Companies Law must maintain books of accounting and related records. These records must allow a true and fair view of company affairs to be drawn up. They must also provide sufficient information to explain company transactions. The records must show all monies received and expended and the reasons for receiving and expending these funds. Sales and purchases and assets and liabilities must be accounted for through these records (Chapter 12).

There are no statutory requirements that financial statements of businesses in general must be audited. Independent auditors must, however, be appointed by companies incorporated under the Companies Law. There are no specific requirements in the tax law for filing of audited tax reports. However, tax authorities commonly insist on audited financial statements to be presented when audits are required by the Companies Law or other relevant legislation. In other cases as well, the failure to produce audited accounts may prejudice a company's case before tax authorities (Chapter 11).

A qualified auditor must be a member of a recognized U.K. body of accountants that is one of the U.K. Institutes of Chartered Accountants or the Chartered Association of Certified Accountants. The Cyprus government may also authorize auditors as having similar qualifications or as having obtained adequate knowledge and experience. This requirement, as noted elsewhere, is not applicable to exempt private companies (Chapter 11).

The Institute of Certified Public Accountants of Cyprus has been formed by some 400 qualified accountants in practice, commerce and industry, and government in Cyprus. The Cyprus institute members are required to follow International Accounting Standards and International Auditing Guidelines as adopted by the institute.

Accounting practices in Cyprus have commonly followed U.K. standards and practices. As noted above, the Institute of Certified Public Accountants of Cyprus adopted the International Accounting Standards. This should cause few problems, since for the most part these sets of standards are similar in content and requirements (Chapter 12).

Reporting for financial statement purposes and tax reporting purposes may call for differing treatments of items of income or expense. While the form and presentation of financial statements is not set out in statute, financial statement disclosure requirements are contained in the Companies Law. Additional disclosures are required by International Accounting Standards. Most disclosure requirements have to do with items that are judged to be material or critical in determining profit or loss for the year and in stating financial position. For example, the bases of valuation of fixed assets, investments and inventories must be disclosed. Companies following the United Kingdom principles may periodically revalue their land and buildings based on appraisals of current value with resulting surplus, which is not distributable, credited into a revaluation reserve (Chapter 12).

GIBRALTAR

Gibraltar, being a U.K. Overseas Territory, has a legal system based on English common and statutory laws to which some modifications have been made for local conditions. The supreme court, the court of first instance and magistrates court constitute the judiciary. Ultimate appeal is to the Privy Council in the United Kingdom. The House of Assembly exercises legislative powers (Deloitte & Touche, 1998h).

The unit of currency is the Gibraltar pound made up of 100 pence. The Gibraltar pound is on a par with the British pound. There are no exchange controls. Funds may be converted to any currency and may be sent across Gibraltar's borders at will (1998h). Both residents and non-residents may hold foreign currency bank accounts (Ernst & Young, 1999f).

Gibraltar company acts are quite similar to the English Companies Act of 1929. A company may be formed with differing shareholder liability arrangements: liability limited by shares, liability limited by guarantee with share capital, liability limited by guarantee without share capital and unlimited liability with or without share capital. A private company incorporated with liability limited by shares requires only one subscriber. In a public company subscribers must number seven as a minimum. A private company must have no more than 50 shareholders and the rights for public subscription and subsequent transfer of shares must be restricted. Private companies need not file financial statements with the registrar of companies (1999f).

At formation all companies must have authorized share capital of a minimum of 100 Gibraltar pounds. Those seeking to incorporate must file appropriate information with the registrar. The Gibraltar address of the company's registered office must be declared so that legal notice can be served on the company. Names and addresses of directors and shareholders need to be registered. A listing indicating how shares were assigned to subscribers must be provided to the registrar. After the incorporation certificate is granted, every company must file an annual return with the registrar.

Foreign corporations seeking to do business by establishing a Gibraltar branch must provide the registrar with a certified copy of the parent company's memorandum and articles of association. The names of parent company directors must also be provided. A Gibraltar agent who can receive legal service in Gibraltar on behalf of the parent company must be appointed (1999f).

Partnerships may be formed in Gibraltar by verbal or written agreement between all partners. The partnership place of business in Gibraltar needs to be registered with the Employment and Training Board and the Registry of Companies and Business Names (1999f).

Trusts have full legal status in Gibraltar law. The Trustee Ordinance governs trusts. The accumulation and life of a trust is 100 years. If nonresidents of Gibraltar are trust beneficiaries, trust income may be exempt from tax. There are no estate taxes, capital gains taxes, wealth or gift taxes in Gibraltar. Stamp tax is not charged on asset transfers from a trust (1999f). Businesses of all forms, including sole traders, carrying on business in the domestic economy must register at the Registry of Business Names. A license must also be obtained from the Trade Licensing Authority by any business in the retail or wholesale trade as well as by caterers, publicans, hoteliers, clubs and canteens (1999f).

Companies are required by the Gibraltar Companies Ordinance to maintain accounting books and related records in good order. The ordinance states that proper books include accounting for money received and expended, for all sales and purchases of goods and for company assets and liabilities. Proper accounting books and records must support the preparation of annual financial statements, including a balance sheet and profit and loss statement. Such annual financial statements must be submitted to the annual general meeting of shareholders. A directors' report explaining the state of company business is required to be attached to the balance sheet. The directors' report must also indicate the dividend payment recommended by the board, together with the total transferred to reserves (1999f).

The Gibraltar Companies Ordinance sets out minimum contents required for the financial statements. A summary of authorized and issued share capital must be included. Liabilities need to be presented with sufficient information such that the nature of the liabilities can be determined. Information on assets must be sufficient for shareholders to distinguish between fixed and floating assets. Disclosure must be made of the methods used to arrive at the valuation of all assets. Any company preliminary expenses not yet written off should be separately disclosed in the financial statements. Expenses incurred in conjunction with issuance of capital shares or debentures must be separately treated in the financial statements. Goodwill, patents and trademarks are required to be presented separately in the financial statements (1999f).

Subsidiary company shares owned by the company must be reported separately. Disclosure must be made of loans made and remuneration paid to directors by either the company or the subsidiary company. Consolidated financial statements are not required. But company's financial statements must disclose how subsidiary profits or losses have been accounted for in the parent company's financial statements (1999f).

Company financial statements must be audited. Company auditors should be appointed by the shareholders at their annual general meeting. As set forth in the Gibraltar Companies Ordinance, the auditor's charge is to report whether all information and explanations required have been obtained and to express an opinion on whether the company balance sheet is properly presented such that a true and correct view of company affairs is presented. This expression of opinion is to be based on the books of account and is to be formed taking into consideration the best information and explanations given to the auditor. In pursuit of sufficient evidence upon which to base the opinions, the auditor must be given access at all times to the accounting and related records. The auditor has the right to seek any information and explanations necessary from company directors and officers (1999f).

Most of the accounting standards and all of the auditing standards issued in the United Kingdom have been adopted by The Gibraltar Society of Chartered and Certified Accountants. Some have been modified for local conditions. The U.K. Accounting Standards Board pronouncements essentially provide generally accepted accounting standards in Gibraltar. Many Gibraltar accountants are members of the United Kingdom's accountancy bodies and therefore follow appropriate professional standards required of all members of those associations.

In the Treaty of Rome, European territories, for which a member state of the European Union has external responsibility, are considered part of the European Union and the European Economic Area unless specifically excluded. Being such a United Kingdom dependent territory, Gibraltar is a part of the European Union. Gibraltar laws must be brought into line with the European community agreements that are adopted by the United Kingdom.

The various European Union Directives must be placed in force. This effort is progressing with assistance from the United Kingdom. Gibraltar was granted derogations in Article 28 of the Act of Accession such that the following do not apply to Gibraltar: the Common Customs Tariff, Harmonization of Turnover Taxes (VAT) and Common Agricultural Policy. Gibraltar adopted the European Union measures in its European Communities Ordinance of 1972. Gibraltar is in the process of instituting both the fourth and eighth European Union directives. The fourth directive deals with company accounts. The eighth directive sets approval and registration procedures for auditors (1999f).

MALTA

Maltese and English are the official languages of Malta. Laws and legal documents are generally prepared in both languages. The business and administrative sectors commonly use English in their activities. The government promotes a free enterprise–based economy by providing planning, infrastructure, utilities and health services. In recent times about 38 percent of total employment in the country has been in the public sector. The government operates public utilities for water, gas, electricity, fuel, telephone and telecommunications. Air Malta and Sea Malta are government owned and operated. There are private medical services and private health centers, but the island's main hospital is government operated. The government's role in tourism has been restricted to maintaining necessary facilities and other infrastructure (Price Waterhouse Coopers, 1999, Chapter 1).

The currency, the Maltese lira, consists of 100 cents. A basket of currencies consisting of the U.S. dollar, the EC dollar and the pound sterling, is used to set the official exchange rate. The Central Bank selects the composition of the currencies within the basket (Chapter 1). The Central Bank maintains exchange controls. The bank monitors payments received from offshore. Its approval is needed for foreign-owned businesses to borrow funds within Malta. Complete exemption from exchange controls is granted for companies wholly foreign owned which carry on all of their business outside of Malta (Ernst & Young, 1999d).

In recent years, GNP has grown at an 8 percent rate, with inflation at 4 percent. The unemployment rate was 4.3 in June 1997. Agriculture and fishing contribute around 3 percent to GDP. The industrial sector manufactures primarily for export and accounts for approximately 25 percent of GDP. Over 200 foreign companies have manufacturing subsidiaries on the islands. The EU agreement allows Maltese industrial products to be marketed freely in the EU, except for textiles, which have a quota system. Tourism produces in the neighborhood of one-quarter of annual export receipts, with about 18 percent of all employment in tourism areas (Price Waterhouse Coopers, 1999, Chapter 1).

Malta encourages new foreign investments, and numerous tax and other incentives are offered. Foreign ownership is not limited in Malta-registered companies, whether operating offshore or in the domestic local economy. Repatriation of capital and profits is readily made, provided that upon entry proper procedures for inbound capital are followed. Special incentives are also offered to foreigners who settle in Malta. Foreign-owned companies, after they are established, commonly enjoy equal rights with Maltese-owned companies. However, foreign investments in the domestic market are generally not approved for operations in areas already adequately served by locals (Chapter 3).

Permitted business forms of organization in Malta are sole proprietorships, joint ventures, branches of overseas corporations, general and limited partnerships and companies, both public and private. All organizational forms are governed by the provisions in the Malta Companies Act of 1995, except for the sole proprietorship and the informal partnership (Chapter 9).

For the sole proprietor there are no requirements for registering the business entity, nor are there specifics about how the organization must be founded and operated. Persons pursuing business in the proprietorship form must, of course, abide by police licensing requirements, which can be administered differently on a case-by-case basis. Sole traders may register by means of special procedures for traders with the commercial court. Traders are required by law to keep adequate records such that accounting to the customs and excise tax authorities can be substantiated (Chapter 9).

In Maltese law a joint venture is known as "association en participation." A written agreement is not required, nor are registrations or filings. The venture is permitted to operate on the basis of private contracts between the parties in association (Chapter 9).

A branch of a foreign corporation may operate in Malta by filing with the registrar. Adequate information and documentation must be provided about the parent overseas company, including copies of documents by which the company was authorized in its home country. A Malta resident must be named to represent the parent company. Accounting standards and practices applicable in the parent corporation's home country may be accepted in Malta as long as they are broadly similar to the Maltese standards (Chapter 1).

Partners in a general partnership have joint and several legal liability for the obligations of the partnership. Partnerships operate under the actual names of the partners. A deed of partnership must be agreed to and filed with the registrar for registration. Changes made in the deed of partnership, such as withdrawals or additions of new partners, must likewise be reported to the registrar.

Limited partnerships must have at least one general partner who retains unlimited liability for partnership obligations. One or more limited partners have their liability limited to their partnership investments (Chapter 9).

The Maltese limited liability company may be a public or a private corporation. The liability of shareholders is limited to whatever payments were made for company shares, assuming payment of all subscriptions. Private companies constitute a majority of companies in Malta. A memorandum and articles of association must be drawn up, generally by lawyers or accountants, which include the company name, the company's Malta office address, a listing of the persons who subscribed to buy shares, the specific objectives for forming the company, and the names of the initial board of directors and company secretary, among other information requirements. A prototype for the memorandum of association is provided in the law. Subscribers must deposit total paid-in capital of the company with an authorized bank.

The incorporation materials are filed with the registrar of companies who, after approving, certifies the company registration and prints an announcement of the new company in the government gazette. For a public company a proper prospectus must be issued as the basis for soliciting for general public subscriptions. The prospectus is required to include an audit report. Subsequent changes to the memorandum and articles of association must be approved at an extraordinary shareholders' meeting (Chapter 9).

Permission must be received from exchange control in the Central Bank for non-residents to purchase Malta company shares. Should non-residents be elected as directors or officers of a Malta company, application for work or resident permits are required and need the approval of the Office of the Prime Minister (Chapter 9).

A company must have at least two shareholders but in special circumstances may have only one. The Company Act sets no maximum on permitted number of shareholders. The value of a share may be set at any amount but, except in special cases, no par shares are not permitted. A premium over the set value of a share may be paid in and is to be carried in a share premium account of the owners' equity section of the balance sheet. All shares are required to be registered. Bearer shares may not be used. Treasury stock transactions may be undertaken only as authorized in the company memorandum or articles of incorporation. Differing classes of shares are permitted with differing voting, dividend and other rights. Under normal circumstances common stock carries unrestricted dividend rights and has voting rights on an equal basis with one another. Preferred stock does not carry voting rights but is entitled to an annual fixed dividend amount or rate. If included in the incorporating documents and bylaws, redeemable shares may be issued. But redemption must come from retained earnings or from a new share issue designated for the redemption (Chapter 9).

Company shares must be prenumbered until such time as the subscription price has been paid into the corporation. Transferring shares requires that a written agreement between the two parties to the transfer be filed with the company. A transfer stamp tax is charged. Private company directors may have the right to refuse to transfer share ownership.

An annual meeting of shareholders is required at which reports by directors and auditors are presented. The normal business to come before Malta corporate shareholders is a consideration of the company financial statements, directors' report and auditor's report. Other business commonly coming before shareholders is election of directors, selection of company auditors and authorization of dividends, which may be paid only out of distributable earnings. Proxy voting is permitted (Chapter 9).

Directors may not compete with the company, nor may they except loans from the company. The law sets forth a number of duties and responsibilities for directors and provides for the joint and several liability of directors. Such liability attaches to the directors as an owner of a business would have in the ordinary conduct of business. Directors appoint the executives of the company. A company secretary is required. The Company Act sets secretarial responsibilities. (Chapter 9).

In the main, Malta limited liability companies are formed as private rather than public organizations. Private companies may have no more that 50 shareholders. Company securities may not be offered to the public. Share transfer rights are restricted. In order to qualify as an exempt company, debentures may be held by no more than 50 persons, and shares or debentures may not be held by another company, except another exempt company. The exempt company may make loans to its directors and may have only one shareholder (Chapter 9).

Accounting records for all businesses in Malta must reflect a true and fair portrayal of financial condition and transactions. The Company Act requires that the International Accounting Standards (IAS) be used by Malta businesses. To assist in the use of IAS, the Malta Institute of Accountants publishes guidance for the use of IAS in Malta which gives consideration to local conditions. With the passage of the Accountancy Profession Act of 1979, Malta established an Accountancy Board. The board's charge includes providing guidance to the government on accounting procedures, standards and profession matters (Chapter 12).

Malta law sets out the form and content of financial statements. A directors' report, income statement, balance sheet, cash flow statement and disclosure notes are commonly included. The statements should be of the comparative type showing the prior year figures as well as the current. Disclosure must be made of authorized capital, premiums paid on shares and any reserves. Both the directors' report and the income statement may be abridged in financial statements of small private companies (Chapter 12).

Included in the income statement must be turnover, cost of sales, gross profit, profit on ordinary activities, interest payable and receivable, investment income, tax expenses, extraordinary items, dividends, changes in reserves, minority interests and any changes made in the basis of accounting. Balance sheets should be sectioned as tangible fixed assets, current assets, current and long-term liabilities, total assets after liabilities, paid in capital and reserves.

The accrual basis of accounting is required. Valuation bases used must be disclosed. Buildings and land amounts may be periodically valued with the credit shown in a nondistributable revaluation reserve. The law requires that tangible fixed assets be allocated to expense over estimated useful life. The lower of cost and net realizable value is used for inventories. LIFO is not acceptable for tax reporting. The acquisition or the merger method of accounting may be used for the purchase of a company. Malta has issued no rulings on the accounting treatment of any resulting goodwill. Goodwill cannot be deducted as an expense in tax reports. Subsidiaries must be consolidated. Any associated companies not consolidated are required to be accounted for under the equity method. Disclosure in the financial statement notes is required for accounting policies used, directors' and auditors' fees, related party transactions, contingent liabilities and capital commitments, among others (Chapter 12).

A minimum of 14 days before the annual meeting, shareholders are required to be provided with the company financial statements, auditor's report and directors' report. The directors' report commonly includes, among other matters, the directors' statements on their responsibility to safeguard company assets and to maintain an effective internal control system (Chapter 11).

A yearly return must be filed by each Malta company with the registrar of companies. The return should contain a shareholder list, detailed information on directors, a summary of share capital and debentures. The annual financial statements, directors' report and auditor's report are also required to be filed each year with the registrar of companies.

By law company auditors must be given access to company books and records. They may require any and all information from the company officers necessary to carry out their audit. Company auditors must be properly notified of each meeting of the shareholders. The auditors have the right to attend and be heard at any general shareholder meeting (Chapter 11).

Any person may be appointed as company auditor who holds a warrant to practice as an auditor under the Accountancy Profession Act or who is a partner in a partnership registered under the act. Auditors for banks or insurance companies must also have the approval of the minister of finance.

A warrant to practice is issued to those who have qualified by completing the accountancy degree at the University of Malta or possess qualifications that the Accountancy Board accepts as being equivalent. The board generally requires applicants in the second category to pass an examination on local law. The qualifications accepted by the board include passing the professional accountancy examinations given by the Malta Institute of Accountants. Those who have professional certifications from foreign countries are also commonly accepted provided that said practitioners pass the Malta Institute of Accountants examination on Malta laws and taxation (Chapter 11).

The Accountancy Board, appointed by the minister of finance, consists of government officials and professionals. Accounting and auditing standards and practices are under the purview of the board. A single publication by the board has been issued. This publication covers procedures to be followed when allegations of negligence, misconduct or dishonesty have been made about an auditor or public accountant.

The board has not issued auditing standards. The Malta Institute of Accountants members are required to use International Standards on Auditing by the International Federation of Accountants (Chapter 1).

Chapter 9

Accounting and Business Environments in the Persian Gulf, the Indian Ocean and the Far East

In evaluating the business, institutional and legal environments of off-shore center hosts, six countries were selected for this chapter from three widely separated areas of the globe. Bahrain and the United Arab Emirates, both important Arab financial centers, are included from the Persian Gulf. In the Indian Ocean, Mauritius and Seychelles have significant regional ties to India and Africa. From the Far East and Pacific Ocean, Singapore and Vanuatu are included, each having a differing role and a differing approach to the offshore center business.

BAHRAIN

Bahrain is recognized as an established tax haven with no restrictions on capital, profits or dividend repatriation. Currency exchange is not controlled. No personal, corporate or withholding taxes are imposed. There are, in fact, no direct taxes. Indirect taxes consist only of import duties on imports held out for sale in Bahrain. There are also some municipal taxes on rents and a petrol tax. Imports and exports have no significant restrictions, but import duties apply to goods that are for sale within the country. Bahrain does not have a free-trade zone (Price Waterhouse Coopers, 1999, Chapter 3).

Restrictions on foreign investment have been relaxed in recent years but foreign ownership of entire businesses is permitted in few areas. Foreigners, other than nationals from Gulf Cooperation Council states, may not own land. Total foreign ownership is possible in offshore banks and in the services sector. Prior approval for business formations is not necessary, but after formation, all businesses must register with the appropriate government agency (Chapter 5).

Full foreign ownership is permitted for exempt or offshore companies, brass-plate companies, closed joint stock companies, branches or representative offices of foreign companies and some companies with limited liability. Foreign ownership is generally restricted to at most 49 percent in other businesses (Chapter 5).

The Bahrain Monetary Agency regulates the financial service area, which has the highest volume of activity in the Middle East. Four types of banks are authorized to operate. Commercial banks have the traditional banking and loan services roles. Offshore banks are permitted to offer full banking services but must not provide services to Bahrain residents. Investment banks are similar to offshore banks, except that they are not authorized to offer checkbook or other current account services (Chapter 7).

Islamic banks may also operate in Bahrain. Both offshore and onshore Islamic banks operate. Their services are in compliance with the rules of Islamic Shari'a. They offer banking services, fund management and Islamic insurance. Bahrain is also a regional insurance center with major international insurers in operation. Annual audited financial statements for all companies operating offshore must be filed with the Bahrain Monetary Agency within 90 days after the close of the fiscal year (Chapter 7).

The Bahrain Stock Exchange has operated since 1989 with 34 companies listed in 1996. The exchange has links with exchanges in Muscat, Oman and Jordan (Chapter 7).

All business entities must complete appropriate registration requirements with the Ministry of Commerce. Operation of sole proprietorship business organizations is permitted only for Bahrain nationals. A Bahrain national in the same line of business must sponsor a foreign company branch or representative office. The foreign parent must be a viable company and must take responsibility for all of the branch's obligations. Prior approval and registration with the Ministry of Commerce is required before operations begin. Such branch or representative office particulars must be entered into the Commercial Register. And the branch must follow procedures set out for other Bahrain businesses. If the unit will be a regional distribution center for goods or services, the Bahrain national sponsor is not required (Price Waterhouse, 1997, 64, 65).

General, limited, or limited by shares partnerships are permitted in Bahrain. In the general partnership form, all partners have unlimited liability for partnership obligations. Creditors may seek collection from either partnership or personal assets of all partners. There are no specific capital requirements. The partnership agreement must specify how profits and losses are to be distributed to all partners. Shares in the partnership may not be transferred to a non-partner without such provision in the partnership agreement. Partners who withdraw from the partnership will be liable only for obligations before withdrawal. New partners will be liable for obligations both before and after their entry into the partnership. No more than 49 percent of the ownership rights may be held by a foreigner (59).

The agreement for a general partnership must contain the partnership name and address, main office and branches, partners' names and nationality, total capital and percentage share for each partner, partners responsible for management and authorized to sign for the partnership, profit sharing arrangements among partners and the partnership fiscal year. The name of the partnership is required to contain at least one partner's name and the designation "and Partners" followed by "Bahrain Partnership Co." At formation, an announcement is entered in the Commercial Register and a summary of the partnership agreement is published in the *Official Gazette* and in a local publication.

Unless otherwise provided in the initial partnership agreement, changes to the partnership agreement must have the agreement of all partners. All partners must agree upon decisions. Each partner has the right to participate in partnership management and may examine partnership books and related records. A non-partner may carry out partnership management. A partner who manages the partnership but is not so named in the partnership agreement may be dismissed by a majority of the partners without partnership dissolution. The partnership is considered dissolved if a partner named in the partnership agreement to manage the partnership is removed by court order as a result of the request of the other partners. Should a partner die or go bankrupt, the remaining partners may carry on the partnership. The general partnership may be dissolved by the unanimous decision of the partners. There are no legislated procedures, methods or content of general partnership books and records. Audited financial statements are not mandated (60).

Limited partnerships are governed by many of the same legal provisions as the general partnership. In the limited partnership, however, there must be at least one partner who maintains unlimited liability for partnership obligations. A limited partnership must have more than 50 percent of capital owned by unlimited partners who are Bahraini nationals. Limited partners are liable only up to the amount of their partnership contribution. Any partner's name that appears in the limited partnership's firm name must be an unlimited partner. Limited partners are not permitted to manage the partnership. Should this occur, unlimited liability for that partner may result. Any partner may apply to the court for approval to wind up the partnership (61).

The third kind of partnership, one limited by shares, combines features of both the general and limited partnerships. There must be at least one general partner with unlimited liability for partnership obligations. Partnership name should contain at least one general partner's name. Procedures and requirements to form the partnership limited by shares are similar to that for a corporation. Although government approval is not required, The Ministry of Commerce has prescribed a model partnership agreement.

The partnership limited by shares requires four or more promoters and must have at least one general and 10 limited partners. Invested capital, totaling at least BD10,000, must be equally divided into par value negotiable shares. Only Bahrain nationals may own partnership shares unless foreign expertise or capital is needed. In no case may foreigners own more than 49 percent of the capital. The partnership must build from earnings a general reserve of 25 percent of total share par value.

The law requires that general partners who will manage the partnership be named in the partnership agreement together with their responsibilities. The salaries and other emoluments for management should be specified in the partnership agreement. By statute no more than 10 percent of net income may be paid to those managing the partnership if their remuneration is specified as a percentage of partnership income. General partners must approve changes to the partnership agreement. Should irregularities develop, a board of control of no fewer than three limited partners is to be elected by all limited partners to oversee partnership management and to call general meetings of the partners. An annual meeting of both general and limited partners is required (63).

There are no specifics on requirements for partnership accounting books and related records. A statutory auditor must be appointed who will report to the general meeting as to whether proper accounts have been kept. Generally, books must be kept that reflect a true and fair financial position and results. In addition, a register of loans, mortgages and debentures must be properly kept by each partnership (64).

Corporate forms permitted in Bahrain are the public joint stock company, the closed joint stock company and the exempt joint stock company. Foreigners may wholly own the later two types of corporations under certain conditions. However, the public joint stock company may not have more than 49 percent of its capital owned by foreigners (46).

The Ministry of Commerce must approve the formation of all public joint stock companies. The ministry has set forth required contents and formats of the memorandum and articles of association which the promoters, one of who must be Bahrainian, must file with the ministry. The main corporate office must be in Bahrain. The company name must be followed by the phrase "Bahrain Joint Stock Company." Foreigners may own no more than 49 percent of company's capital shares (76).

Shares must be issued in Bahraini currency. Total capital must be divided into shares of equal value. Share value may be between BD1 and

BD100. Capital as a minimum must total BD500,000. Voting and non-voting, preferred and convertible shares are not permitted. Founding shareholders are required to subscribe to at least 7 percent of the total capital but may subscribe to no more than 20 percent prior to issuance of a public prospectus. Upon approval the prospectus must be published in the *Official Gazette* and one other publication for five days before subscriptions begin. The subscription period may be from 15 days to three months duration and may be extended with ministry approval. All shares must be fully subscribed for the incorporation to go forward. All subscribers must be resident in Bahrain. The ministry may allow the promoters to lower total capital for any unsubscribed shares or to subscribe to them (77).

An initial shareholder meeting must be held no later than 45 days after the end of the subscription period at which the board of directors and company auditors are elected. At this meeting, the promoter's report is made to the shareholders and the incorporation is declared complete by the shareholders. The Directorate of Commerce and Company Affairs must receive minutes of the meeting, documentary evidence that procedures were proper, and a list of subscribers with subscription totals (50).

Only after subscriptions are fully paid in may debentures be issued. Such issuance can be only to Bahrain nationals and only through a national bank after proper debenture prospectus and other procedures are followed. The value of the debentures may not be greater than the total of paid-in capital. Additional shareholder capital may be raised subsequent to the initial issuance through an audited prospectus and procedures similar to those for the initial offering. Capital may only be decreased at an extraordinary general shareholder meeting where an auditor's report explains the need for such decrease (51).

The board of directors has responsibility for the affairs of the company. The board should consist of three to 12 members who have renewable three-year terms. Directors must own shares valued at BD2,500 and must assign such shares to secure third-party claimants. Public servants are not eligible to sit on the board, except where the government is involved (51).

Director remuneration may not exceed 10 percent of net profit after reserves and expenses. Directors may not be involved with other similar businesses and must not have direct or indirect interests in contracts or other transactions of the corporation. The corporation may not loan or guarantee a loan for directors. Any individual may be a director of no more than three corporations and managing director of one.

A quorum of the board consists of half of the directors. The board is prohibited from selling the place of corporate business, mortgaging company assets or making loans that exceed three years duration (52).

An annual shareholder meeting is required in which all shareholders may attend and participate. However, the bylaws may specify a minimum number of shares must be owned to participate in the meeting (53).

Shares of the closed joint stock company may not be offered to the public. Should five or more promoters guarantee that the corporation will meet requirements of the Commercial Companies Law, an Amiri Decree is not necessary for approval of the formation of a closed stock company. Capital must total at least BD200,000. Full payment of all subscribed shares must be deposited in a bank authorized by the Ministry of Commerce. A summary of company information must be inserted in the Commercial Register and must appear in the *Official Gazette* and one other publication. If the closed joint stock company is an industrial or distribution company, foreigners are permitted to completely own the capital (47–48).

Exempt companies may operate only offshore. Main company offices must, however, be situated in Bahrain. The exempt company must have Bahrain Monetary Agency approval for entering into the financial markets. An exempt company may not hold property or land in Bahrain. Maximum corporate life is 25 years; however, the Ministry of Commerce may approve extensions (54).

Bahrain does not legislate the content or form of accounting books and records. Businesses use accounting systems of their own choice. The language used is also not legislated. English and Arabic are most common. Shareholders details must be kept in register form by corporations, limited liability companies and partnerships limited by shares. Registers must kept by corporations for board of directors meeting minutes and for liabilities owed (74).

Corporations, limited liability companies and partnerships limited by shares are required to undergo an annual audit of their financial statements. Financial service sector units must present annual audited financial statements to the Bahrain Monetary Agency. The auditor is mandated to attend shareholder annual meetings where the audit report is read (74).

The Bahrain accounting profession is regulated by the 1996 Legislative decree. Auditors must obtain licensing before practicing in the country. A code of ethics along with required academic and other required preparation is set forth in the decree.

There has been no promulgation of auditing procedures or standards in Bahrain. In practice, auditors choose the audit standards that they wish to follow. Choice commonly takes local customs and usage into consideration. The Commercial Code does specify the form and content of the audit report for corporations, limited liability companies and partnerships limited by shares. Bank audit reports are mandated by the Bahrain Monetary Agency (75).

The Commercial Companies Law requires boards of directors of corporations and limited liability companies to issue a report about their entity each year. The report must be published and must contain a balance sheet, profit and loss statement, auditor's report and a summary report in local newspapers no less than 15 days prior to the annual shareholder meeting. The financial statements must be filed with the Ministry of Commerce (76).

The statute requires that generally accepted accounting principles be followed for the financial statements. Bahrain does not have a government or other group responsible for such principles. International Accounting Standards are preferred by the government (74) The international standards are followed by most of the large businesses in Bahrain. The Bahrain Monetary Agency requires banks and other financial companies to follow International Accounting Standards. The banks in the offshore center must file annual audited financial statements no later than 90 days after close of their fiscal year (64).

The nation's accounting professional group, the Bahrain Society of Accountants, is open to all accountants and auditors in Bahrain. Only Bahrain nationals may sit on the society's board of directors. The society remains in an early stage (75).

UNITED ARAB EMIRATES

The public sector is dominant in the United Arab Emirates. Cooperation between the public and private sectors remains limited. The boundaries of each sector have been set up. UAE nationals make up no more than 5 percent of the workforce. However, nationals hold high positions in government and in quasi-government organizations. Expatriates make up the remainder of the workforce. A foreign worker must be sponsored by an employing organization to be granted a resident visa. Residence visas are strictly controlled. Trade unionism is not permitted (Price Waterhouse Coopers, 1999, Chapter 2).

Arabic, the official national language, and English are both used in the business environment (New Zealand Trade Development Board, 1999, 1). Population was in the 2.3 million range in 1998. Per capita GDP was U.S.$23,800 (1).

The country in many ways operates more through its individual Emirates than as a federal unity. Individual Emirates set their own goals and plans consistent with their own comparative advantages. Each Emirate is responsible for its own industrial development policy. Most are in the process of attempting to stimulate their industrial development through creation of industrial development zones. Free-trade zones have been successful in Dubai, attracting over 1,000 companies, and other Emirates, likewise, have established free zones where full foreign ownership is permitted. The federal and local governments have essentially adopted a laissez-faire approach to trade (Price Waterhouse Coopers, 1999, Chapter 2).

With Bahrain, Kuwait, Oman, Qatar and Saudi Arabia, the UAE was a founding member of the Gulf Cooperation Council. The goal is to develop closer economic and trade relations. While the long-range goal is to form a single market, progress has been slow. Nevertheless, advances have been made on immigration between countries, citizen rights between countries and lowering or eliminating customs duties. A unified investment law is under development (Chapter 2).

The UAE joined the General Agreement on Tariffs and Trade in 1994 and was accepted as a member of the successor World Trade Organization. For its region the UAE has a very open foreign trade policy, with both federal and local governments favoring foreign investments. There are no protective duties. Only a small number of products are restricted, usually for health and safety. A 4 percent customs duty is standard (New Zealand Development Board, 1999, 7). Some essential items are exempt from customs duty (Price Waterhouse Coopers, 1999, Chapter 2).

There are no corporate or personal income taxes, except on oil-producing companies and branches of foreign banks in Abu Dhabi, Dubai and Sharjah. Although each Emirate has legislation for taxation of companies, it is not enforced and is not expected to be in the foreseeable future. Enterprises set up in the free zone areas are granted at least 15-year tax exemption guarantees (Chapter 13).

The currency is fully convertible. No restrictions exist on the repatriation of capital or earnings. The unit of currency is the UAE dirham (Dh), which has 100 fils. The UAE government fixes the value of the dirham to the U.S. dollar periodically (Ernst & Young, 1999i).

The country's policies restrict foreign ownership of domestic businesses. Foreign ownership is limited to a maximum 49 percent participation in businesses under jurisdiction of the Federal Commercial Companies Law. Ernst & Young, United Arab Emirates, indicates that in reality the practice is for local investors to hold all of the capital in both public and private companies (Ernst & Young, 1999i). Foreign investors may not be general partners in any partnership. Foreigners are not permitted to operate as sole proprietors. Branches of foreign companies may be 100 percent foreign owned. Enterprises in free zones may also be wholly owned by foreigners (Price Waterhouse Coopers, 1999, Chapter 9).

Foreign branches must be registered with the Ministry of Economy and Commerce, the local Chamber of Commerce and the local Emirate authority that regulates business. Other firms that have UAE nationals as majority shareholders must register with the ministry and the local Emiri authority. Firms setting up in free zone areas must register with the individual free zone authority. Off-the-shelf procedures for setting up companies do not exist in the UAE (Chapter 9).

Business organizations permitted in the UAE are: sole proprietorships, public shareholding companies, private shareholding companies, limited liability companies, general partnerships, limited partnerships, partnerships limited by shares, joint participation (ventures), foreign company branches, and free-trade zone companies. Sole proprietorships are open only to UAE nationals (Ernst & Young, 1999i).

Federal Commercial Company Law No. 8 of 1984 lays out the specific requirements for the number of directors and shareholders, minimum capital levels and incorporation procedures for each type of business. The law provides the governing rules for the conversion, merger and dissolution of companies. As discussed above, companies in the UAE must have a minimum of 51 percent local equity participation. However, in practice, for both public and private companies, the local equity participation is normally 100 percent (Ernst & Young, 1999i).

Commercial Company Law No. 8 of 1984 provides that a public company's shares must be at least 55 percent held in general public hands. Shareholders' liability is limited to paid in amounts. Total minimum capital for a public company was set at Dh10 million. One-fourth of the subscription must be paid at initiation. Shares are not permitted to be issued below their nominal value. A share register must be kept with details of shareholders and holding. All shares must have equal rights unless specifically changed by the Articles of Association. Companies with limited liability can be initiated with between two and 50 shareholders. Company board of directors must consist of from three to 15 members, a majority of whom are UAE nationals. Minimum capital of such companies is Dh150,000. Banking and insurance sectors may not use the limited liability company form (Price Waterhouse Coopers, 1999, Chapter 9).

Private companies must observe essentially the same statutory provisions as public companies. However, private companies need to have a minimum of three shareholders and minimum capital of Dh2 million.

General partnerships, limited partnerships and partnerships limited by shares are also authorized and governed by the Federal Commercial Company Law No. 8 of 1984. Partnerships are required to register at the Chamber of Commerce and the municipality of the Emirate in which they operate. A partnership agreement is required to govern the partners and their business affairs. Corporations are eligible to be partners as well as individuals (Ernst & Young, 1999i).

A general partnership must have two or more UAE nationals jointly and severally liable for partnership obligations. The partnership names must contain only names of partners. Approval of all partners is required to transfer an interest in the partnership unless provided otherwise by the partnership agreement. One or more natural persons who are not required to be partners may undertake partnership management. The partnership is considered dissolved upon the death, insanity, bankruptcy or withdrawal of a partner unless remaining partners unanimously agree to continue the partnership and that information is registered in the commercial register (Ernst & Young, 1999i).

Limited partnerships must have at least one general partner whose liability is unlimited for partnership debts and one or more limited partners who have liability limited to contributed capital. There is no minimum capital specified by law. General partners are required to be UAE nationals. Limited partners are prohibited from managing the partnership or acting in the name of the partnership. The limited partnership is not dissolved at the death, insanity, bankruptcy, withdrawal or dismissal of a limited partner unless a provision for such is written in the partnership agreement. The processes for initiating a limited partnership are similar to a general partnership (Ernst & Young, 1999i).

A partnership limited by shares has general unlimited liability partners and partners whose liability is limited to subscribed capital. Minimum capital required is Dh500,000. The general partners must be UAE nationals. Annual audit of the financial statements is mandated. In general, rules for the public shareholding company apply as well to partnerships limited by shares (Ernst & Young, 1999i).

Two or more natural persons registered legally in the UAE may form a joint venture. A contract is drawn up between the parties to govern their business affairs.

A branch of a foreign company may be set up in the UAE. A local sponsor or service agent is required. Branches are required to register with the Chamber of Commerce in the local Emirate and the Economic Department of the relevant municipality. They must also register with the Ministry of Economy and Commerce by providing appropriate information and documentation (Price Waterhouse Coopers, 1999, Chapter 9).

Free-trade zones for foreign companies have been established. In these zones, incorporation is permitted for 100 percent foreign-owned limited liability entities. Such corporate entities may conduct activities inside the free zone in accordance with the terms of a special license and outside the free zone in accordance with applicable laws and regulations. The company is required to maintain a registered office in the free zone.

The free-trade zone company is a separate legal entity. Minimum capital of Dh1 million is needed. There may be as few as one shareholder. A director and a secretary who must reside in Dubai are necessary. The company must appoint a locally licensed auditor. Audited financial statements must be filed with the government no later than three months following the end of its financial year. The corporation is required to have net assets of at least 75 percent of its share capital (Ernst & Young, 1999i).

Every business operating in UAE is required to register with the Ministry of Economy and Commerce. The business must also register with the municipality or the appropriate Economic Department and the Chamber of Commerce of the Emirate in which business is undertaken. A number of business sectors require government approval. For example, banks and other financial organizations need Central Bank approval. Businesses operating in the insurance field require approval from the commissioner of insurance in the Ministry of Economy and Commerce. And the Ministry of Finance and Industry must approve manufacturing businesses. Registration of oil and gas sector companies must follow special procedures in each Emirate. These registrations must be renewed annually with payment of annual fees. Tax returns need only be filed for those companies that are in the oil and gas sector and are branches of foreign banks (Price Waterhouse Coopers, 1999, Chapter 9).

Annual audits are required for banks, insurance sector companies, both public and private shareholding companies, limited liability companies, branches of foreign companies, partnerships limited by shares and companies whose articles of incorporation require annual audits (Ernst & Young, 1999i).

There is no federal tax legislation in the UAE. Each Emirate has issued decrees for taxation but in practice these are not enforced. Taxes must be paid only by companies in the oil and gas sector and by branches of foreign banks. For the oil and gas companies the tax rates are set in concession agreements with the government. The branches of foreign bank rates of taxation are by agreements with Emirate rulers where they operate (Ernst & Young, 1999i).

Boards of directors should insure that the company's annual accounts and reports are proper and correct. Such reports must be signed by the board chairman and be presented at the general shareholders' annual meeting.

UAE has no promulgated accounting and auditing standards. The International Accounting Standards and International Standards on Auditing are commonly followed. The Commercial Law provides that business books of account depend upon the scope and character of the business carried on. The account books should accurately reflect financial position. The accrual method of accounting is commonly applied. The fundamental accounting concepts followed in the UAE include going concern, consistency, prudence, matching and the historical cost convention. All public shareholding companies and banks must publish their annual audited financial statements in the local press. The UAE regulates form, content and disclosure of financial statements only for banks and insurance companies. These standards are set by the Central Bank (Ernst & Young, 1999i).

By law and ministerial directives public and private shareholding companies, limited liability companies and branches of foreign companies must file annual audited financial statements with the Ministry of Economy and Commerce. In certain Emirates limited liability companies and branches of foreign companies may be required to file audited accounts to renew their trade licenses.

While there is no local professional association of accountants, the profession is strong in the UAE and includes, as noted elsewhere, most of the global accounting firms. Practicing accountants must be registered under Federal Law No. 22 of 1995. A Federal Register of Accountants and Auditors is maintained. Only those registered are permitted to perform audits required by statute (Ernst & Young, 1999i).

MAURITIUS

The economy of Mauritius has long operated under free enterprise principles. The country has been rewarded, in the view of the Diamonds, with annual average growth rates in the 6 to 8 percent range since the 1980s. Foreign trade advanced to $3.7 billion in 1992 from $672 million in 1982. The Diamonds also took note of the rapid expansion in the industrial sector and steady gains in tourism over this 10-year period. The annual balance of payments surplus has averaged $188 million since 1985 (Diamond and Diamond, 1998, 13).

The Bank of Maritius, established in 1967, plays a strong role in the economy, both in current and future planning (15). The country currency is the Mauritian rupee, which is divided into 100 cents. The average exchange rate in 1997 was U.S.$1 to 20.56 rupees (Economist Intelligence Unit, 1999). Since suspension of the Exchange Control Act in 1993, foreign exchanges do not require Bank of Maritius approval (Ernst & Young, 1999g). The Stock Exchange of Mauritius Limited began operations in 1989. By 1998 there were 39 listed companies with total market capitalization of U.S.$1.5 billion (Eland Systems Limited, 1998).

The legal system of Mauritius is a hybrid from English and French systems of law (Attorneys Taxplanning Companies Trusts, 1998). The English procedures are used in the civil and criminal law, while the French Napoleonic Code is followed for substantial laws of the country. Companies' laws are patterned after their U.K. equivalents. The Mauritius populace is largely bilingual, speaking English and French (1998).

The Companies Act of 1984 permits domestic partnerships, branches of foreign companies and the incorporation of public companies or private companies. Companies may have liability limited by shares, by guarantee or both. It is also possible to form a Mauritius company with unlimited liability. The provisions of the Companies Act of 1984 apply to offshore companies as well as resident. However, the 1984 law is modified by provisions passed in the 1992 Offshore Business Activities Act and the 1994 International Companies Act. All forms of business may be granted a Mauritius Offshore Certificate that allows them to operate as offshore companies.

The Baltic Banking Group in its report on tax havens (1998) believes that Mauritius has good tax haven investments at inexpensive cost. Mauritius companies may, as noted above, be formed under the International Companies Act of 1994, which provides complete tax exemption. Shares in such corporations may be no par, and the shares may be issued to bearer. The government does not require that information be filed before granting corporate or exempt status. Information is not available to the public about exempt companies. Companies must have a registered office and designate a representative who must keep required documentation at his office. Mauritius has a number of double taxation treaties. The double taxation treaties are available for companies that are formed under the Business Activities Act of 1992 (1998).

A private international company (IC) must not have capital exceeding $1 million. The beneficial owners must be non-residents. The IC must operate only outside of Mauritius (Ernst & Young, 1999g). The private international company is not permitted to raise funds from the public. Company information, including beneficial ownership, need not be publicly disclosed. The government does not require that shareholder or directors meetings be held. If all shareholders sign, an agreement may restrict the powers and activities of the corporate directors. A company secretary is optional. Annual financial statements or returns need not be filed with the government. Shelf company registrations may be used. Shares may be issued at no par and to bearer (Diamond and Diamond, 1998, 2). Banks and insurance companies may not operate as private international companies (19)

The public offshore company may raise capital from public offerings. Beneficial ownership must be disclosed to regulators. Par value registered shares only may be issued. A Mauritian resident must be appointed as corporate secretary. Two directors are required, and neither may be a corporation. Information disclosure at formation is extensive. A complete three-year business plan must show projected cash flows and profit expectations. Sources of funding, bank references, audited statements for three years and a business history are included. (21). Annual financial statements are required by the Mauritius Offshore Business Activities Authority (MOBAA) (4). Auditors are required to be members of the Institute of Chartered Accountants of England and Wales, Scotland and Ireland or of the Institute of Certified Accountants (21).

Both offshore and domestic companies must maintain a registered

Mauritius office which is publicly open for four hours each business day. Company books and publicly available registers of officers, shareholders and debenture holders must be kept at this registered office. For either the IC or the public offshore company only one shareholder is required at formation. In the case of the IC this shareholder is required to be a Mauritius registered agent (18).

The Trust Act of 1992, as modified by the Income Tax Act of 1995 and the Finance Act of 1996, permits the establishment of a variety of trusts, both resident and offshore. Trusts may be created by oral declaration, written instrument, a will or codicil. Creators of trusts may designate a protector and may file in written form their wishes. Trust instruments may state that the trust is revocable; otherwise, established trusts become irrevocable. Two trustees need to be appointed by the creator to manage the trust, one of whom is either resident in Mauritius, is an offshore bank or is an MOBAA-approved offshore company. Trustees must file a trust declaration with the MOBAA which need not disclose the beneficiaries or the settler unless they are residents in Mauritius. Beneficiaries do, however, have to be identifiable by name, class or relationship. The settler can retain control over the trust by establishing a private trust corporation that can be the trustee (4).

Unlike many offshore centers, an offshore bank in Mauritius may be qualified to do business both offshore and in the domestic economy. Such banking companies must be well qualified. Among many other requirements, banks must file annual audited financial statements with the Central Bank that must also be publicly published (8).

There are no withholding taxes required in Mauritius. Taxable incomes of both resident and foreign branches are in general computed in accordance with generally accepted accounting principles. Provisions are not allowed. Inventory valuation may be at cost, market or replacement values. Depreciation is allowable for long-term fixed assets at rates established by the government. An investment allowance may be taken in the first year of assets service as well. There is no carry back of losses, but they may be carried forward at any amount over an indefinite future (Ernst & Young, 1999g).

SEYCHELLES

The Seychelles system of justice is founded on English Common Law, French civil law and customary law. The country has a court of appeal and a supreme court. The legislature is unicameral with 22 elected members and 12 awarded seats distributed among the political parties based on each party's share of the votes garnered in the election of the legislature (ABC Country Book of Seychelles, 1999).

The unit of currency is the Seychelles rupee (SR), which is divided into

100 cents. The rupee exchange rate uses a weighted basket of eight currencies which, it is thought, better represent the country's trading partners (Economist Intelligence Unit, 1998, 59). There are no foreign exchange controls, and disclosure of foreign currency transactions is not required. Funds may be freely transferred worldwide in any nation's currency. Bank accounts may be kept in any currency (Diamond and Diamond, 1998, 16). Any nation's currency may be used to invoice transactions. Importing does not require a government license. Export proceeds must be deposited in an authorized bank (22).

Since independence in 1979, the government has been deeply involved in control of and ownership in the economy. The Ministry of Planning and Development details continuous five-year development plans, which are updated yearly. Economic and budget policy is the province of the Ministry of Finance. The Monetary Authority administers the money supply and bank system. While local branches of foreign banks operate in the Seychelles domestic market, the government owns the two local banks: the Development Bank of Seychelles and the Seychelles Savings Bank. The Development Bank is charged with funding developmental projects. The Seychelles Savings Bank operates savings and current bank accounts (Library of Congress, 1994b).

The first parastatal company began operation in 1979. By 1988 the number of parastatal companies had expanded to 35. The Library of Congress in its country study reported that in 1991 the government employed 38 percent of the labor force. Parastatals employed 26 percent, leaving 36 percent in the private sector. In recent years the government seems to be moving toward an increase in the private sector of the economy through privatization (1994b).

The Companies Act of 1972 applies to local business units that carry on business in and are resident in Seychelles. The normal tax schedule applies to the Seychelles income of these units (Diamond and Diamond, 1998, 3). Legislation permitting offshore companies, offshore trusts and international trade zone companies was enacted in December 1994. Such international companies may not do business in the domestic economy of Seychelles. The Seychelles laws are similar to offshore laws in the Bahamas and the British Virgin Islands (Seychelles, 1998).

The Seychelles International Business Authority was created to administer most aspects pertaining to offshore businesses. Companies seeking to operate as Seychelles offshore units must file with the authority's registrar. Formation of an offshore company can be made only through a registered agent, and the certificate of incorporation may only be issued to a registered agent. The authority's registrar unit is said to be efficient. The registrar maintains offices in the United States and the United Kingdom, through which incorporations may be carried out. Corporate names are approved in minutes through an automated process. Appli-

cations for incorporation filed with the registrar must include memoran-
dums and articles of association. Approval is usually granted with two
hours of filing (1998).

Formation of an international business company requires only one
shareholder. And there need be only one director. There is no minimum
capital requirement. Shares may be issued to bearer. Beneficial ownership need not be revealed. There are no requirements to file accounting
statements with the government. The law guarantees confidentiality.
Any civil legal proceedings involving an international business company
are dealt with in judicial chambers (1998).

For the international business company no taxes are levied in Seychelles. The amount of the initial annual licensing fees will remain the
same for the life of the international business company, shielding the
company from any future increases which may be made (1998). Recent
changes in the laws pertaining to banks and insurance companies have
added provisions to license offshore banks and offshore insurance-
related companies.

Seychelles recognizes international trusts as enforceable and valid. Setting up an international trust in Seychelles must be handled through a
licensed trustee. There were two licensed trustees in 1998. Only non-
residents of Seychelles are eligible to form a trust. The law that the settler
chooses to govern the trust holds valid, whether the choice was declared
or implied (1998).

Settlers may name themselves or the trustee as trust beneficiary. Neither the name of the settler nor beneficiary need be disclosed. Secrecy is
protected in that the law prohibits information about an international
trust from being disclosed, except for cases of drug or arms trafficking
and money laundering. And even in these cases, disclosure may be made
only by an injunction from the Seychelles supreme court upon the application of the Seychelles attorney general (1998).

The trust is protected against invalidation based on any claims of heirs
under foreign laws or rules designed to force heirship. The Seychelles
trust may own bank accounts in Seychelles. Corporate shares may also
be owned and traded by the trust. A trust may, however, not involve
land within Seychelles. There are no limits on accumulation of income
within the trust (1998).

The Business Tax Act governs corporate income tax in Seychelles. The
financial statements of a company prepared under generally accepted
accounting principles must be modified as specified in the tax law to
compute taxable income. Any interest received from financial institutions
is exempt from taxation. Rental income from residences is not taxed. All
business expenses incurred to earn taxable income may be deducted. The
inventory methods that are acceptable for tax purposes are the lower of
cost or market value, or the replacement value. Any provisions made for

financial statement purposes are not included in the tax report (Ernst & Young, 1999h).

Depreciation rates are specified in the tax law by category of asset. Accelerated depreciation may be elected for any class of assets. The election must be made by the due date of the tax return and remains in effect for the life of the specified asset class. In any year a full year's depreciation may be taken in the year of acquisition for assets acquired before June 30. For assets purchased after June 30 depreciation is taken on a pro rata basis for the time owned. With the exception of expenditures for buildings, expenditures made for capital assets of up to SR5,000 may be deducted in full in the year purchased (1999h).

There are no carry backs for tax losses. Tax losses may be carried forward for five-years. Depreciation which is included in the prior period losses may be carried forward indefinitely if income in the five-year period is not sufficient to absorb the total of such depreciation. Every company must submit an individual tax return and pay taxes accordingly. Consolidated tax returns are not permitted (1999h).

SINGAPORE

Singapore has a total land area of 626 square kilometers. A causeway links Singapore to Malaysia. The climate is tropical, moderated by the sea. A United Kingdom Crown Colony from 1946, Singapore became separate and independent in 1965 with a legal system based in English Common Law and a parliamentary system. The government has been stable since established (Price Waterhouse Coopers, 1999, Chapter 1).

The multiracial population approximated 2.9 million in 1995, consisting of about 78 percent Chinese, 14 percent Malay and 7 percent Indian. Population density is 4,535 persons per square kilometer. A successful public housing program has resulted in modern housing for about 87 percent of the population. Healthcare is also operating at a high level, with both public and private medical sectors contributing to a high standard of healthcare services. While a number of languages are spoken, Malay is the national language. English is used for administration and predominates in business (Chapter 1).

Singapore has grown economically at a high rate during the last two decades. Per capita GNP in 1995 was S.$34,459, which was a 10-fold increase over GNP in 1970. The important sectors of the economy consist of financial and business services, which provide 28 percent of the GDP, manufacturing, 25 percent and commerce, 17 percent. The nation is highly dependent upon foreign trade. The financial and business services sector and the manufacturing sector are seen as the growth areas in the future. However, the transport and communications sectors have been steadily increasing as a part of GDP.

The Singapore dollar, which is divided into 100 cents, floats against a trade-weighted basket of Singapore's major trading partner currencies. In 1996 the Singapore dollar was equated to U.S.$1.409 (Price Waterhouse Coopers, 1999, Chapter 1).

The economy is based on free enterprise. Foreign investors are welcome. There are no restrictions on foreign ownership of businesses or employment of foreign expertise. Capital may be imported and profits repatriated without restriction. In fact, the economy is dominated by foreign investors. Government-owned enterprises remain a significant force in the economy. The government of Singapore has set a policy to divest public ownership of business organizations (Chapter 2).

The government policy is to continue to develop an external economy by promoting overseas investments by local companies and multinational companies based in Singapore. Government policy also seeks to increase Singapore's regional presence and business. Six free-trade zones and a freeport, which have virtually no import or export duties, are operating as an international manufacturing and trading center (Chapter 8). An international financial center is encouraged by a number of incentives. The Association of Southeast Asian Nations (ASEAN), of which Singapore is a member, is working toward an ASEAN Free Trade Area by 2003 through progressive tariff reductions to nil and the elimination of quotas and other nontariff barriers to trade (Chapter 6).

Business enterprises are commonly formed under the Companies Act and are permitted to take the legal form of a sole proprietorship, general or limited partnership, joint venture, branch of a foreign company or a company. Specific industries are regulated under a number of Singapore statutes: Banking Act, Insurance Act, Securities Industry Act, Finance Companies Act and Futures Trading Act (Chapter 9).

A sole proprietor or a partnership may engage in nearly any business. Such businesses must register with the Registry of Companies and Businesses. Should the business be a foreign corporation, a local citizen or permanent resident must be named as manager to take responsibility for the business and assume the liabilities of the owner of the business.

General partnerships may have individuals or companies as partners. Partners need not be resident in Singapore. No more than 20 persons may be included in the partnership. Partners are jointly liable for the obligations of the partnership, even from personal assets. Although not required for a general partnership, a written partnership agreement is common to set forth rights and obligations. A written agreement must be drawn up for a limited partnership, however, which specifically provides for at least one partner to retain unlimited liability for partnership obligations. This kind of limited partnership is rare in Singapore (Chapter 9).

A joint venture may be undertaken by either an incorporated or unincorporated entity. The corporate form is commonly used where a long-term relationship is planned. If the joint venture is not expected to be ongoing, the partnership form is commonly used.

A representative office of a foreign company may be established in Singapore. Such an office may promote or carry on liaison in the foreign company's interest, but it may not carry on any other business. The representative office must register with the Trade Development Board or with other appropriate authorities, depending upon the nature of the business involved. Accounting records and tax returns are not ordinarily required (Chapter 9).

Foreign companies may establish branch operations in Singapore by filing proper documents with the registrar of companies. Upon satisfactory completion of the filings, the registrar issues a certificate of registration. A registered office in Singapore is required where the company must exhibit its name and place of incorporation. Such information is required on letterhead, billheads and other official publications.

Each such branch of a foreign corporation must name at least two natural persons who are resident to act as agents for the company. These agents are personally responsible for acts of the foreign branch in Singapore. The branch must file annual reports with the registrar that consist of the certified true copies of parent company financial statements, together with copies of all documents that the parent must file in its home country and certified true copies of the branch financial statements. These documents must be audited. The audit may be conducted by an auditor qualified in the parent company's home country (Chapter 9).

The registrar of companies in the Ministry of Finance administers the companies and securities acts of Singapore (David Tong, 1993, 25). Public or private companies may be formed. For private companies there may be no more than 50 shareholders. The rights of transferring ownership may be limited (84). Prior to offering securities for public sale, a prospectus must be prepared and submitted to the registrar.

A business may be incorporated in several alternate forms. It may be a limited liability company that is limited by shares or by guarantee. Or a company may be formed in Singapore that has unlimited liability. The business form most used is a company limited by shares. The remaining two forms of business are used almost exclusively by trade associations or professional organizations (Price Waterhouse Coopers, 1999, Chapter 9).

A company may be formed as either a private or a public corporation. A private company must not sell its securities to the public at large. Shareholders may be no more than 50 in number, and share transfer rights may be restricted. Should a private company have 20 or fewer shareholders, it is considered an exempt private company The exempt private company may not be owned by another corporation. Under the

Company Act an exempt company does not have to file copies of its accounts with the registrar of companies to be made available to the public, nor do the restrictions on company loans to directors apply to the exempt private company (Chapter 9).

A public company will, by definition, hold its securities for public sale. The registration requirements for such public sale must be properly filed with the registrar of companies, including a prospectus detailing company affairs.

Two or more people can undertake incorporation under the Singapore Companies Act by completing the formation procedures and subscribing to at least one share each. A proposed name for the company is first filed for two months with the registrar of companies. Next, a memorandum of association or articles of incorporation with bylaws is filed with the registrar. The act provides standard articles which may be used in lieu of being individually prepared. The registrar will issue a certificate of incorporation when all requirements are satisfied (Chapter 9).

Foreigners may wholly own corporate shares or debentures. A minimum of two registered shares with a par or nominal value must be issued. A maximum for the number of shareholders has not been set. Bearer shares are not permitted. Issued capital may not exceed authorized capital. No par shares are not authorized for use. After incorporation, another corporation may be the sole shareholder.

Common or ordinary shares, preferred shares and redeemable preferred shares may be issued. Convertible securities are authorized. Companies may increase capital shares by vote of shareholders, but to reduce capital requires the approval of the court. Premiums may be paid on capital shares, but a discount needs court approval. In general a company may not purchase its own shares for treasury stock. Transfer of a public company's stock is almost always without restriction. Liability of shareholders is only for par value of purchased or subscribed shares (Chapter 9).

A company must have two or more directors, of whom one must be resident in Singapore. Corporations may not be directors of other corporations. Directors are not required by statute to own shares, although such a requirement may be placed in the bylaws. A statutory meeting of shareholders is required at company formation for the shareholders to receive a statutory report for the incorporators. An annual general meeting of shareholders of a public company is required at which the annual report on accounts is approved, declaration of dividends is made and directors and company auditors are elected. This meeting may be held anywhere. Directors meet as necessary. Dividends, by statute, may only be paid from profits. The Company Act sets forth winding up rules for dissolution of companies (Chapter 9).

Each company must keep a registered Singapore office where statutory records are on file. Accounting books and records must support an annual return filed with the registrar of companies. All solvent companies, except exempt companies, must file annual audited financial statements and a report of the directors (Chapter 9). Auditors must be independent of the company and are required to be approved company auditors under the Company Act. In practice only certified public accountants are appointed as company auditors. Such auditors must meet statutory requirements in the Code of Professional Conduct and Ethics for certified public accountants (Chapter 11).

The primary legislation for the accounting profession is the Singapore Accountants Act of 1987, which views accountants as practicing or nonpracticing. Nonpracticing accountants are employed in industry, government or public accountants. Coopers & Lybrand reported that in 1991, 637 public accountants were practicing in Singapore, which was about 9 percent of the total accounting profession. The Institute of Public Accountants of Singapore was established by the 1987 act and was given the authority to develop and promulgate audit and accounting standards in Singapore (Coopers & Lybrand, 1991, 61).

The Public Accountants Board was also established with the responsibility to register and oversee accountants (David Tong, 1993). To be registered as a public accountant applicants must complete a professional examination, have required amounts of experience, complete preregistration courses and must have demonstrated proficiency in local laws (2, 7).

Company accountants must be independent of audit clients as required by the Accountants Act and by the institute's rules. Accountants may offer their services to the public as sole proprietors or in partnerships. A wide range of services are offered by public accountants: auditing, accounting, tax, liquidation of companies, corporate secretarial services and business advisory services (Price Waterhouse, 1993, 98).

International Auditing Standards adapted as needed for local conditions have been adopted by the institute. For all practical purposes the audit standards are similar to those used in the United States. The auditor's report on the financial statements essentially follows the British standards by reporting on whether or not the financial statements present a true and fair view. In addition, reports must be made to the company audit committee on the auditor's review of internal control within the company and on compliance with requirements of the Company Act. Should the auditor note deficiencies that have not been adequately addressed by the company, a report must be made to the registrar of companies. Should the auditor find serious fraud or dishonesty, a report must be made to the minister of finance. Under the Company Act, the auditors are provided with access at all times to company records and the right to be unobstructed in the conduct and completion of the audit (David Tong, 1993, 9).

The institute has promulgated Statements of Accounting Standards, which must be used for financial statements. These adopt the International Accounting Standards Committee's International Accounting Standards. A series, Statements of Recommended Accounting Practice, is also issued by the institute that may be used. Generally accepted accounting principles of other countries are also used when Singapore's prescribed procedures are silent (9).

There are a number of differences between accounting practices and principles in the United States and Singapore. For example, real property is permitted to be valued upward for appraisal values above cost. The costs of interest on long-term construction projects are expenses rather than added to cost of the asset. Affiliated companies that are controlled by a parent company are not consolidated where such control is intended to be temporary (70). Discontinued business segments are not separately reported (80).

VANUATU

Vanuatu was administered from 1906 to 1980, as a joint Anglo-French condominium under its former name New Hebrides. As discussed elsewhere in this volume, independence was achieved in 1980, when a democratic government with a single-chamber, 46-member parliament was elected. The nation is now a Commonwealth of Nations and United Nations member country. English Common Law is the basis for the legal system as is the Company Act, which governs the nation's business (Price Waterhouse, 1992b, 2).

Over 40 languages are in use. Bislama, an offshoot from English, is the official national language. English and French are both in wide use. The climate is tropical to subtropical (3). Agriculture is the principle economic sector, where about four-fifths of the population is employed. Services are becoming more important, increasing rapidly in recent years. Offshore banking and finance, tourism and flag-of-convenience shipping all are growing sectors (4).

The offshore financial center is large and active. The country is a pure tax haven where no personal or corporate income tax, estate tax, gift tax or capital gains tax are levied against residents or non-residents. There are no exchange controls. The secrecy laws are extensive. Vanuatu has no tax treaties with other countries (5).

Businesses may be formed as sole proprietorships, partnerships, trusts, joint ventures and companies. The first two forms, proprietorships and partnerships, do not have any form of limited liability for their business obligations. Owners have unlimited liability. Neither a partnership nor a proprietorship need be registered with a government agency unless the name of the business is not the name of the owners. In this case registering the business name with the registrar of companies (42) must follow the Business Names Act. Joint ventures do not require a separate form of business but rather operate as one of the other acceptable forms of business listed above.

In using the trust form or business organization, the legal ownership of assets may be transferred by means of a trust deed to a trustee for the trust beneficiaries. This form may be used to carry on finance and business activities. Filing with a government agency is not required, nor need the results of administering the trust be reported to a government agency (45).

The Company Act allows three classes of incorporations: local, overseas and exempted. Such entities may be either public or private. There must be at least seven shareholders for a public company, with at least two directors. The number of shareholders needed to form private company is at least two. There may be no more than 50 shareholders in a private company. The minimum number of directors for a private company is one. Should the private company be wholly owned by another corporation, then one shareholder only is permitted.

A local company, after obtaining a business license from the minister of finance, may do business in the domestic economy. Reports and related materials must be filed appropriately with the registrar of companies. Such filings are open for public inspection, including the identity of the company's beneficial ownership (42).

An overseas company may be formed to do business outside of Vanuatu. A permit to carry on such business must be obtained from the minister of finance by filing articles of incorporation and all related materials. Two residents of Vanuatu need to act as agents for the overseas company in Vanuatu (38). Annual reports on the accounts must be filed with the registrar of companies but need not be audited (42).

Exempted companies are permitted to do business only outside of Vanuatu, but such offshore business activities may be directed from within the country. A registered office must be maintained by the company in Vanuatu. At least one shareholder is mandated. There must also be one director and a company secretary. At least one shareholder meeting per year must be held in Vanuatu. All of the exempted corporation's official filings and documentation is barred from being publicly disclosed. This includes barring any court proceedings of the company or company affairs from public disclosure. The exempted company must file an annual report with the registrar of companies. There are no audit requirements (39).

Adequate books of account with related records must be kept by all companies in order that true and fair financial statements are prepared.

Such records should be maintained at the company's registered office in Vanuatu. Both local private companies with sales that exceed VT2 million and all public companies must appoint auditors. Such appointments must be made by shareholders at the annual meeting. All companies that hold licenses under the banking, trusts or insurance regulations must appoint auditors. This requirement includes the exempt companies that hold licenses for banking, trust or insurance activity (40).

Auditors for all local companies are simply required to have a valid business license in the same manner as all Vanuatu businesses under the Business Licenses Act. There are no other preparation or professional requirements, nor does Vanuatu have locally promulgated auditing standards. Although not legally required, auditors commonly adhere to the International Auditing Guidelines. Likewise, Vanuatu authorities have not promulgated accounting standards.

Accountants in public practice in Vanuatu are usually members of the Institute of Chartered Accountants in Australia or the New Zealand Society of Accountants. The Australian organization appears to be dominant. The basis for financial statements, reporting and disclosure tend to follow the pronouncements of the organization in which the particular public accountant holds membership. This is permissible as long as all of the requirements of the Company Act have also been upheld. Some accounting firms use the International Accounting Standards Committee pronouncements when accounting principles from a particular country are not required (53).

Part IV

Implications for Growth and Change

Chapter 10

Offshore Financial Centers, Accounting Services and the Global Economy

This volume has reviewed the role of major accounting firms in a selection of jurisdictions that are recognized as offshore financial centers or are moving in that direction. The purpose has been to better understand what such firms can hope to accomplish in such settings. In choosing from the plethora of actual or would-be centers, the presence of active accounting firms has been a factor, since it is known that the firms have been locating their outlets or offices internationally so as to best serve their international clients.

In the view of the current authors, major international accounting firms and presumably other major international purveyors of business and economic support services have much to offer clients, both public and private. Beyond such direct impacts facilitative services can be expected to have positive influences upon the global economy as well as upon the jurisdictions that house them. Of course, offshore service centers have been recognized as impacting the global scene. In the present context it is also time to consider the impact of the services housed upon their host jurisdictions as well as to consider whether or not small economies can or should opt for material betterment by seeking to become offshore business or financial centers and hosts to various business service purveyors such as the major accounting firms. The concerns referred to here will be considered in the context of the groupings of offshore financial centers that have been the focus of this volume.

WESTERN HEMISPHERE LOCATIONS

When one speaks of offshore financial centers in the New World, the focus turns almost instinctively to the Caribbean Basin region. As mentioned earlier (Chapter 4) that region could almost be considered to be an impacted area. Many of its small jurisdictions have been or are attempting to become offshore financial centers. In its discussion of the area the present volume has been selective rather than all inclusive.

Among jurisdictions discussed, the Bahamas and the Cayman Islands stand out as harboring major concentrations of international banking activities. Bermuda has gained recognition as a host for captive insurance operations. Antigua and Barbuda are moving towards expanding their involvements in offshore endeavors, as is Barbados.

Although independent from Great Britain since 1981, Antigua and Barbuda as a nation has adopted British Common Law. That legal framework, together with various other traditions dating from colonial days, has set the stage for successful forays into offshore activities as a workable component of the nation's development strategy. Such a strategy includes a state-of-the-art transportation and communications infrastructure and a literate labor force. Beyond such matters the government's resolve to create an environment receptive and encouraging to international business is also an important factor. Indeed, the government has worked with the private sector to improve the climate for offshore banking and corporate endeavors by introducing helpful legislation (Chapter 4). Beyond such initiatives, as mentioned earlier (Chapter 4), "first rate professional services are widely available, including banking, law, accounting and management resources" (Netforce Group Plc, 1998, 1).

KPMG is among the major international accounting firms active in Antigua and Barbuda, where it offers an extensive menu of corporate services. Included in its offerings are professional services relating to the establishment, maintenance, administration and cessation of business entities (KPMG, 1997b, 1). The firm's services related to the establishment of businesses are extensive. In the maintenance area KPMG can maintain a registered office and corporate records and can supply corporate secretarial, advisory and compliance services (2).

With regard to administration, the firm can arrange for relocation support and for staff recruitment and orientation and can also supply a business or mailing address (2). It can also arrange for the banking of funds received and for the payment of creditors and can also arrange for the maintenance of company correspondence, taxes and telephone calls (2). Beyond such matters it can arrange for the preparation of periodic statements concerning cash movements, assets and liabilities and the receipt of various forms of income.

Its traditional auditing and accounting services are performed by professionals with extensive knowledge of national, regional and international markets as well as expertise in risk analysis (1997c, 1). It conducts audits and reviews vis-à-vis various business operations and can also perform compliance reviews. The firm can also help in developing internal audit departments and stands ready to train both management and employees in issues relating to finance and accounting (1). KPMG also offers a broad menu of tax services in Antigua and Barbuda.

Another major firm active in the country is Price Waterhouse Coopers. Prior to its merger with Coopers & Lybrand, Price Waterhouse dealt in various services in Antigua and Barbuda. Included were auditing, accounting, tax, management consulting and corporate secretarial and trustee services (Price Waterhouse, 1991a, 100).

Clearly, the availability of such services as those offered by KPMG and Price Waterhouse would make Antigua and Barbuda much more attractive to international business operations. The services in question seem capable of significant contributions to the nation's domestic economy as well.

As an offshore financial center, the Bahamas occupies a rather prominent position among such jurisdictions in the Western Hemisphere. In 1998 financial services accounted for roughly 11 percent of the nation's GDP (Internet Bahamas Ltd., 1998, 2). Legislation was passed in 1990 designed to enhance the nation's position as a trading and financial center. In 1993 it was reported as boasting 415 licensed banks and trust companies, not to mention five retail banks (1998, 1, 2).

Among major accounting firms active in the country was Price Waterhouse, which offered "traditional accounting and auditing services as well as management and financial consulting services both domestically and internationally" (McKee, Garner and AbuAmara McKee, 1998, 35). That firm was serving smaller clients, nonprofit organizations, individuals and government agencies (Price Waterhouse, 1992a, 119).

That firm offered a wide range of business services, including assistance in developing corporate plans and strategies and in choosing computer systems. It was also active in offering assistance with financial restructuring as well as with mergers and acquisitions. It stood prepared to offer investment and trade advisory services and advisory services to government, including help in the privatization area (120–121). It was able to carry out organization and personnel management studies and could assist with recruitment of managerial and staff personnel. The firm was also equipped to perform evaluation and compensation studies to assist with employee development and training. Its offerings were suggestive of the extent of possible activities on the part of major accounting firms in a setting like the Bahamas.

Barbados is yet another Caribbean jurisdiction moving towards an expansion in the hosting of offshore financial activities. During the 1990s that nation has entered a restructuring process which has included a phased removal of restrictions on financial markets, the dismantling of price controls and import licensing, comprehensive tax reforms, trade liberalization and privatization (Arthur, 1997, 85). The nation has also been introducing other measures to boost competitiveness and emphasize productivity (85).

Arthur identified the intent to adopt "an open outward looking export oriented approach to the management of . . . economic affairs" (85). He indicated that efforts were being made to turn the nation into a dynamic, open and outward-oriented modern competitive economy, able to sustain itself and prosper due to its response to stimuli and its acceptance of drastic far-reaching changes across the board (87).

KPMG is a major accounting firm which has been very active in Barbados. Among facilitative services offered by that firm are assurance and accounting services, consulting services, corporate and financial services and tax services. The firm stands ready to advise on organizational and market issues and on information technology (1997b). It is also able to train management and employees vis-à-vis financial and accounting matters and can assist in preparing share offers, prospectuses and company information for the placement of shares (1997b).

The firm can help in improving efficiency with respect to customer demand by enhancing internal systems and processes in order to cut costs, improve quality and reduce cycle time (1997c, 1). It is also able to assist with the application of technologies with an eye to maximizing operational and financial efficiency.

KPMG also provides financial advisory and financial management services and can deal with strategy, privatization and economic impacts and policy advice (1997c, 1). The firm also deals with resource and operations management, human resource management and the management of change (1997c, 1–2). It can help with information technology, strategy and architecture, which involves the alignment of technology and business goals, as well as systems selection and implementation. Among enabling technologies are such things as technology and information risk management and emerging technologies, including groupware, data warehousing and business intelligence (1997c, 2). The firm also has an active service base in matters relating to taxation. In the corporate sphere the intent is to assist with corporate objectives while minimizing tax burdens.

Deloitte & Touche has also been active in Barbados. It has been making contributions in the nation's offshore financial sector, where it professes to have been "a leader in attracting overseas investors who have formed international business companies, exempt insurance companies, offshore banks and foreign sales corporations" (Deloitte Touche Tohmatsu International, 1996b). It is prepared to assist clients with incorporation, the generation of corporate directors, fiduciary administration and operating support (1996b).

Price Waterhouse was also active in Barbados. "Its clients include businesses of all forms and sizes, government agencies, nonprofit organizations, and individuals, and it is organized so that decisions affecting clients are made by partners, who have full professional authority" (1994, 120). The firm claimed notable experience in services to hospitality, manufacturing, banking, insurance, construction and service industries (120–121). Such assistance was provided to both onshore businesses and offshore investments (121). It offered "corporate administration in support of offshore companies, including acting as local agent and dealing with staff supervision, reinvoicing and banking needs" (121). It assisted with executive recruitment and offered advice on all aspects of offshore business. It also helped with insolvency and deals in trustee and trust administration services. Beyond such matters it arranged the incorporation of companies, offer corporate secretarial services and general business advisory services (121).

Although Bermuda is often thought of as an upscale tourism destination, the international business industry has exceeded tourism as that jurisdiction's biggest revenue producer (Forbes' Bermuda on Line, 1995–1996a, 1). Included in the international business category are activities such as captive insurance, reinsurance investment, shipping and other international companies as well as aircraft and ship registration and leasing, collective investment plans, foreign sales corporations, international arbitration, trusts, professional services for international business and intellectual property and software (1).

The activities listed above make up the financial services industry, the collective name for the "establishment or incorporation or registration and servicing in Bermuda of a large number of business-partnerships and bodies corporate—not owned or operated by Bermudians, falling within the exempted companies category" as well as "the regulation and other servicing, on a comprehensive local and international scale, of their partnership and corporate requirements, as well as those of their principals, by a number of highly specialized Bermudian based businesses" (2).

The authors referred to above endorse Bermuda as having excellent communications and telecommunications as well as relationships with accountants, bankers and law firms (2). They also suggest that in terms of business dealings, corporate personnel can get just about any type of work done in Bermuda for affiliates, subsidiaries or parent companies in the United States, Canada, Europe or any other foreign jurisdiction (3). The economy has a good base of imported and local professionals and a well-educated, stable, business-oriented workforce (3).

Bermuda is host to many multinational business organizations including 84 of the top *Fortune* 100. By the end of 1995 Bermuda boasted a registration list of 8,600 international companies. It was the world's largest market for captive insurance companies, with some 65 percent of the worldwide complement of some 2,700 captives (4).

Ernst & Young is among the major accounting firms operating in Bermuda, where it provides assistance in auditing, management consulting and information services. It also offers actuarial services, tax services, fund administration and corporate recovery and insolvency (Ernst & Young Bermuda, 1996). In terms of auditing the firm also conducts reviews aimed at identifying areas of potential risk. Under the management consulting designation the firm deals with business process reengineering and capacity planning consulting for short-term performance resolution and long-term system resource planning (1996). The firm also offers assistance in the planning of computer utilization and information technology planning for firms in need of help with their technology infrastructure (1996).

The firm can also conduct feasibility studies and offers insurance and reinsurance company appraisals. It supplies financial modeling and reporting and is able to conduct strategic and feasibility studies (1996). It stands ready to help with product development and risk management and can provide second opinions and conduct dynamic financial analysis. Among other service offerings, the firm can maintain offshore bank accounts and offshore general ledgers, and can handle subscriptions and redemptions and communication with existing and potential investors (1996). It also offers comprehensive corporate recovery and insolvency services. Indeed, its partners have acted as liquidators to various insurance and reinsurance companies (1996).

KPMG was the first international accounting firm to establish an office in Bermuda and boasts nine partners and a local staff in excess of 100 (KPMG, 1996) It can advise on accounting and financial management and matters pertaining to taxation. Indeed, its overall offerings make it competitive with other major accounting firms operating in Bermuda and internationally.

Another Caribbean jurisdiction featured in the current volume is the Cayman Islands. The Cayman Islands enjoy worldwide recognition as an offshore financial center. Of course, major accounting firms are quite active there. A good example is Deloitte & Touche, which operates with four partners and a staff of 40. The firm boasts a client list composed of overseas individuals and corporations as well as key local businesses in banking, insurance, the construction of investment funds, real estate, tourism and transportation (Deloitte Touche Tohmatsu Internatural, 1996b). Beyond the accounting area the firm is active in management consulting.

EUROPEAN LOCATIONS

The present volume has bypassed Switzerland and various other locations in mainland Europe in favor of examining various smaller and perhaps more recent entrants to the field of offshore finance. Among jurisdictions chosen were the Channel Islands, the Isle of Man, Cyprus, Gibraltar and Malta. All of those jurisdictions have had some historical link to Great Britain, links that still have parts to play in their business climates.

Jersey and Guernsey in the Channel Islands are both important players in offshore financial circles. Jersey has been described as having a "highly sophisticated infrastructure of trust companies, banking services, accountants, lawyers etc." (Baltic Banking Group, 1998). Guernsey has been identified as having many companies providing a whole range of trustee management, financial and corporate planning and administrative services (Rowe, 1990, 34). The services envisioned by Rowe included international accountants, banks and other organizations and also independent specialist corporate administrators (34). The economies of both Jersey and Guernsey are highly dependent upon financial center activities (Diamond and Diamond, 1998, 35). Both jurisdictions remain offshore with respect to Europe and Great Britain in terms of taxation, immigration and financial services (35).

Rowe acknowledged that international accountants and banks have the benefit of global connections but are frequently constrained by territorial presence, especially in the face of certain trading and confidential considerations (1990, 34). He pointed to the inflexibility of large organizations due to internal rules and suggested the advantage of independent corporate and trust management companies that "are often able to offer an unbiased, highly personalized and confidential service to their personal and corporate clients" (34–35). As mentioned earlier (Chapter 5), the type of services alluded to by Rowe can often be provided by major accounting firms operating in various jurisdictions. Such organizations functioning in Guernsey and Jersey benefit from the stability and independence of those jurisdictions.

Deloitte & Touche are among international accounting firms active in the Channel Islands. "By drawing on world wide resources, we can advise on the following: preparation of business plans; advice on management buy-outs and other transactions; due diligence for acquisitions, both locally and internationally; advice and assistance for companies planning UK stock market flotations" (Deloitte & Touche, 1999, 2). The firm encourages its audit teams to service a wide range of clients with an eye to broadening their experience, thus helping it to offer "a highly commercial, risk-focused service" (3). The firm is active in forensic accounting, undertaking investigations and valuations. In the investigative mode it stands ready to trace funds through international bank networks, while its valuation activities include matrimonial, professional negligence and general commercial disputes (5).

Ernst & Young is another major accounting firm active in the Channel

Islands, where it has offices in both Guernsey and Jersey. Through its Guernsey office it offers accountancy services as well as other forms of assistance such as business consultancy, statutory and secretarial services, tax planning and the developing of compliance and business plans (1998a, 1). It claims to be one of the leading professional service firms in Jersey (1998a).

In the Isle of Man the financial services sector is the largest subsector of the economy. That jurisdiction's banking industry has been seen to be dominated by branches and subsidiaries of the main British clearing banks (Baltic Banking Group, 1998). In addition to banking, the island has a growing insurance sector with 15 life insurance companies (*Isle of Man*, 1998). "There is a vast choice of schemes, policies and services available ... including insurance protection, regular savings schemes, capital investments, pensions, stand alone investment funds, asset management, offshore personalized portfolio bonds and trusts" (1998). The Isle of Man boasts the first free-trade zone to be established in the British Isles (Diamond and Diamond, 1998, 37).

Moore Stephens International is a rather large accounting firm active in the Isle of Man. That firm is a major player internationally and "can call upon a detailed understanding of financial matters, whatever they are—wherever they are" (1998a). The firm can provide comprehensive audit and accounting services and can advise on taxes, business administration, financial planning and cash flow as well as VAT (1998a).

Pannell Kerr Forster International Association is another accounting organization active in the Isle of Man. Its management consulting arm is Pannell Kerr Forster Management Consultants. The firm provides a wide range of services to both public and private sector clients (Pannell Kerr Forster, 1996–1998a). Service offerings include "objective consulting services ... in all aspects of project planning and marketing, general economic development, organizational services, the use of technology and financial control" (1996–1998a). The firm deals with large public projects as well as assistance to small private firms. Many of its projects are carried out in cooperation with other specialists such as consulting engineers, architects, planners, agricultural consultants and others (1996–1998a).

As suggested earlier (Chapter 5), such an interfunctional exposure illustrates how deeply the facilitative activities of such a firm can penetrate an economy. The organization can assist a variety of business and economic activities including healthcare, central and local governments, large engagements in developing countries, education, financial models for major projects, information technology and systems, franchising and private financial initiatives (1996–1998a).

The organization's role in assisting governmental agencies seems significant in as much as it offers "advice in establishing procedures and structures necessary to adapt to a more commercial role and affecting change, including advice on resource accounting and budgeting ... and the private finance initiative" (1996–1998b). The organization is also willing to assist local authorities in implementing legislation, particularly the compulsory tendering regulations recently extended to professional services (1996–1998b). As mentioned earlier (Chapter 5), the services in question seem to pertain to circumstances in the United Kingdom, but the organization may be able to offer similar services elsewhere.

The Pannell Kerr Forster organization through its global network may also be a significant player through its involvements in developing nations, where it advises public and private sector clients on financial and strategic problems and the lack of managerial skills common to such locations (1996–1998b). The organization can also advise universities concerning information technology and issues related to information systems. It can also assist with development and costing methodologies concerned with teaching and learning in higher education. Beyond such matters it can provide "value for money studies to grant maintained and private secondary schools" (1996–1998b).

The organization reviews complex project forecasting and financing models with an eye to accuracy and reliability. In the area of strategic and operational consultancy it can help with all aspects affecting performance, profitability improvement, product profitability analysis, cost reduction, financial feasibility studies and fund raising (1996–1998b). It is also involved in information technology and computer consultancy. It appears as though the organization impacts events in the domestic economy of the Isle of Man, not to mention external constituencies.

Despite having been divided since 1974, Cyprus has done reasonably well economically and has been described as a high-income service economy (Wilson, 1992, 4). On the island the Greek Cypriots are seen as the more successful (Library of Congress, 1991). Since the late 1970s the service sector has been the leading component of the Greek Cypriot economy (1991). Although tourism has been the main cause of service expansion, the other branches of the service sector such as transportation, storage, telecommunications, finance, insurance, real estate and business services have also experienced steady growth (1991).

Another dynamic component of the service sector consists of offshore enterprises. In assessing the potential of Cyprus with respect to offshore business, Wilson points to the fact that much offshore business activity can be carried out through telecommunications (1992, 80). Since most aspiring offshore centers have telecommunications facilities, he sees those as offering no distinct advantage to Cyprus (1992, 81). Rather, he sees interest from offshore companies as stemming from two possible sources. First of all, he points to Western businesses with strong Middle Eastern interests that could benefit from establishing a regional headquarters service base or center for coordinating operations (82–83). Secondly, "there are companies in the Middle East which can benefit from carrying out certain activities with a regional or international orientation from a less regulated or more secure base outside their home country" (83).

Wilson suggests that Western enterprises have a regional base geared to observe and manage ordering and to arrange the shipment of goods as well as to deal with invoicing and payment (83). According to him, financial management functions may be considerable and may also benefit from a regional base by client knowledge and quicker market intelligence (83).

The Diamonds, writing about Cyprus, allude to various benefits available to foreign companies, which include low operating costs, efficient local clerical workers, excellent communications, a good strategic location and legislation based upon English Common Law (1998, 7). However, they acknowledge that the difficulties between Greece and Turkey have deterred some investors (7).

Offshore companies are expanding in number on Cyprus, with three-quarters of the number involved in trading, contracting, investments, and consulting and management services (7). The Diamonds report that the government sees the nation as a suitable setting for banks, captive insurance, holding companies and printing and publishing, in addition to advertising, marketing, offshore reinvoicing, royalty, trust and employment companies (7–8). Elsewhere, it has been suggested that "clear policies adopted in connection with offshore banking and financial services as well as modern legislation . . . on international trusts give Cyprus major advantages and total flexibility as an international business and financial center" (Eracleous & Eracleous, 1998a, 3).

The Diamonds describe Cyprus as a major link in Eastern and Western trade (1998, 8). Architects and engineers are being encouraged to set up headquarters there for projects in the Middle East and the Arabian Gulf. The island has also enjoyed an influx of firms fleeing the difficulties in Beirut, although some of those firms are returning to Lebanon (8). Eracleous & Eracleous have described the island as ideal for the establishment of shipping firms (1998a, 6), noting that the country ranks fourth in the world vis-à-vis ship registrations (3). The Diamonds have identified the island's main ports (Limassol and Larnaca) as major container transshipment centers in the eastern Mediterranean (1998, 35).

Prior to its recent merger with Price Waterhouse, Coopers & Lybrand saw itself as the largest organization of chartered accountants and management consultants in Cyprus (1998a). It provided special services to offshore clients, standing ready to offer services required for the establishment and management of offshore entities (1998b). Such offerings included services involving offshore company administration, the opening and operation of company bank accounts and complete accounting and financial reporting services, not to mention taxation and audit services. The firm offered financial advice on all business concerns and was ready to assist with getting residence and work permits and locating office and residential space. Beyond such matters it assisted with executive search and recruitment and with nominee and trustee services (1998b).

The firm was very involved in financial and management consulting (1998c). It also stood ready to assist with project management consulting (1998f). "Project management reduces risk by helping to maximize return on investment, ensuring that the project achieves desired goals and that those goals correspond to the business objective" (1998f).

Price Waterhouse was also very active in Cyprus, where its services fell into three major categories, which included audit and accountancy, taxation and management consulting (Price Waterhouse, 1991b, 159). In addition to the audit requirements in operation in Cyprus, the firm saw their audits as constructive, cost-effective aids to management (159). Under the management consulting label the firm was offering design and implementation of accounting systems, feasibility studies, computerization, assistance relating to the establishment of businesses and help with human resource concerns. Clearly the post-merger firm of Price Waterhouse Coopers can be expected to be a major influence in the economy of Cyprus.

Gibraltar, a dependent territory of the United Kingdom, occupies a historically strategic position on the southern coast of Spain. Although small in land area and limited in natural resources, its strategic importance may well be maintained and perhaps even enhanced through offshore financial activities. The territory has enjoyed substantial investments in infrastructure and now boasts "a wide selection of offshore space, warehouses, light industrial areas and residential accommodations" (Deloitte & Touche, 1998a). The Diamonds have suggested that the revenues of the territory derive mainly from financial services, supplies for visiting ships, entrepot trade, tourism, transshipment and a government-sponsored lottery (1998, 21). Indeed they describe the territory as gearing up as an offshore financial center.

Deloitte Touche Tohmatsu International is one of the major accounting firms active in the territory (1998b). According to the firm, all of its services are guided by common global principles that impact the way in which they perform their tasks (1998c). Their services cover audit and accountancy, tax, consulting and reconstruction and insolvency. Through a subsidiary the firm offers offshore services. As mentioned earlier (Chapter 5), specific offshore service offerings include the incorporation of Gibraltar-registered companies and the registration of branches of foreign companies registered in the territory.

The final European jurisdiction considered in this volume is Malta, a small nation composed of three islands in the Mediterranean. Malta is host to 170 foreign and 230 domestic manufacturers but additional industrial growth is constrained by serious water and electricity shortages (Diamond and Diamond, 1998, 20–21). The nation boasts 2,200 registered offshore companies but is phasing out offshore companies over a nine-year period in hopes of becoming a financial center for both domestic and foreign companies with an "onshore" designation (1998, 1). As noted earlier (Chapter 5), many existing companies are Russian or Eastern European.

Price Waterhouse has been represented in Malta since 1977, providing a full range of professional services to both national and international clients (Price Waterhouse, 1991c, 190). "A significant portion of the practice is devoted to serving the special needs of foreign multinational companies doing business in Malta, including those operating in the oil and gas industry" (191). Services provided included audit and business advisory, tax, management consulting and offshore services (191).

The merged firm of Price Waterhouse Coopers and other major accounting firms may well be in an advantageous position to facilitate international business linkages through Malta due to the large complement of Russian and Eastern European firms located there. Specifics related to this set of circumstances deserve ongoing observation.

LOCATIONS SELECTED AT LARGE

Since space hardly permits the coverage of each and every actual or aspiring offshore financial center in existence, it was decided to consider a selection of centers from various locations in settings that have not been highlighted in regional coverage. In Chapter 6, six jurisdictions were discussed. Included were Bahrain and the United Arab Emirates because of their significance to the Middle East, Mauritius and Seychelles in the Indian Ocean, and Singapore and Vanuatu from the Asia Pacific theater of operations. It is hoped that this selection can provide insights into the real and potential significance of offshore financial centers and the accounting services available in or through them.

The last quarter of the twentieth century has seen the emergence of Bahrain as an important financial center in the Arab world. As noted earlier (Chapter 6), the Diamonds have identified this jurisdiction as having eclipsed Beirut as the Arab money capital (1998, 1). That status was supported through the licensing of 50 large banks to become offshore banking units and 21 to serve as investment banks. Nugent and Thomas have alluded to yet another rather important role being adopted by Bahrain in "attempting to discern a way to blend the rich traditions of the Arab and Islamic cultures indigenous to the Gulf with the values of urban industrialized Western societies" (1985, 5).

Coopers & Lybrand has seen Bahrain as the commercial hub of the Gulf since it has adjusted its framework to support both investments and business ventures (1996, 3). The nation enjoys strong international transportation linkages. Indeed, it "has been the entrepot for the region and is also a distribution center" (McKee, Garner and AbuAmara McKee, 1999, 69). It is seen as one of the most diverse economies of the Gulf, boasting that area's largest concentration of manufacturing firms and the largest community of international bank branches (Arab World Online, 1997a, 1).

As mentioned earlier (Chapter 6), Bahrain has been described as the Middle East's preeminent financial hub and as a key player in world financial and banking services (Arab Net, 1997, 1). Arab Net became even more explicit describing Bahrain as "an international and regional interbank money market centered on its offshore banking sector" (1). Bahrain is host to international law firms, insurance companies, certified public accountants and various consultants (McKee, Garner And AbuAmara McKee, 1999, 70). According to Arab Net, the presence of such activities stimulates the appearance of other related financial establishments (1997, 1).

Among various business services available in Bahrain are those offered by major accounting firms. Coopers & Lybrand was one of the Big Six active in Bahrain, where it operated as Coopers & Lybrand/Juwad & Habib & Co. Its service offerings included management consulting, information technology services and human resource consulting. It also offered financial services, business assurance, business recovery and insolvency, litigation support services and company formation (McKee, Garner and AbuAmara McKee, 1999, 76). Various major accounting firms are active in Bahrain and, of course, enhance that jurisdiction's stature as an offshore financial and business service center.

The United Arab Emirates share Bahrain's linkage function between the Arab world and the global economy. The Emirates boast transportation and communications linkages that support a range of competitive offshore financial services. The governments of various Emirates are seeking investments of expertise and capital (Ernst & Young, 1990, 3). Free-trade zones have been established and financial reporting requirements at both federal and local levels are minimal (3). Beyond energy-related activities the economy is comprised of utilities, communications, construction, banking and financial services, manufacturing projects and tourism (4).

The United Arab Emirates enjoy a significant presence on the part of major accounting firms. Ernst & Young is quite prominent among such firms. Although the firm sees its main business in the Middle East as the auditing of financial statements (1997b), it does claim to have one of the world's largest management consulting practices (1997c). Among consulting services offered by it are business planning and control, financial planning and control and performance improvement (1997c).

RSM International is another major accounting firm active in the United Arab Emirates. That organization is well aware of both local and international issues affecting their clients' industries and organization (1998a). Clients vary from startup companies to very large multinational organizations, many of which are publicly traded (1998a). In the tax area the firm is experienced in offering extensive services to multinational firms and can provide export-related services (1998a). RSM International is very active in consulting, dealing with international business development, international information technology, international cash and financial management and global human resources (1998).

In the Indian Ocean, Mauritius and Seychelles are listed in some circles as offshore financial centers. Neither appears to be as active in that regard as do some of the other jurisdictions that have been featured in the present volume. Nonetheless, they are of interest in the present context because of their location and because they may be representative of a new range of rather small jurisdictions opting to host offshore activities as a means of economic expansion.

The Library of Congress has cited Mauritius as having developed a rather diverse and prosperous economy (1994a). Some of that success was attributed to export processing zones (1994a). The same study suggested that the government has planned further economic diversification for the 1990s, including the development of the country as a center of offshore banking and financial services (1994a).

Elsewhere, it has been suggested that "Mauritius provides an ideal environment for banks, insurance and reinsurance companies, captive insurance managers, trading companies, ship owners or managers, fund managers and professionals to conduct their international business" (Moonesamy, 1996). Among offshore activities that can be conducted are banking, insurance and funds management, not to mention international financial services, operational headquarters and international consultancy services (1996).

Offshore business opportunities also include shipping and ship management, aircraft financing and leasing, international licensing and franchising and international trading (1996). Beyond those activities are international data processing and information technology services, offshore pension funds, international assets management and international employment services (1996).

Price Waterhouse Coopers is quite active in Mauritius. Robert Bigugnon, the firm's country leader, sees the merged firm as offering enormous scope and scale in what he terms critically important emerging markets as well as a faster deployment of new products and services as the result of a more efficient management of a larger investment pool (Price Waterhouse Coopers, July 1, 1998).

The merged accounting firm began with a client base of 1,000 companies, and had the intent of providing a full range of business advisory services to leading national and local companies and public institutions (July 1, 1998). Intended services include audit, accounting and tax advice and management, information technology and human resource consulting. The firm also provides financial advisory services, including assistance with mergers and acquisitions, business recovery, project finance and litigation support (July 1, 1998). The firm in Mauritius also provides service to Madagascar and Seychelles as well as other islands in the Indian Ocean and portions of Eastern Africa (July 1, 1998).

Seychelles has also become active in offshore financial activities. The government has been interested in creating an enabling environment for business, whether domestic, offshore or international (Seychelles, 1998). Seychelles has adopted laws similar to those in the Bahamas and the British Virgin Islands. A freeport and export processing zone have been established in hopes of attracting economic activity. The country is promoting itself as a serious financial and business hub. As mentioned earlier (Chapter 6), satellite communications, an established banking sector, together with professional management service companies add support to the offshore aspirations of the nation. Price Waterhouse Coopers service interests in Seychelles through their practice in Mauritius. It remains to be seen whether Seychelles can become a strong offshore financial center. Beyond Mauritius it has little regional competition. No doubt the major accounting firms would have much to contribute if the nation's international linkages were to increase.

Singapore has great potential as a major player in the world of international finance. That nation is a trading and distribution hub for Southeast Asia and is a major transshipment link between the region and the world at large (State of Hawaii, 1999. 1). The government seeks the development of Singapore as an international banking center and wishes to regionalize local operations in order to counter inherent internal limits to growth. The nation is seen as "building upon its traditional strengths in entrepot trade and shipping, while gradually diversifying into banking and financial services and other high-value-added sectors" (British Club, 1999).

As referred to earlier, Lessard has suggested that Singapore has transformed itself from a home-based banking center in the 1960s to a regional center (Chapter 6). Beyond that he suggested that the country has ambitions towards becoming an international financial center as well as a regional or perhaps international capital center (Chapter 6). The latter, he suggested, "not only engages in the financing of businesses, but also in the management and control of operations, including not only the creation of entrepreneurial capital, but also strategic roles in corporate growth and restructuring through joint ventures, alliances, internal expansion and mergers and acquisitions" (1993, 200).

Writing in 1990, Chungsoo Kim and Kihong Kim ranked Singapore as third in Asia as an international financial center behind Tokyo and Hong Kong (184). Lessard saw financial dealings as a positive influence in Singapore. "Financing of crossborder trade and investment within the Asian-Pacific region and between that region and the rest of the world, attracted foreign non-financial corporations into the region" (1993, 203). According to Lessard, large foreign banks followed their customers and established branch networks (203). He was quite accurate in suggesting that a foreign bank well established in Singapore could provide contacts, advice and financial services to domestic clients interested in Asian markets (203).

As mentioned earlier (Chapter 6), various business service groups by locating in Singapore might well attract both domestic and foreign business clients wishing to operate in the region. Lessard saw seven areas of growth for the financial sector as reported by the Economic Review Committee as early as the mid-1980s. Those included risk management, fund management, capital markets, untested securities market, financial and commodities futures, financing of third country trading and reinsurance (203).

According to Bavishi, all of what had been termed as the Big Six accounting firms were active in Singapore in 1991. Beyond those he identified seven other rather large accounting firms as present (1991, Appendix B, 19).

A Price Waterhouse manual for Singapore illustrates how extensive the operations of a major accounting firm can be. In Singapore the firm was serving "a large number of major local and international organizations as well as many smaller clients, public sector entities, non profit organizations and individuals" (1990, 162). The firm was serving an extensive clientele, which included "financial institutions, insurance companies and both multinational and local businesses in the industrial, commercial and service sectors" (163). Clearly, a firm with such a diverse clientele would be capable of generating major impacts in the nation's economy and beyond.

Moores Rowland International is another major firm active in Singapore. As mentioned earlier (Chapter 6), MRI has members in every region of the world equipped to make it easier and more profitable for clients to engage in international trade. Assistance with business organization in foreign countries and help with tax structures are among services offered. The firm can also help with legal and banking contracts in foreign locations and with international business information and advice on information technology. Beyond such matters the firm offers foreign market assessments and export strategies (1998a). It seems clear that what the firm is doing in Singapore should help to enhance the role of that nation as an offshore financial and business center.

According to Bavishi, various major accounting firms have been active in Vanuatu. The firm of Moores Rowland has labeled Vanuatu as the South Pacific's premier tax haven (1998a, 1). The nation is also an extremely active financial center with extensive business and financial facilities (1). Moores Rowland sees the country as a dualistic economy comprised of a small holder subsistence agricultural sector and a small monetized sector. The latter is based upon established plantations, ranches and associated trading, manufacturing, banking and shipping services, together with the tourist industry (2).

The nation boasts an offshore business and financial center dating from the 1970s. "The financial center produces significant government revenue through business license fees, insurance, banking and trust company licenses, annual company registration fees, stamp duties and other small fees" (2). The center also generates foreign exchange through capital transfers, professional fees and interest (2).

Moores Rowland "provides accounting, auditing, management and consulting services to government, offshore clients, local business and individuals from around the world" (1998b, 1). It provides wholesale company incorporation services to finance, legal and tax guidance professionals (1). It sees itself as a central figure in the offshore financial centers of the Pacific and offers a complete range of professional accounting services as well as various other facilitative business services (1). It offers banking services via the Pacific Bank Limited. Those services include offshore bank accounts in any currency, credit card services, mutual funds and portfolio management, not to mention back-to-back financing, back-to-back deposits and trusteeships (1). What the firm is providing through its service menu in Vanuatu speaks to the significance of major accounting firms in such settings.

Chapter 11

Some Final Reflections

All of the jurisdictions that have been featured in this volume are either well established as offshore financial centers or are taking steps to encourage offshore financial activities. Although they are situated in various parts of the world, all have had historical links to Great Britain and in general have adopted British legal and governmental institutions. All are very small in terms of population, and thus must rely upon external sources for the bulk of needed manufactured goods.

Of course, the need to import such significant quantities of finished goods necessitates exports if trade imbalances are to be avoided. All small economies face variations of this issue. In the past many solved their trade imbalances through the export of primary products. This was the route pursued by various Caribbean jurisdictions, including some that have been featured in the present volume. Achieving trade balances and/or material improvements through primary exports has not been effective, since the prices of primary products have not risen as rapidly in world markets as have those of manufactured goods, a fact that has been known by economists for some time (Nurkse, 1967).

If the world's smallest economies find it difficult to encourage an expansion of material well-being through primary production for export, other means must be found. In various larger economies that other means has taken the form of manufacturing for export. However, that alternative may not be readily available to the smallest economies due to constraints revolving around labor and other needed resources. Among the jurisdictions reviewed in this volume, Singapore may be the lone exception. As one of the "Asian Tigers," that nation achieved rather impressive progress through manufacturing for export (McKee and Garner, 1996).

Although secondary pursuits have often been seen as a logical progression for economies seeking to move beyond a dependence upon primary products, service industries have also been recognized as potential generators of employment and foreign exchange. Indeed, it has been suggested that services that are traded internationally can be a source of growth and prosperity for smaller economies (Amara, 1994a and 1994b).

Concentrating on a selection of Caribbean jurisdictions, Amara found that material progress was being achieved through an emphasis on international service sectors, notably tourism and offshore finance. Through concentrating on such activities, various economies in the Caribbean Basin were found to be successfully deemphasizing primary production for export, notably plantation crops, in favor of the new service emphasis. Although there are certainly downside risks in the new emphasis, the opportunity costs of moving in that direction seemed slight since major manufacturing endeavors were hardly viable alternatives. Thus, Amara concluded that development could be pursued with some success through the service option in the Caribbean economies that she investigated.

For the service option to be successful, economies considering it would require receptive and encouraging legal and business environments. How those concerns apply in the case of international tourism is beyond the parameters of the current volume. However, legal and institutional environments supportive of offshore financial activities have been given considerable attention. For any jurisdiction wishing to play a role in the global economy as an offshore financial center some requirements seem self-evident. For example, a good transportation and communications infrastructure is indispensable, as is a stable government and a safe environment. Given such prerequisites, offshore financial centers emerge in keeping with the needs of multinational business interests in the global economy.

Among the jurisdictions that have been discussed in this volume, legal environments generally have roots in English Common Law, a circumstance which provides the global business community with a basis of understanding. Indeed, legal systems, the prevalence of other British institutions and the use of the English language contribute to facilitating the international linkages needed in offshore financial centers. This of course does not suggest that English roots are a prerequisite for success as an offshore financial center. It does support the position that would-be offshore financial centers have an advantage if they share language, legal systems and cultural linkages with nations occupying strong positions in the global economy. Such linkages contribute to confidence building among multinational business interests.

It is clear that success as an offshore financial center can serve as the basis for substantial economic progress for a small nation. The services offered in and through such centers are among those that can contribute to redressing trade imbalances in such nations. Beyond that, of course, procedures and practices in place in the offshore financial sector may generate a demonstration effect in the domestic economy of the host jurisdiction. Although there are positive benefits to small jurisdictions able to successfully develop offshore financial sectors, there is hardly an unlimited market for such facilities. As more jurisdictions seek to enter the market for offshore services, that market will become more competitive.

In another context it was suggested that regulations aimed at international concerns are proportionally more significant among smaller economies (McKee, Garner and AbuAmara McKee, 1998, 126). Such rules are important to the generation of strong business climates (126) and thus to facilitating the expansion of international business and economic linkages. "The compatibility of domestic laws and procedures with the operation of international business interests will encourage or retard such operations" (McKee and Garner, 1996, 137).

It is clear that the actual or emerging offshore financial centers that have been featured in this volume are aware of international realities. Some have taken steps to ease the tax burdens of multinational businesses and foreign personnel. Nonetheless, foreign interests are frequently faced with various domestic procedures and requirements that may differ from those they may be accustomed to. If they wish to operate in the jurisdictions in question, they must follow the prescribed procedures. Such procedural frameworks may well be reassuring to international business interests, since they do establish parameters that can be relied upon. At the same time they do constitute constraints. It seems clear that any jurisdictions wishing to encourage international business linkages would be well advised to avoid the overregulation of business operations.

The international economy is replete with cadres of business and legal service providers which act as facilitators of international business. These providers are skilled in helping their clients in the navigation of the institutional anomalies of operating in multiple jurisdictions (McKee, Garner and AbuAmara McKee, 1998, 126). Among such cadres of facilitators are the major international accounting firms. Those firms are very active in helping both their business clients and the host jurisdictions that have been featured in this volume.

The major accounting firms are known to locate internationally in keeping with the needs of their international clients (McKee and Garner, 1992). It is almost a truism to suggest that their presence in smaller jurisdictions illustrates linkages that those jurisdictions have to the global economy. Of course, the firms facilitate such linkages, or more accurately, they facilitate the functioning of internationally oriented business units present in or operating through such jurisdictions. Their presence seems to signal international involvements, but more than that it facilitates and nurtures such involvements, and may well support their extension in number and complexity.

No one would suggest that the jurisdictions that have been featured in this volume are offshore financial centers because of the presence of the major accounting firms. Rather, the firms are present because of the international involvements of the small economies in question. Many small insular jurisdictions have enjoyed little or no involvement on the part of the accounting firms simply because their business and economic needs have not created the demand for it.

Although the jurisdictions featured in this volume display variations vis-à-vis their functioning as offshore financial centers, they all enjoy the involvement of the accounting firms. Although the services offered by the firms are extensive, some are geared more strongly in the direction of supporting international activity. This support for international activity is perhaps the most important element in a cadre of very significant impacts rendered by the major accounting firms in and through offshore financial centers.

By facilitating the operations of international business interests, the firms are improving the operation of the global economy, while simultaneously strengthening the relations of their host offshore centers to that economy. In the host centers, what the firms are offering renders those centers more attractive to offshore business, both as places to locate their facilities and places through which to operate. This in turn improves the economic climate, performance and prospect of the centers in question.

As suggested earlier, the firms serve as settings where aspiring local accountants and business-oriented personnel can gain on-the-job training and experience. Whether or not such employees ultimately pursue careers within the firms themselves or elsewhere in the local business community, their experience contributes to the strength of the local economy.

Without redetailing the extensive service offerings of the firms at this juncture, it seems safe to suggest that those offerings permeate almost all aspects of local business, while at the same time assisting and even promoting international business dealings. In cases where the firms serve as consultants to government agencies their influence seems even more pervasive. This is not to say that the firms are the element that insures the success of a jurisdiction as an offshore financial center. Nonetheless, their impacts can be very significant.

This volume has featured a selection of jurisdictions with some claim to being offshore financial centers. Certainly, it is less than all inclusive. In their most recent review (1998) the Diamonds have featured in excess of 60 centers. The jurisdictions chosen for attention in this volume show considerable variations in the extent of their offshore involvements.

The Bahamas, the Cayman Islands and Bermuda are well recognized as focal points for offshore activity. The same can be said for the Channel Islands and the Isle of Man. In the Asia/Pacific region Singapore is certainly an important financial center and entrepot. In the Arab world Bahrain and the United Arab Emirates are very significant links to the global economy. Cyprus has also developed links to the Arab world in competing for business interests that had traditionally been housed in Lebanon. Malta and Gibraltar are staking claims as seats for offshore activities in the European theater of operations. In the Indian Ocean Mauritius and Seychelles have emerged as aspiring offshore centers. The extent of their ultimate success may well be dependent upon the functions they develop vis-à-vis neighboring jurisdictions on the African continent. In the Caribbean Barbados and Antigua and Barbuda have shown some success in developing offshore sectors, and the same can be said of Vanuatu in the Pacific.

Although the centers featured above have various historical and institutional linkages to the United Kingdom, they are very diverse geographically and also differ in size, not to mention the scope of their economies. All of this hardly suggests that the door is open for unlimited new aspirants to the offshore field. In an already crowded field that can hardly be the case. It cannot be said either that aspirants need only attract the accounting firms and the latter will do the rest. As mentioned more than once, the firms only locate in response to client needs. The point is that where they actually do locate, they can have very positive impacts.

Bibliography

ABC Country Book. (1999). *ABC Country Book of Gibraltar* (On-line). Available: http://www.theodora.com/wtb/gibraltar

ABC Country Book of Mauritius. (1999). *Mauritius Economy 1994* (On-line). Available: http://www.theodora.com/wfb/mauritius_economy.html

ABC Country Book of Seychelles. (1999). *Seychelles* (On-line). Available: http://www.theodora.com/wfb/seychelles_people.html

AbuAmara McKee, Yosra, David L. McKee and Don E. Garner. (1997). "Accounting Services and Growth in the Islamic World: Some Evidence from the Mediterranean and the Middle East." In Abbass F. Alkhafaji and Zakaria El-Sadek (eds.), *International Business Strategies: Economic Development Issues*. Apollo, Pa.: Closson Press, 59–63.

Amara, Yosra A. (1994a). "Externally Traded Services and the Development of Small Economies." In David L. McKee (ed.), *External Linkages and Growth in Small Economies*. Westport, Conn.: Praeger, 7–14.

Amara, Yosra A. (1994b). "Services and Growth in Small Developing Countries." In David L. McKee (ed.), *External Linkages and Growth in Small Economies*. Westport, Conn.: Praeger, 17–26.

Amara, Yosra A., Don E. Garner and David L. McKee. (1995). "A Taxonomy of Accounting Service Impacts upon Caribbean Economies." In Abbass F. Alkhafaji (ed.), *Business Research Yearbook: Global Business Perspectives*, Vol. II. Lanham, Md.: University Press of America, 52–56.

American Institute of Certified Public Accountants. (1991). *International Accounting and Auditing Standards*. New York: American Institute of Certified Public Accountants.

Anderson, Robert E. and Albert Martinez. (1998). "Supporting Private Sector Development in the Middle East and North Africa." In Nemat Shafik (ed.), *Prospects for Middle Eastern and North African Economies: From Boom to Bust and Back?* New York: St. Martin's Press, 178–193.

Anon. (1998). *The Free Port of Mauritius* (On-line). Available: http//pub. intnet.mu/iels/freeport_mau.htm

Antigua & Barbuda. (1998). *Offshore Banking* (On-line). Available: http:// www.antigua-barbuda.com/offshore.html

Arab Net. (1997). *Bahrain Business: Financial Services* (On-line). Available: http:// www.arab/net/bahrain/business/hn/financial.html

Arab World Online LLC. (1997a). *Country Profile: State of Bahrain* (On-line). Available: http://www.awo.net/country/overview/overview/crbah.asp

Arab World Online LLC. (1997b). *Country Profile: United Arab Emirates* (On-line). Available: http://www.awo.net/country/overview/cruae.asp

Arthur, Owen. (1997). "Preparing for the New Global Economy." *Caribbean Affairs*, Vol. 7, No. 6, 85–93.

Askari, Hossein, Maha Bazzari and William Tyler. (1998). "Policies and Economic Potential in the Countries of the Gulf Cooperation Council." In Nemat Shafik (ed.), *Economic Challenges Facing Middle Eastern and North African Countries: Alternative Futures*. New York: St. Martin's Press, 225–255.

Attorneys Taxplanning Companies Trusts. (1998). *Latest News* (On-line). Available: http://www.mmv.se/uj/tips.html

Bahamas: Economic Trends and Outlook. (1998) (On-line). Available: http:// tradecompass.com/library/books/com-guide/BAHAMAS02.html

Baltic Banking Group. (1998). *Tax Havens A to Z* (On-line). Available: www. BalticBankingGroup.com

Bavishi, Vinod. (1991). *International Accounting and Auditing Trends*, 2nd ed. Princeton, N.J.: Center for International Analysis and Research.

Bendelow, Edmund. (1996). "Cleaning up Offshore—An Opinion." *Offshore Financial World* (On-line). Available: http://www.itl.net/business/ofw/ Jersey/articles/bail2.html

BKR Damianou & Co. (1998a). *Audit and Accounting Services* (On-line). Available: http://www.damianou.com/services.html

BKR Damianou & Co. (1998b). *Cyprus . . . The Offshore Superhighway to Russia* (On-line). Available: http://www.damianou.com/offshore-ent.html

British Club. (1999). *The Singapore Economy and Currency* (On-line). Available: http://www. expatsingapore.com/general/economy.htm

Bromley, Simon, (1994), *Rethinking Middle East Politics*. Austin: University of Texas Press.

Buckley, Peter J. and Jeremy Clegg (eds.). (1991). *Multinational Enterprises in Less Developed Countries*. New York: St. Martin's Press.

Castle, Leslie and Christopher Findley (eds.). (1988). *Pacific Trade in Services*. Sydney: Allen & Unwin.

Cayman Web World. (1996–1997). *Advantages of the Cayman Islands as an Offshore Financial Centre* (On-line). Available: http://cayman.com.ky/finance.htm

Charles, S. (1993). "Conceptualizing Services Sector Productivity." *Social and Economic Studies*, Vol. 42, No. 4, 95–113.

Clifton Gunderson L.L.C. (1998a). *International* (On-line). Available: http:// www.cliftoncpa.com/international/index.html

Clifton Gunderson L.L.C. (1998b). *Client Services* (On-line). Available: http:// www.cliftoncpa.com/services/index.html

Cohen, Stephen S. and John Zysman. (1987). *Manufacturing Matters: The Myth of Post-Industrial Society*. New York: Basic Books.

Columbus Group Plc. (1998). *Cayman Islands* (On-line). Available: http://www.wtg-online.com/country/ky/gen.html

Coopers & Lybrand. (1991). *International Accounting Summaries*. New York: John Wiley and Sons.

Coopers & Lybrand. (1998a). *Spotlight on the Cyprus Firm* (On-line). Available: http://www.cy.coopers.com/cycom/coopers/facts/cyinfo.htm

Coopers & Lybrand. (1998b). *Special Services to Offshore Clients by the Cyprus Firm* (On-line). Available: http://www.cy.coopers.com/cycom/coopers/offshore/index.htm

Coopers & Lybrand. (1998c). *Financial and Management Consulting by the Cyprus Firm* (On-line). Available: http://www.cy.coopers.com/cycom/coopers/ourservi/financial.htm

Coopers & Lybrand. (1998d). *Information Technology Consulting by the Cyprus Firm* (On-line). Available: http://www.cy.coopers.com/cycom/coopers/ourservi/infotech.htm

Coopers & Lybrand. (1998e). *Computer Software Services by the Cyprus Firm* (On-line). Available: http://www.cy.coopers.com/cycom/coopers/ourservi/computer.htm

Coopers & Lybrand. (1998f). *Project Management Consulting by the Cyprus Firm* (On-line). Available: http://www.cy.coopers.com/cycom/coopers/ourservi/project.htm

Coopers & Lybrand. (1998g). *Business Recovery Services by the Cyprus Firm* (On-line). Available: http://www.cy.coopers.com/cycom/coopers/ourservi/recovery.htm

Coopers & Lybrand. (1998h). *Human Resources Consulting by the Cyprus Firm* (On-line). Available: http://www.cy.coopers.com/cycom/coopers/ourservi/human.htm

Coopers & Lybrand. (1998i). *Operations and Quality Management by the Cyprus Firm* (On-line). Available: http://www.cy.coopers.com/coopers/ourservi/logistics.htm

Coopers & Lybrand. (1998j). *Services by the Cyprus Firm* (On-line). Available: http://www.cy.coopers.com/cycom/coopers/ourservi/ourservi.htm

Coopers & Lybrand Consultants (East Asia). (1997). *Consulting Services* (On-line). Available: http://www.asiamcs.coopers.com?servicesbody.htm

Coopers & Lybrand International. (1996). *Bahrain: A Guide for Businessmen and Investors*. Bahrain: Coopers & Lybrand Jawad Habib & Co.

Coopers & Lybrand International. (1997). *Coopers & Lybrand: Bahrain* (On-line). Available: http://www.cooperslybrand.com.bh/

Cuttiford, Nicholas. (1990). "Jersey's Major Role in International Finance." *Offshore Investment*, No. 15, 32–33.

Cyprus. (1998). *Cyprus—A Center for International Business* (On-line). Available: http://www.cosmosnet.net/azias/cyprus/bus-main.html

Damianou & Co. (1995–1998a). *Cyprus . . . The Offshore Superhighway to Russia* (On-line). Available: http://www.damianou.com/offshore-ent.html

Damianou & Co. (1995–1998b). *Audit and Accounting Services* (On-line). Available: http://www.damianou.com/services.html

Daniels, P.W. (1993). *Service Industries in the World Economy* Oxford: Blackwell Publishers.

David Tong and Company. (1993). *The Accounting Profession in Singapore.* New York: American Institute of Certified Public Accountants.

DeBendt, J. (1996). "Business Services: Markets and Transactions." *Review of Industrial Organization*, Vol. 11, No. 1, 19–33.

Deloitte & Touche. (1998a). *About Gibraltar* (On-line). Available: http://www.deloitte.gi/aboutgib.htm

Deloitte & Touche. (1998b). *Deloitte & Touche in Gibraltar* (On-line). Available: http://www.deloitte.gi/dtingib.htm

Deloitte & Touche. (1998c). *Our Services* (On-line). Available: http://www.deloitte.gi/audit.htm

Deloitte & Touche. (1998d). *Offshore Services.* (On-line). Available: http://www.deloitte.gi/offshore.htm

Deloitte & Touche. (1998e). *Gibraltar as a Finance Centre* (On-line). Available: http://www.deloitte.gi/finance.htm

Deloitte & Touche. (1998f). *Tax Advantages in Gibraltar* (On-line). Available: http://www.deloitte.gi/taxadv.htm

Deloitte & Touche. (1998g). *Trusts* (On-line). Available: http://www.deloitte.gi/trusts.htm

Deloitte & Touche. (1998h). *Gibraltar Companies* (On-line). Available: http://www.deloitte.gi/gibcomp.htm

Deloitte & Touche. (1998i). *Insurance* (On-line). Available: http://www.deloitte.gi/ins.htm

Deloitte & Touche. (1998j). *Banking* (On-line). Available: http://www.deloitte.gi/banking.htm

Deloitte & Touche. (1999). *Deloitte & Touche Jersey* (On-line). Available: http://www.itl.net/business/ofw/Jersey/adverts/touche/p1.html

Deloitte Touche Tohmatsu International. (1994). *The Bahamas: International Tax and Business Guide.* New York: Deloitte Touche Tohmatsu International.

Deloitte Touche Tohmatsu International. (1995). *Cayman Islands: International Tax and Business Guide.* New York: Deloitte Touche Tohmatsu International.

Deloitte Touche Tohmatsu International. (1996a). *United Arab Emirates.* New York: Deloitte Touche Tohmatsu International.

Deloitte Touche Tohmatsu International. (1996b). *Information Folder, Latin America and the Caribbean.* New York: Deloitte Touche Tohmatsu International.

Deloitte Touche Tohmatsu International. (1996c). *The Bahamas International Tax and Business Guide.* New York: Deloitte Touche Tohmatsu International.

Diamond, Walter H. and Dorothy B. Diamond. (1998). *Tax Havens of the World,* 3 vols. New York: Matthew Bender.

Dufey, Gunter and Ian H. Giddy. (1978). "Financial Centers and External Markets." *Appendix 2 of The International Money Market.* Englewood Cliffs, N.J.: Prentice-Hall, 35–47.

The Economist. (March 22, 1997). *Supplement: A Survey of Management Consultancy.*

Economist Intelligence Unit. (1998). *Country Profile: Seychelles.* London: The Economist Intelligence Unit.

Economist Intelligence Unit. (1999). *Country Profile: Mauritius Seychelles.* London: The Economist Intelligence Unit.

Eland Systems Limited. (1998). *Financial Services: Mauritius* (On-line). Available: http://www.barint.on.ca/mauritius/t_finserv.html

El-Erain, Mohamed A. and Susan Fennell. (1997). *The Economy of the Middle East and North Africa*. Washington, D.C.: International Monetary Fund.

Enderwick, Peter. (1991). "Service Sector Multinationals and Developing Countries." In Peter J. Buckly and Jeremy Clegg (eds.), *Multinational Enterprises in Less Developed Countries*. New York: St. Martin's Press, 292–309.

Eracleous & Eracleous. (1998a). *Cyprus—A Place for Doing Business* (On-line). Available: http://www.eracleous.com?business.htm

Eracleous & Eracleous. (1998b). *Cyprus International Trusts* (On-line). Available: http://www.eracleous.com/cyofftru.htm

Eracleous & Eracleous. (1998c). *Information on Cyprus Double Tax Treaties* (On-line). Available: http://www.eracleous.com/treaties.htm

Eracleous & Eracleous. (1998d). *Information on Cyprus Offshore Companies* (On-line). Available: http://www.eracleous.com/cyoffco.htm

Eracleous & Eracleous. (1998e). *Our Services* (On-line). Available: http://www.eracleous.com/services.htm

Ernst & Young. (1990). *Doing Business in the United Arab Emirates*. New York: Ernst & Young International, Ltd.

Ernst & Young. (1995). *Doing Business in the Cayman Islands*. Cayman Islands: Ernst & Young.

Ernst & Young. (1995–1997). *Doing Business Around the World* (On-line). Available: http://www.eyi.com/cgi-bin/foliocgi . . . /query=*/doc/{tl}/pageitems ={body}?

Ernst & Young. (1997a). *The Middle East Practice* (On-line). Available: http://www.eyi.com/mideast/meinfo.htm

Ernst & Young. (1997b). *Audit & Related Services* (On-line). Available: http://www.eyi.com/mideast/meaudit.htm

Ernst & Young. (1997c). *Management Consultancy* (On-line). Available: http://www.eyi.com/mideast/memcs.htm

Ernst & Young. (1997d). *Accounting & Financial Services* (On-line). Available: http://www.eyi.com/mideast/meaccnt.htm

Ernst & Young. (1997e). *Taxation* (On-line). Available: http://www.eyi.com/mideast/metax.htm

Ernst & Young. (1997f). *Middle East Taxation* (On-line). Available: http://www.eyi.com/mideast/Mebbtaxb.htm

Ernst & Young. (1997g). *Business Community Training* (On-line). Available: http://www.eyi.com/mideast/metrain.htm

Ernst & Young. (1998a). *The Island of Jersey* (On-line). Available: http://www.eyjersey.co.uk/jersey.htm

Ernst & Young. (1998b). *The Bailiwick of Guernsey—Executive Summary* (On-line). Available: http://www.guernsey-ey.com/dbigg/htm/exec_summ.html

Ernst & Young. (1998c). *The Economy* (On-line). Available: http://www.guernsey-ey.com/dbigg/htm/economy1.htm

Ernst & Young, (1998d). *General* (On-line). Available: http://www.guernsey-ey.com/dbigg/htm/general1.htm

Ernst & Young. (1998e). *Our Services* (On-line). Available: http://www.guernsey-ey.com/services/htm/sectioncontent.htm

Ernst & Young. (1999a). *Doing Business in the Cayman Islands* (On-line). Available: http://www.doingbusinessin.com

Ernst & Young. (1999b). *Doing Business in Bermuda* (On-line). Available: http://www.doingbusinessin.com

Ernst & Young. (1999c). *Doing Business in Barbados* (On-line). Available: http://www.doingbusinessin.com

Ernst & Young. (1999d). *Corporate Tax Guide: Malta* (On-line) Available: http://www.doingbusinessin.com/start/index.cfm?country=malta

Ernst & Young. (1999e). *Doing Business in Guernsey* (On-line). Available: http://www.guernsey-ey.com

Ernst & Young. (1999f). *Gibraltar Information* (On-line). Available: http://www.gibnet.com/ey/index.htm

Ernst & Young. (1999g). *Doing Business in Mauritius* (On-line). Available: http://www.doingbusinessin.com

Ernst & Young. (1999h). *Doing Business in Seychelles* (On-line). Available: http://www.doingbusinessin.com/start/index.cfm

Ernst & Young. (1999i). *Doing Business in the United Arab Emirates* (On-line). Available: http://www.doingbusinessin.com/start/index.cfm?country=unitedarabemirates

Ernst & Young Bermuda. (1996). *Services* (On-line). Available: http://www.ey.bm/Services.htm

Euromoney. (May 1989). *Supplement: Treasure Islands.*

Fairbairn, T'eo. (1985). "Economic Prospects for the Pacific Islands." In Robert C. Kiste and Richard A. Herr (eds.), *The Pacific Islands in the Year 2000.* Manoa: Working Paper Series, Pacific Islands Study Program, Center for Asian and Pacific Studies, University of Hawaii, in collaboration with the Pacific Islands Development Program, East West Center, Honolulu, 44–69.

Falvey, R.E. and N.A. Gemmell, (1996). "Formalization and Test of the Factor Productivity Explanation of International Differences in Service Prices." *International Economic Review,* Vol. 37, No. 1, 85–102.

Falvey, R.E. and Norman Gemmell. (1995). "Explaining International Differences in the Share of Services in Real Expenditure." *Economic Letters,* Vol. 47, No. 1, 59–62.

Feketekuty, Geza. (1988). *International Trade in Services.* Cambridge, Mass.: Ballinger Publishing Company.

First American Legal Corporation. (1998). *Isle of Man* (On-line). Available: http://www.falc.com/ver09981location/manx.htm

FND. (1998). *Mauritius* (On-line). Available: http://www.fnd.cz/maurit2.htm

Forbes' Bermuda on Line. (1995–1996a). *A Profile of Bermuda's International Business Industry: Now Producing More Revenue Than Tourism* (On-line). Available: http://www.berbiz.com/finprof.htm

Forbes' Bermuda on Line. (1995–1996b). *Bermuda's Banking Environment, Banks and Global Banking Networking* (On-line). Available: http://www.berbiz.com/finbank.htm

Forbes' Bermuda on Line. (1995–1996c). *Bermuda's Insurance Market: A World Leader* (On-line). Available: http://www.berbiz.com/finins.htm

Forsyth, David J.C. (1990). *Technology Policy for Small Developing Countries.* New York: St. Martin's Press.

Francois, J.F. (1990). "Producer Services: Scale and the Division of Labour." *Oxford Economic Papers*, Vol. 42, No. 4, 715–729.

Freeport of Mauritius. (1998). *The Freeport* (On-line). Available: http://pub.intnet.mu/iels/freeport_mau.htm

Gerakis, A.S. and O. Roncesvalles. (1983). "Bahrain's Offshore Banking Center." *Economic Development and Cultural Change*, Vol. 31, No. 2, 271–293.

Gibraltar. (1998). *Gibraltar* (On-line). Available: http://surf.germany.eu.net/bookland/compendia/cia/gi.html

Goe, W.R. (1991). "The Growth of Producer Services Industries: Sorting Through the Externalization Debate." *Growth and Change*, Vol. 22, No. 4, 118–141.

Gordon, R.A. (1981). *Tax Havens and Their Use by US Taxpayers—An Overview (The Gordon Report)*. Washington, D.C.: Internal Revenue Service.

Grant Thornton International. (1998). *Grant Thornton International* (On-line). Available: http://www.gti.org/index.htm

Harker, Patrick T. (ed.). (1995). *The Service Productivity and Quality Challenge*. Boston: Kluwer.

Harrington, James W., Alan D. MacPherson and John R. Lombard. (1991). "Interregional Trade in Producer Services: Review and Synthesis." *Growth and Change*, Vol. 22, No. 4, 75–93.

Harrison, Bennett and Barry Bluestone. (1988). *The Great U-Turn*. New York: Basic Books.

Heely, James A. and Roy L. Nersesian. (1993). *Global Management Accounting: A Guide for Executives of International Corporations*. Westport, Conn.: Quorum.

Internet Bahamas Ltd. (1998). *The Bahamas as an Offshore Business Center* (On-line). Available: ysiwyg://10/http://flamingo.bahamas.net.bs/business/index.html

Isle of Man. (1998). (On-line). Available: http://www.iii.co.uk/news/international/centres/cent02.htm

Iwata, Kazumasa. (1988). "Liberalisation of Trade in Financial Services." In Leslie Castle and Christopher Findley (eds.), *Pacific Trade In Services*. Boston: Allen & Unwin.

Jequier, Nicolas and Yao-Su Hu. (1989). *Banking and the Promotion of Technological Development*. New York: St. Martin's Press.

Johns, R.A. and C.M. LeMarchant. (1993). *Finance Centres: British Isle Offshore Development Since 1979*. London: Pinter Publishers.

Johnson, Harry G.. (1976). "Panama as a Regional Financial Center: A Preliminary Analysis of Development Contribution." *Economic Development and Cultural Change*, Vol. 24, No. 2, 261–286.

Kim, Chungsoo and Kihong Kim. (1990). "Asian NIE's and Liberalization of Trade in Services." In H.E. English (ed.), *Pacific Initiative in Global Trade*. Vancouver: Institute for Research on Public Policy, 181–198.

KPMG. (1997a). *Ken Hewitt Discloses New Focus for KPMG Barbados* (On-line). Available: http://www.kpmg.bb/future.htm

KPMG. (1997b). *Assurance & Accounting Services* (On-line). Available: http://www.kpmg.bb/aa/default.htm

KPMG. (1997c). *Consulting Services* (On-line). Available: http://www.kpmg.bb/consult/default.htm

KPMG. (1997d). *Corporate & Financial Services* (On-line). Available: http://www. kpmg.bb/fs/default.htm

KPMG. (1997e). *Tax Services* (On-line). Available: http://www.kpmg. bb/tax/default.htm

KPMG. (May 1997f). *Barbados* (On-line). Available: http://www.kpmg.bb/

KPMG. (1997g). *Bermuda: Products and Services* (On-line). Available: http://www.kpmg.bm/bm_svcs.htm

KPMG Fakhro. (1997). *List of Services Provided by KPMG Fakhro* (On-line). Available: http://php.indiana.edu/~hqasem/kpmg/kpmgserv.html

KPMG International. (1997a). *Industry* (On-line). Available: http://www. kpmg.com/indust.html

KPMG International. (1997b). *Services* (On-line). Available: http://www. kpmg.com/services.html

KPMG International. (1997c). *Statistics* (On-line). Available: http://www. kpmg.com/stsas.html

KPMG International. (1997d). *World Wide Presence* (On-line). Available: http:// www.kpmg.com/wwpres.html

KPMG International. (1997e). *KPMG International Contact Partners* (On-line). Available: http://www.kpmg.com/mideast.html

KPMG Peat Marwick. (1991). *Investment in the Cayman Islands.* Grand Cayman: KPMG Peat Marwick.

KPMG Peat Marwick Antigua. (1997a). *An Overview* (On-line). Available: http://kpmgantigua.com/overview.htm

KPMG Peat Marwick Antigua. (1997b). *Corporate Services* (On-line). Available: http://kpmgantigua.com/fs.htm

KPMG Peat Marwick Antigua. (1997c). *Audit and Accounting Services* (On-line). Available: http://kpmgantigua.com/audit.htm

KPMG Peat Marwick Antigua. (1997d). *Tax Services* (On-line). Available: http://kpmgantigua.com/tax.htm

KPMG Peat Marwick Antigua. (1997e). *Corporate Services: International Business Companies* (On-line). Available: http://kpmgantigua.com/ibc.htm

KPMG Peat Marwick Antigua. (1997f). *Corporate Services: Offshore Banking* (On-line). Available http://kpmgantigua.com/offshore.htm

KPMG Peat Marwick Antigua. (1997g). *Corporate Services: International Insurance* (On-line). Available: http://kpmgantigua.com/insure.htm

KPMG Peat Marwick Antigua. (1997h). *Corporate Services: Trusts* (On-line). Available: http://kpmgantigua.com/trust.htm

KPMG Peat Marwick Antigua. (1997i). *Management Consulting Services* (On-line). Available: http://kpmgantigua.com/consult.htm

Lessard, Donald R. (1993). "Singapore as an International Financial Centre." As excerpted in Richard Roberts (ed.) (1994), *Offshore Financial Centres.* Aldershot, England: Edward Elgar Publishing Company, 200–235.

Lessard, Donald R. and Adrian E. Tschoegl. (1988). "Panama's International Banking Center: The Direct Employment Effects." *Journal of Banking and Finance,* Vol. 12, 43–50.

Library of Congress. (1991). *Cyprus—A Country Study* (On-line). Available: http://lcweb2.loc.gov/frd/cs/cytoc.html

Library of Congress. (1994a). *Mauritius—A Country Study* (On-line). Available: http://lcweb2.loc.gov/frd/cs/mutoc.html

Library of Congress. (1994b). *Seychelles—A Country Study* (On-line). Available: http://lcweb2.loc.gov/frd/cs/sctoc.html

Lindbeck, A. (1975). "The Changing Role of the Nation State." *Kyklos*, Vol. 28, 23–46.

Maritimelink Network. (1998). *Bahamas: Economic Trends and Outlook* (On-line). Available: http://tradecompass.com/library/books/com_guide/BAHA-MASO2.html

McKee, David L. (1988). *Growth, Development and the Service Economy in the Third World*. New York: Praeger.

McKee, David L. (ed.). (1994). *External Linkages and Growth in Small Economies*. Westport, Conn.: Praeger.

McKee, David L., Yosra A. Amara and Don E. Garner. (1995). "International Services as Facilitators." *Foreign Trade Review*, Vol. XXIX, No. 4, 254–264.

McKee, David L., Yosra AbuAmara McKee and Don E. Garner. (1997a). "Some Reflections on Accounting Services in the Global Economy." In Jerry Biberman and Abbass Alkhafaji (eds.), *Business Research Yearbook: Global Business Perspectives*, Vol. IV, 35–39.

McKee, David L., Yosra AbuAmara McKee and Don E. Garner. (1997b). "The Positive Functions of Offshore Financial Centers." *Journal of Global Competitiveness*, Vol. 5, No. 1, 406–413.

McKee, David L. and Don E. Garner. (1992). *Accounting Services, the International Economy, and Third World Development*. Westport, Conn.: Praeger.

McKee, David L. and Don E. Garner. (1996). *Accounting Services, Growth and Change in the Pacific Basin*. Westport, Conn: Quorum.

McKee, David L., Don E. Garner and Yosra AbuAmara McKee. (1998). *Accounting Services and Growth in Small Economies: Evidence from the Caribbean Basin*. Westport, CT.: Quorum.

McKee, David L., Don E. Garner and Yosra AbuAmara McKee. (1999). *Accounting Services, the Islamic Middle East and the Global Economy*. Westport, Conn.: Quorum.

McKee, David L. and Clem Tisdell. (1990). *Developmental Issues in Small Island Economies*. New York: Praeger.

Merren, Orren. (1995–1997). *Caylaw Corporate Services Ltd.: Legal Aspects of Doing Local Business in the Cayman Islands* (On-line). Available: http://www.caylaw.ky/law/articles/localbus.htm

Molyneux, Douglas and William R. Storie. (1998). *Research and Information Paper on the Dramatic Growth of Offshore Mutual Funds*. Hamilton, Bermuda: William R. Storie & Co. Ltd.

Moonesamy, S. (1996). *Financial Services* (On-line). Available: http://www.barint.on.ca?mauritius/t_finserv.html

Moore Stephens. (1998a). *The Firm* (On-line). Available: http://www.moore-stephens.com/company/firm.htm

Moore Stephens. (1998b). *Services* (On-line). Available: http://www.moore-stephens.com/services/index.htm

Moore Stephens. (1998c). *Audit* (On-line). Available: http://www.moore-stephens.com/services/audit.htm

Moore Stephens International. (1998). *Moore Stephens International* (On-line). Available: http://www.moore-stephens.com/company/international.htm

Moores Rowland. (September 1997a). *Welcome to Moores Rowland—Vanuatu* (On-line). Available: http://www.mooresrowland.com/welcome.html

Moores Rowland. (September 1997b). *Services Offered by Moores Rowland* (On-line). Available: http://www.mooresrowland.com/services.html

Moores Rowland. (September 1997c). *Other Offshore Entities* (On-line). Available: http://www.mooresrowland.com/bank. html

Moores Rowland. (September 1997d). *Vanuatu: The South Pacific's Premiere Tax Haven* (On-line). Available: http://www.mooresrowland.com/vanuatu. html

Moores Rowland. (September 1997e). *Offshore Trusts* (On-line). Available: http://www.mooresrowland.com/trust.html

Moores Rowland. (1998a). *About MRI* (On-line). Available: http://www.mri-world.com/Pages/about.html

Moores Rowland. (June 1998b). *Offshore News & Links* (On-line). Available: http://www. mooresrowland.com/news.htm

Moss, Mitchell L. (1988). "Telecommunications and International Financial Centers." *Information and Behavior*, 3, Chap. 13, 239–252.

New Zealand Trade Development Board. (1999). *Country Profiles* (On-line). Available: http://www.tradenz.govt.nz/intelligence/profiles/unitd_arab_emirates.html

Netforce Group Plc. (1998). *Offshore Business in Antigua and Barbuda* (On-line). Available: http://www.antigua-barbuda.com/offshore.html

Nugent, Jeffrey B. and Theodore H. Thomas (eds.). (1985). *Bahrain and the Gulf: Past Perspectives and Alternative Futures*. New York: St. Martin's Press.

Nurkse, Ragner. (1967). *Problems of Capital Formation in Underdeveloped Countries and Patterns of Trade and Development*. New York: Oxford University Press.

O'Farrell, P.N. (1994). "Manufacturing Demand for Business Services." *Cambridge Journal of Economics*, Vol. 19, No. 4, 523–543.

O'Farrell, P.N. and L.A.R. Moffat. (1995). "Business Services and Their Impact upon Client Performance: An Exploratory Interregional Analysis." *Regional Studies*, Vol. 29, No. 2, 111–124,

O'Farrell, P.N., L.A.R. Moffat and P.A. Wood. (1995). "Internationalization of Business Services: A Methodological Critique of Foreign-Market Entry-Mode Choice." *Environment and Planning A*, Vol. 27, No. 5, 683–697.

Offshore Investment. (September 1986). "21 Places an International Investor Should Know About." *Offshore Investment*, No. 1, 33–47.

Offshore Investment. (November/December 1986). "21 Other Places an International Investor Should Know About." *Offshore Investment*, No. 2, 33–47.

Offshore Investment. (October 1990). "The Channel Islands Move Up Market in an Era of Change." *Offshore Investment*, No. 15, 25–27.

Ohmae, Kenichi. (1990). *The Borderless World: Power and Strategy in the Interlinked Economy*. New York: McKinsey & Company.

O'Malley, Shaun F. (1992). "Accounting Across Borders." *Financial Executive*, Vol. 8, No. 2, 28–31.

Pacific Basin Economic Council United States Member Committee. (1998).

Destination ASEAN (On-line). Available: http://www.pebcus.org/daintro.htm

Park, Y.S. (1982). "The Economics of Offshore Financial Centers." *Columbia Journal of World Business*, Vol. XVII, No. 4, 31–35.

Pannell Kerr Forster. (1996–1998a). *Activities* (On-line). Available: http://www.pkf.com/uk/pkfactiv.html

Pannell Kerr Forster. (1996–1998b). *Management Consultants* (On-line). Available: http://www.pkf.com/uk/pkfa.html

Pannell Kerr Forster International. (1995–1998). *Pannell Kerr Forster International Association* (On-line). Available: http://www.pkf.com/index.html

Picciotto, S. (1983). "Jurisdictional Conflicts, International Law and the International State System." *International Journal of the Sociology of Law*, Vol. 11, No. 1, 11–40.

Price Waterhouse. (1990). *Doing Business in Singapore*. New York: Price Waterhouse World Firm.

Price Waterhouse. (1991a). *Doing Business in Antigua and Barbuda*. New York: Price Waterhouse World Firm.

Price Waterhouse (1991b). *Doing Business in Cyprus*. New York: Price Waterhouse World Firm.

Price Waterhouse (1991c). *Doing Business in Malta*. New York: Price Waterhouse World Firm.

Price Waterhouse. (1992a). *Doing Business in the Bahamas*. New York: Price Waterhouse World Firm.

Price Waterhouse. (1992b). *Doing Business in Vanuatu*. New York: Price Waterhouse World Firm.

Price Waterhouse. (1993). *Doing Business in Singapore*. New York: Price Waterhouse World Firm.

Price Waterhouse. (1994). *Doing Business in Barbados*. New York: Price Waterhouse World Firm.

Price Waterhouse. (1996). *Doing Business in the United Arab Emirates*. New York: Price Waterhouse World Firm.

Price Waterhouse. (1997). *Doing Business in Bahrain*. New York: Price Waterhouse World Firm.

Price Waterhouse Coopers. (July 1, 1998). *Price Waterhouse Coopers: The World's Largest Professional Services Organisation, Born Today* (On-line). Available: http://www.mauritius-online.com/coopers/index.html

Price Waterhouse Coopers. (1999). *Doing Business and Investing Worldwide* (CD-ROM). New York: Price Waterhouse Coopers.

Riahi-Belkaoui, Ahmed. (1994). *Accounting in the Developing Countries*. Westport, Conn.: Quorum.

Roberts, Richard (ed.). (1994a). *International Financial Centres: Concepts, Development and Dynamics*. Aldershot, England: Edward Elgar Publishing Company.

Roberts, Richard (ed.). (1994b). *Offshore Financial Centres*. Aldershot, England: Edward Elgar Publishing Company.

Robinson, Peter (1989). "Information Technology and the Relationships among OECD Countries." In Meheroo Jussawalla, Tadayuki Okama and Toshihiro Araki (eds.), *Information Technology and Global Interdependence*. Westport, Conn.: Greenwood Press.

Romanoff, E. and S.H. Levine. (1993). "Information Industry Dynamics and the Service Industries." *Environment and Planning A*, Vol. 25, No. 3, 305–316.

Roper, John. (1990). "Misconceptions about the Channel Islands." *Offshore Investment*, No. 15, 28–31.

Rowe, Richard. (1990). "Manifold Advantages of a Guernsey Base." *Offshore Investment*, No. 15, 34–35.

RSM International. (1998a). *An Introduction to RSM International* (On-line). Available: http://206.121.62.9/rsmiweb.nsf...1982c80256523005803cf? OpenDocument

RSM International. (1998b). *RSMI Overview* (On-line). Available: http://206. 121.62.9/rsmiweb.nsf/0c...e7048862564ce0047668a?OpenDocument

RSM International. (1998c). *Consulting Services* (On-line). Available http:// 206.121.62.9/rsmiweb.nsf/82...a187d862564e5005a2372?OpenDocument

RSM International. (1998d). *Tax Services* (On-line). Available: http:// 206.121.62.9/rsmiweb.nsf/82...6dd30862564d5005b2a04?OpenDocument

RSM International. (1998e). *Audit & Accounting* (On-line). Available: http:// 206.121.62.9/rsmiweb.nsf/82...alcbf862564d5005b0156?OpenDocument

Segal-Horn, Susan. (1993). "The Internationalization of Service Firms." *Advances in Strategic Management*, Vol. 9, 31–55.

Seychelles. (1998). *The New Business Center* (On-line). Available: http:// www.seychelles.net/siba/lochis.html

Singapore Department of Statistics. (1998). *Economy* (On-line). Available: http: //www.tdb.gov.sg/bizspore/sp_2.html

Sletmo, Gunnar K. and Gaven Boyd (eds.). (1993). *Pacific Service Enterprises and Pacific Cooperation*. Boulder, Colo.: Westview Press.

Starchild, Adam. (1996). *Switzerland: Gateway to Global Investment*. The Libertarian Library. (On-line). Available: http://www.cyberhaven.com/libertarian/ swisgate.html

State of Hawaii. (1999). *Country Profile: Singapore* (On-line). Available: http: //www.hawaii.gov/dbedt/ert/cp/singa.html

Straw, J.F. (Jim). (1997). *Offshore Banking Is Not an Evil*. The Libertarian Library (On-line). Available: http://www.cyberhaven.com/libertarian/offbank. html

Thrift, Nigel. (1987). "The Fixers: the Urban Geography of International Commercial Capital." In Jeffrey Henderson and Manuel Castells (eds.), *Global Restructuring and Territorial Development*. London: Sage, 203–233.

Tordoir, Pieter. (1995). *The Professional Knowledge Economy: The Management and Integration of Professional Services in Business Organizations*. Boston: Kluwer Academic.

Tucker, Ken and Mark Sundberg. (1988). *International Trade in Services*. New York: Routledge.

Walter, Ingo. (1990). *The Secret Money Market*. New York: St. Martin's Press.

William R. Storie. (1995). *Towards 2000: Trends in the Alternative Markets*. Hamilton, Bermuda: William R. Storie & Co. Ltd.

William R. Storie & Co. Ltd. (1995). *A Discussion Paper on the Offshore Group or*

Association Captive Insurance Company: The Use, the Advantage, the Concern.
Hamilton, Bermuda: William R. Storie & Co. Ltd.
Wilson, Rodney. (1992). *Cyprus and the International Economy.* New York: St. Martin's Press.
Zimbalist, Andrew. (1991). "Institutions of the Service Economy II: Free Zone and Banking Center." In Andrew Zimbalist and John Weeks, *Panama at the Crossroads: Economic Development and Political Change in the Twentieth Century.* Berkeley: University of California Press, 65–84, 183–187.

Index

About the Authors

DAVID L. McKEE is Professor of Economics in the Graduate School of Management at Kent State University, where he specializes in development economics and economic change. His most recent books, coauthored with Don E. Garner and Yosra AbuAmara McKee, are *Accounting Services, the Islamic Middle East and the Global Economy* (1999) and *Accounting Services and Growth in Small Economies* (1998), both published by Quorum Books.

DON E. GARNER is Professor and former Chair of the Department of Accounting at California State University, Stanislaus. He is a certified public accountant and a certified internal auditor as well as a specialist in auditing and accounting.

YOSRA ABUAMARA McKEE is an adjunct faculty member in economics at Kent State University. Her work on international trade and services, economic integration and regional development has been aired in various professional publications and presentations.

CPSIA information can be obtained at www.ICGtesting.com
Printed in the USA
LVOW071613070112

262635LV00002B/2/P